1996

The Judiciary

The Judiciary

The Supreme Court in the Governmental Process

SEVENTH EDITION

Henry J. Abraham

James Hart Professor of Government and Foreign Affairs
University of Virginia

Allyn and Bacon, Inc.

Boston • London • Sydney • Toronto

Library of Congress Cataloging-in-Publication Data

Abraham, Henry Julian, 1921–
   The judiciary : the Supreme Court in the governmental process.

   Bibliography; p.
   Includes index.
   1. United States. Supreme Court. I. Title.
KF8748.A2 1987   347.73′26   86-14048
ISBN 0-205-10312-X   347.30735

Series editor: Judith Shaw
Production coordinator: Helyn Pultz
Editorial-production service: TKM Productions
Cover coordinator: Linda Dickinson
Cover designer: Susan C. Hamant

Printed in the United States of America

10 9 8 7 6 5 4 3 2 1   90 89 88 87 86

To Peter

Contents

☆☆☆

Preface

To the First Edition

Despite a growing awareness by the American public of the significant role played by the judiciary, the latter is still the least known, the least understood, and the most maligned of the three branches of the United States government. That this is not a surprising state of affairs does not gainsay the need to try to provide insight and material that may help to alleviate the problem. There is some evidence of a growing body of serious commentary on the judiciary, in general, and the Supreme Court, in particular—but much of it has been produced with either little or no regard for the nonprofessional reader or student, and a good deal of it is difficult or expensive to obtain. The purpose of this little book is to avoid these problems by presenting a brief but meaningful analysis of the judicial function as seen through the role of the Supreme Court of the United States in the governmental process. It is both an explanatory and an evaluative presentation, but I have endeavored to be objective in an area where far too much reaction is still based upon the answer to the question "whose ox is being gored?" This work is by no means a wholly uncritical study of the Supreme Court and its functions, but I happen to believe strongly that, on balance, the Court has played not only a crucial but an indispensable role in the growth and evolution of our Republic.

Designed for use by the general public as well as by students of government and politics at all levels, the book tells its essential story in three chapters: The first treats the dual system of courts in the United States and the jurisdiction and institutional setting of the Supreme Court. The second deals extensively with what has clearly become the Court's most important function: its role in the delineation and preservation of basic individual freedoms in our democratic society. The chapter does this topically by an analysis and explanation of both historical and legal aspects, in particular stressing the judicial role in the interpretation and application of constitutional mandates to the national government and the states in such vital areas as religion, expression, and political and racial equality, with a thorough consideration of the general problem of substantive and procedural due process of law. The third chapter, after explaining the selection of judges and justices, concentrates on three significantly difficult and vexatious problems in the Supreme Court's function: its ultimate power of judicial review, its role as a "line-drawer," and that of a public policymaker.

My greatest debt in the writing of this work is to Professor William M. Beaney who, as editor of the Allyn and Bacon Series of which this is the first publication, provided both the essential encouragement and necessary criticism; I am deeply grateful to him. Among the many others who stimulated and aided in a variety of ways, I should like to single out Professor, now Congressman from Iowa, John R. Schmidhauser, who read the entire manuscript; Mrs. Helen White, who typed it with her usual efficiency; Mr. John R. DeRemigis, who conceived the Allyn and Bacon Series; the Oxford University Press for its generously granted permission to adapt for Chapters 1 and 3 material used in my *The Judicial Process: An Introductory Analysis of the Courts of the United States, England, and France* (New York, 1962); Miss Nancy L. Schnerr and Mrs. Sylvia G. Balis of the Statistics Department, who provided a necessary "hiding place" for me to write in peace; my faithful and hard-working research assistants, Rocco D'Amico and Paul Lutzker; and, *bien entendu*, my wife, Mildred, who has been loyally at my side through many a complex writing episode.

And, like an earlier one to his older brother, the book is cheerfully dedicated to a very young man who helped, too—in his own manner.

To the Seventh Edition

As this happily still smallish tome enters its third decade, and is still used widely, it seemed appropriate to engender a number of fairly extensive changes in both format and substance. Thus, responding to repeated suggestions, I have rearranged the chapter sequence by moving erstwhile Chapter 4 to follow Chapter 1 in order to have these two discussions on court organization, procedure, and staffing in logical tandem. What was formerly Chapter 2 now becomes Chapter 3, and the old Chapter 3 will be captioned Chapter 4. Hence, the two civil rights and liberties chapters will complete the book rather than split the two on the judicial process.

All four chapters have been thoroughly revised through mid-1986. New sections on privacy, racial and gender discrimination, and religion have been added and major alterations have been effected to reflect the current status of our constitutional law.

I continue to be profoundly grateful for the ongoing support of *The Judiciary* and the encouragement that has been tendered to me by both colleagues and students whose constructive criticism has been invaluable. A special "thank you" goes to Barbara A. Perry, Gregor Baer, and Linda McClain.

As with all of its predecessors, the seventh edition is dedicated with love and pride to our son, Peter, who was two years old when the first edition appeared, and who, now a college graduate and embarked on his own career, remains a loyal fan of *his* book.

H. J. A.

1

American Courts in Practice

Most Americans know less about the judicial branch of their government than they do about its other two branches, the legislative and the executive. This is particularly regrettable because it is to the courts that Americans turn almost eagerly when they seek solutions to difficult and delicate problems of public concern that the legislative and executive branches are unable or unwilling to handle. The legislative branch has been especially guilty of avoiding troublesome matters of public policy. While publicly flaying the courts—especially the Supreme Court and frequently with intemperate language if not vilification—the legislative branch has been quite willing to "pass the buck." Thus we Americans legalize or "judicialize" our politics. Alexis de Tocqueville recognized this 150 years ago when he opined that, sooner or later, in the United States every political question inexorably becomes a legal question. And so it has been on a seemingly ever-expanding scale.

Two illustrations of pressing and controversial public policy that ultimately landed in the lap of the United States Supreme Court are desegregation and legislative districting. Although the Court[1] had done its best to avoid the issues (and it can be argued properly so), time ran out. When these two delicate matters reached the bar of the Court, there was evidently near-unanimity among the American people in the first matter and sizeable majority opinion in the second that a stand had to be taken by the highest tribunal in the American judicial structure. Thus came about the monumentally significant Supreme Court decisions in *Brown* v. *Board of Education*[2] and *Baker* v. *Carr*[3]—decisions that triggered revolutionary changes in the social, economic, and political structure and texture of America's body politic. As will be explained in Chapter 4, the *Brown* decision (together with its implementation decision one year later[4]) held that state-mandated segregation by race in public schools constitutes a violation of the equal protection of the laws clause of the Fourteenth Amendment to the United States Constitution. This violation was to be eradicated "with all deliberate speed," under the banner of a "prompt and reasonable start."[5] (Earlier[6] and later[7] decisions also ruled that various other types of state authorized or sanctioned racial segregation violated the Fourteenth Amendment.)

The *Baker* case held that the question of deliberate mal-, mis-, or non-apportionment of representative districts in the several states—a matter the Court understandably purposely avoided as "a political question" until the 1962 decision—was a justiciable controversy in the federal courts, and that "invidious discrimination" in the drawing of district lines might well constitute a violation of the equal protection and/or due process of law clauses of the Fourteenth Amendment.

---

[1]Throughout this work, references to "the Court" will signify the United States Supreme Court unless otherwise specified.

[2]347 U.S. 483 (1954).

[3]369 U.S. 186 (1962).

[4]349 U.S. 294 (1955).

[5]*Brown* v. *Board of Education of Topeka, Kansas*, 349 U.S. 294 (1955).

[6]E.g., *Sweatt* v. *Painter*, 339 U.S. 629 (1950); *Shelley* v. *Kraemer*, 334 U.S. 1 (1948); *Morgan* v. *Virginia*, 328 U.S. 373 (1946).

[7]E.g., *Cooper* v. *Aaron*, 358 U.S. 1 (1958); *Watson* v. *Memphis*, 373 U.S. 526 (1963); *Peterson* v. *Greenville*, 373 U.S. 244 (1963); *Griffin* v. *Prince Edward County School Board*, 377 U.S. 218 (1964); *Green* v. *School Board of New Kent County*, 391 U.S. 430 (1968); *Alexander* v. *Holmes County, Miss., Board of Education*, 396 U.S. 19 (1969); *Norwood* v. *Harrison*, 413 U.S. 455 (1973); *Keyes* v. *School District #1, Denver, Colorado*, 413 U.S. 189 (1973).

Baker proved to be the vehicle that ultimately permitted judicial extensions of the reapportionment matter in *Wesberry* v. *Sanders* (applying the "one-man–one-vote" principle to *congressional* districts)[8] and, even more dramatically, in *Reynolds* v. Sims (requiring representation based on *population,* with the apportionment to reflect the principle of "approximate equality" for *both* houses of state legislatures).[9] This principle was extended to the county and city levels in subsequent decisions, ultimately to embrace all *elected* bodies exercising *general* governmental powers.[10]

It is probably regrettable that the desegregation and redistricting issues were not resolved by the executive or legislative branches of the government, especially by the latter; but these two political bodies had either purposely failed to act, were unable or unauthorized to act, or for a variety of reasons had been unsuccessful in acting. The responsibility fell to the judiciary of the United States, with the Supreme Court at its zenith—that institution which, in the words of Chief Justice Earl Warren, "must always stand ready to advance the rights of. . .minorities, if the executive and legislative branches falter."[11] And falter they have on sundry occasions.

Let us now briefly examine the structure and operation of the judiciary in the United States, with particular emphasis on the federal bench.

The Dual System of Courts in the United States

Because we are governed by a *federal* system in the United States, the fifty state governments, as well as the national government, make and enforce law. Consequently, there exist, side by side, either two separate systems of courts or fifty-one, depending upon one's view of how separate and distinct the several state systems are. For present pur-

---

[8]376 U.S. 1 (1964).

[9]377 U.S. 533 (1964).

[10]E.g., *Avery* v. *Midland County,* 390 U.S. 474 (1968) and *Hadley* v. *Junior College District of Metropolitan Kansas City,* 397 U.S. 50 (1970). But elected *judicial* bodies were exempt (*Wells* v. *Edwards,* 409 U.S. 1095, 1973) and so were certain but not all special-purpose governmental bodies, such as some school boards; e.g., *Rosenthal* v. *Board of Education of Central High School,* 420 U.S. 985 (1975) and *Ball* v. *James,* 451 U.S. 355 (1981).

[11]As quoted in *The Philadelphia Inquirer,* October 4, 1968, p. 1.

poses, however, we will adopt the concept of two distinct judicial systems that are created by the two basic authorities under our federal structure, the national and state constitutions. Although these two systems may, and often do, come together at the bar of the final interpretative authority of the federal Supreme Court, they are nonetheless wholly distinct bodies, each applying its own basic constitution and laws and actions based thereon.

Legal procedures vary not only between civil and criminal cases, but also among the various jurisdictions. Generally, however, the following represent typical procedural steps:

Civil Cases	*Criminal Cases*
1. Plaintiff brings suit against defendant	1. Apprehension by agents of government
2. Summons	2. Preliminary examination
3. Pleadings	3. Grand Jury or "Information"
4. Trial	4. Arraignment and pleading
5. Verdict	5. Trial
6. Judgment and sentencing	6. Verdict
7. Appeal	7. Judgment and sentencing
8. Enforcement	8. Appeal
	9. Execution of sentence

When the two judicial systems do "converge" at the level of the United States Supreme Court, they do so only because litigants have been able to raise a substantial federal question in the state courts. (The Supreme Court itself determines what is "substantial.") Moreover, litigants must have exhausted all proper remedies at the state level in order to have proper "standing" before the Supreme Court. In all but a handful of cases, the Supreme Court has complete discretionary authority to accept or reject a petition for review. With the exception of this appellate pathway to the Court, and the technical and confusing matters of injunctive relief and habeas corpus proceedings, the two systems constitute separate entities that must, and almost invariably do, respect each other's jurisdictional lines. These lines may be, but only infrequently are, reinforced by Congress in accordance with its constitutionally granted power to establish "inferior courts," that is, lower federal courts.[12]

THE STATE JUDICIARY

Each and every state constitution either establishes a judicial branch, wholly or partly, or it authorizes its legislature to provide one. However, so much variation in nomenclature as well as structure exists among the judicial systems of the fifty states that it is necessary to create a composite that will give a picture of a typical state system. The well-structured, unified court system of Florida or the simple four-tiered one of Virginia might well serve as a commendable "model" state court system. In practice, however, there are more subdivisions.

The Justice of the Peace

The subdivision at the bottom of the typical state judicial hierarchy is the legendary *J.P.*, the *justice of the peace*, also known as *magistrate* or *squire*. Although usually elected, he or she may be appointed, and generally serves for a term of two to six years in a jurisdiction, normally a county, city, township, or town. He or she is a judicial "jack-of-all-trades" who handles a host of minor civil matters and criminal misdemeanors. Since much, if not all, of the J.P.'s income more often than not depends upon the fees received for his or her labors, the average justice of the peace, who is not necessarily always trained in the law, has demonstrated a remarkable tendency toward convictions. For example, Pennsylvania convictions in 1968 averaged 93 percent in civil and 83 percent in criminal cases—by no means atypical percentages for these courts.[13] There are indications that genuine concern exists with the current status of this minor court;[14] reforms have been effected in a number of states, but it is

---

[12]Article III, Section 1, Paragraph 1.

[13]See my *The Judicial Process: An Introductory Analysis of the Courts of the United States, England, and France*, 5th ed. (New York: Oxford University, 1986), pp. 143–145.

[14]In 1975 the Court granted review on the question of whether a non-lawyer jurist could constitutionally sit in a jail-carrying criminal case (*North* v. *Russell*, 422 U.S. 1040). It ruled "yes" some months later (6:2—provided that the defendant have an opportunity through an appeal to obtain a second trial before a judge who is a lawyer: *North* v. *Russell*, 427 U.S. 328, 1976).

doubtful that they will soon take place on a general scale. Like so many time-honored traditions, that of the J.P. has been able to survive as much because of inertia as tradition.

The Municipal Court

At the next higher subdivision in the state judiciary hierarchy is the *municipal court,* sometimes called *traffic court, court of small claims, night court,* or *police court.* Whatever it is called, the municipal court is generally a court of original, rather than appellate, jurisdiction, and is the first official state "court of record" (a term designed to identify those tribunals presided over by judges rather than magistrates). Its jurisdiction is relatively restricted, often with a ceiling of $150 (Texas) to $3,000 (Louisiana) in civil cases and minor criminal cases, but this varies from state to state, as does its basic jurisdiction. Its judges are almost always trained lawyers.

The County Court

Third in ascending order in the judicial hierarchy lies a court of fairly general jurisdiction, more often than not known as the *county court,* because its broad, original civil and criminal jurisdiction is customarily limited to one or more counties. Juries are usually present in this court. Some of the host of associated tribunals at the county court level are: *quarter sessions, common pleas, oyer and terminer, orphans, probate, domestic relations, juvenile, equity, surrogate,* and *chancery.* All these courts at the county level have original jurisdiction in the various areas roughly indicated by their names.[15]

The Intermediate Court of Appeals

Although in many states appeals from the county court go directly to the state supreme court, the pressure of work at the latter tribunal's level has often necessitated the creation of an intermediate court of appeals. That court may also be known as the *appellate division* (such as in New York) or the *superior court* (such as in Pennsylvania). Very much in the fashion of the United States Court of Appeals, it is the

---

[15]Oyer and Terminer is a criminal court with jurisdiction over capital crimes and other felonies; Quarter Sessions is a court that meets four times a year for criminal cases below the felony level; Chancery specializes in equity matters; and Surrogate is a court similar to Probate, which adjudicates matters involving wills, deeds, and estates.

first, and usually final, stop for appeals that come up from the courts below in accordance with statutory requirements. In the larger states, such as New York, Pennsylvania, and California, it performs a valuable job of disposing of appeals with considerable dispatch.[16]

The Final Court of Appeals

In almost all states the highest court in the judicial hierarchy is known as the *supreme court.* In New York and Maryland, however, it is called the *court of appeals;* in Maine and Massachusetts it is known as the *supreme judicial court,* and in West Virginia as the *supreme court of appeals.* Whatever its name, its decisions constitute the law of the state and are thus final and binding on the hierarchy below, which, as already described, is comprised of local as well as statewide tribunals. Only if all these remedies have been exhausted, and if a *substantial federal* question is present, do litigants have an opportunity to apply for, but not to count upon, review by the highest court of the land. The pathway of appeals from the state courts to the federal courts omits any way station in the lower federal hierarchy (except in a very few complicated jurisdictional situations that need not concern us here). *If* the United States Supreme Court is willing to hear a case, or, in those very rare instances, when it must, that case will move directly to it from the highest state court—all remedies below having been duly exhausted.

THE FEDERAL JUDICIARY

Two Types. There are two types of federal courts, the *constitutional* courts and the *legislative* courts. Our chief concern is with the former, and particularly with the three original[17] constitutional courts, the *United States district courts,* the *United States courts of appeals,* and the *United States supreme court.*

The distinction between the two types of federal courts is in their functions as well as in the constitutional authority under which they were or are created. Broadly speaking, the constitutional courts are established under the judiciary article of the United States Constitu-

---

[16]Some states use certain specialty courts that function separately from the regular judicial hierarchy, e.g., Pennsylvania's *Commonwealth Court.* Created in 1970, its sole function is to hear cases relating to the tasks of government agencies.

[17]The Supreme Court is stipulated specifically in Article III of the U.S. Constitution. The other two courts were established by the Judiciary Act of 1789.

tion, Article III; the legislative courts, on the other hand, owe their existence to Article I, the legislative article of the Constitution. What, then, are the several significant differences between these two types of tribunals?

Distinctions. One key difference is that the legislative courts possess certain functions of a non-judicial or at least quasi-judicial nature, such as administrative and quasi-legislative as well as judicial tasks, whereas the constitutional courts are presumably confined to strictly judicial roles. A second is that although the legislative courts are part and parcel of the constitutional appellate structure for certain specific purposes, their *raison d'être* is to aid in the administration of particular congressional statutes.

A third difference between the two types of courts is that unlike the constitutional courts, the legislative tribunals are empowered to render *advisory opinions*, that is, rulings upon the propriety or constitutionality of governmental action in the absence of a bona fide case or controversy requiring *such* a ruling for a case's disposition. In effect, this function was established as early as 1793, when President George Washington addressed a letter to the members of the Supreme Court asking them for an opinion on the authority given to him by the Constitution to decide certain questions involving the United States's policy of neutrality in the war then in progress in Europe. Chief Justice John Jay, the Court's first and rather reluctant head, responded for his Court that not only would it not, *it could not,* tender legal *advice,* and that its role was confined to the decision of cases that arose in the course of bona fida litigation. However, both types of courts (and the constitutional courts only since 1934) are statutorily empowered to render so-called *declaratory judgments.* Declaratory judgments differ from advisory opinions in that there exists an actual controversy; an advisory opinion deals with an abstract or hypothetical question. A declaratory judgment enables courts of all types to enter a final judgment between litigants in an *actual controversy,* and defines their respective rights under a law, contract, will, or any other official document, *without,* however, attaching any consequential or coercive relief to that otherwise binding judgment.[18]

---

[18]For examples of declaratory judgment action by constitutional courts, see *Nashville, Chicago & St. Louis Railway* v. *Wallace*, 288 U.S. 249 (1933); *Tileston* v. *Ullman*, 318 U.S. 44 (1943); *Steffel* v. *Thompson*, 415 U.S. 452 (1974); and *Roe* v. *Wade*, 410 U.S. 113 (1973).

A fourth, and theoretically the most crucial, difference between constitutional and legislative courts relates to the constitutionally expressed safeguards of tenure, salary, and—by implication and effect—independence that accrue to the constitutional courts by virtue of the provisions of Article III, Section I, of the Constitution, which reads:

> *The judges, both of the Supreme and inferior courts, shall hold their offices during good behavior, and shall, at stated times, receive for their services, a compensation, which shall not be diminished during their continuance in office.*

No such safeguards exist for the courts created under the legislative article of the Constitution, which simply says in Article I, Section 8, Clause 9, that Congress shall have power "To constitute tribunals inferior to the Supreme Court." Judges of the constitutional courts, then, are removable only when they no longer "behave well," which, in effect, clothes them with life tenure. Removal, other than by death, resignation, or retirement, can thus come about solely via the impeachment and conviction process, an unlikely but certainly not unheard-of or unresorted-to procedure. To date, as a result of bills of impeachment duly voted by the House of Representatives and sent on to the Senate for trial, nine impeachment trials have been held involving federal judges. Seven of these were against judges on the United States District Court, one against a judge on the now-defunct United States Commerce Court (a legislative court), and one, in 1804–1805, against an associate justice of the Supreme Court of the United States, Justice Samuel Chase. Of these, five resulted in acquittals, four in convictions, probably only two of which were justified legally.[19] If Congress chooses to do so, as indeed it has frequently seen fit, it may extend "good behavior" tenure to legislative court judges as well, but it is under no constitutional obligation to do so.

This congressional discretionary authority also applies in the case of the constitutional injunction against reduction of judicial salaries while in office (Article III, Sec. 1), but Congress would hardly be

---

[19]For a fuller description and discussion, see my *The Judicial Process*, pp. 44–50. To convict, a two-thirds majority of the members of the Senate present and voting (there being a quorum on the floor) must find the accused guilty on at least one count of the offense(s) charged. But only a majority of members of the House is needed to vote a bill of impeachment for subsequent Senate trial.

likely to reduce these in any case.[20] Although not by any means minuscule, the mid-1986 salaries of federal judges (tied to the cost-of-living index as of 1975, but limited to an annual increment of 4.8 to 8.6 percent) were not necessarily higher than those of some state judges (e.g., highest court jurists were paid $92,500). They ranged from $78,700 for judges of the United States District Court to $108,400 for the Chief Justice of the United States. His associates on the Supreme Court received $4,300 less.

In view of the constitutional prohibition against "diminishing compensation" during their term in office, an intriguing problem by implication soon faced the justices of the highest constitutional court in the land in connection with the matter of intergovernmental tax immunity, that is, the problem of clarifying the extent of implied restrictions upon the taxing power which derive from the nature of our federal system of government. In other words, did the Constitution place limitations upon the power of the two prongs of the federal system, the national (federal) government and the several states, to tax each other's instrumentalities, property, and activities? This is not the place to go into the details of this complicated problem, but as the immunity doctrine began to develop (its initial and great pronunciamento came in Chief Justice Marshall's decision in the monumental case of *McCulloch* v. *Maryland*[21]), it became quite clear that the jurists would not only *not* view with favor the taxation of federal officials by the states, nor that of state officials by the federal government,[22] but not even that by the federal government of *its own* officials! This immunity doctrine was continued, and even enlarged, until the 1930s. But by then the long and strong protests by Justice Oliver Wendell Holmes, Jr., and Justice Louis D. Brandeis—who had *volun-*

---

[20]An intriguing development in this connection was the partly successful suit by 140 federal district and appellate judges in 1976 and 1978, which charged that due to inflation their constitutional safeguard against salary reduction during tenure had been violated. The appeal was initially rejected by the United States Court of Claims in 1976 (*Atkins* v. *United States*, 556 F.2d 1028) and by the Supreme Court in 1977 (Ibid., 429 U.S. 939). However, the 1978 suit was adjudicated by the Supreme Court in December 1980, which provided a partial victory: The 1977 and 1980 increases, ruled the highest tribunal, 8:0, could stand because the statutes involved *had already taken effect;* but those merely *promised* in 1978 and 1979 could not because Congress had properly acted to cancel them ere they had taken effect (*United States* v. *Will*, 449 U.S. 200).

[21]4 Wheaton 315 (1819).

[22]*The Collector* v. *Day*, 11 Wallace 113 (1871).

tarily paid to the federal government what they would have to pay had their salaries been considered taxable, and who were later joined by Justice Harlan F. Stone—coupled with new congressional legislation and new personnel on the Court, brought about the cessation of intergovernmental tax immunity for the salaries of both federal and state employees.[23]

FEDERAL LEGISLATIVE COURTS

As indicated earlier, all of these courts are created under the legislative article of the Constitution, which expressly extends that enabling power to Congress (Article I, Section 8, Clause 9). Utilizing that power, Congress has thus seen fit from time to time to establish sundry legislative courts. These were created partly to have "more flexible" tribunals than the three major constitutional courts (the United States Supreme Court, the Courts of Appeals, and the District Courts); partly to remove some of the crushing workload of cases from the latter tribunals; and partly as a result of technical needs in particular areas of public life—the rationale for the *United States Court of Military Appeals*, for example. What Congress does, then, is to combine this basic legislative power to establish tribunals inferior to the Supreme Court with the famous "implied powers" or "elastic clause" (I–8–18) of the Constitution *and* the specific congressional authority in which it may establish the legislative court. For example, in the case of the Court of Military Appeals, Congress could have used any one of the half-dozen of its overall war powers (I–8–11 through 16), but it chose to rely predominantly upon its power "To make rules for the government and regulation of the land and naval forces" (I–8–14). Congress employed its power "To regulate commerce with foreign nations, and among the several States, and with the Indian tribes" (I–8–3) to create the now-defunct *United States Commerce Court;* the taxing power (I–8–1) for the *United States Customs Court* (since 1980 known as the *Court of International Trade*), the status of which it changed in 1956 to that of a constitutional court, and for the *United States Tax Court*, which it transformed from an administrative agency under the Internal Revenue Service to a legislative court in 1969; and its special power over territories and other property belonging to the United

---

[23]See *Helvering* v. *Gerhardt*, 304 U.S. 405 (1938) and *Graves* v. *New York* ex rel *O'Keefe*, 306 U.S. 466 (1939).

States (IV–3–2) to establish the various territorial courts.[24] The newly-established (1982) *United States Claims Court* (see fn. 24, below) is the latest illustration of a legislative tribunal.

FEDERAL CONSTITUTIONAL COURTS

The three most important, and presumably best-known, federal courts are the three original *constitutional* courts, the United States District Courts, the United States Courts of Appeals, and the United States Supreme Court. Created under Article III of the Constitution (the Supreme Court is the only one expressly mentioned in the basic document), the three remained the only constitutional courts in the American judicial hierarchy until the "transformation" of the three erstwhile legislative courts.[25] The federal constitutional courts remain *the* basic courts in our system, and they adjudicate by far the major proportion of cases arising under the Constitution. The Supreme Court was established by Article III of the Constitution; it remained

---

[24]As will have become apparent, the number of legislative courts has declined with the passing of the years: some have been discontinued (the Commerce Court in 1915); some have been transformed into United States district courts on attaining statehood (Alaska and Hawaii in 1958 and 1959, respectively); others were transformed—sometimes temporarily—into constitutional courts (in addition to the already mentioned Customs Court, the *United States Court of Claims* and the *United States Court of Customs and Patent Appeals*, in 1953 and 1958, respectively). (Note also the special *Foreign Intelligence Surveillance Court*, created in 1978.) But under a 1982 reorganization the Court of Claims *trial* functions were placed into a new *United States Claims Court* of 16 members. Its *appellate* jurisdiction was transferred to the new *United States Court of Appeals for the Federal Circuit* of 12 members. The former was constituted as a legislative court, the latter as a constitutional one. A point of additional interest here is that in 1933 the Supreme Court ruled that the United States District Court for the District of Columbia *and* the United States Court of Appeals for that district are to be regarded "at the same time" constitutional *and* legislative courts (*O'Donoghue* v. *United States*, 289 U.S. 516)—but our analysis will, for the sake of order and clarity, treat them as components of the constitutional hierarchy. In effect, the *territorial courts* might also be regarded as a combination of the two types of courts; but they are commonly viewed as legislative courts because of their diversified yet specific jurisdiction. They were created for, and are located in, such diverse areas as Guam (1900), Puerto Rico (1900), the Virgin Islands (1917), and the Mariana Islands (1978). For additional data on legislative courts see my *The Judicial Process*, pp. 149–155.

[25]See pp. 11–12 and fn. 24.

for Congress to create the balance of the basic hierarchy under powers given to it by Article I. It did this in one of the first pieces of legislation of the First Congress, the Judiciary Act of 1789. It was passed under the leadership of Senator Oliver Ellsworth, who had been a delegate from Connecticut to the Constitutional Convention, and who was destined to succeed Chief Justice Jay as the second Chief Justice of the United States.

Overall Jurisdiction

It is a tribute to the succinctness and comprehensiveness of the Constitution in general, and Article III in particular, that the general jurisdiction of the federal judiciary is spelled out in considerable detail in direct and understandable language. Its second section makes clear that the judicial power of the United States ". . .shall extend to *all Cases* [italics mine], in Law,[26] and Equity,[27] arising under this Constitution, the Laws of the United States, and Treaties made, or which shall be made under their Authority. . . ." The italicized portion emphasizes one of the most significant aspects of the judicial process—already mentioned in connection with the discussion of advisory opinions[28]—namely, that federal constitutional court jurisdiction is limited to bona fide cases and controversies. In brief, this requirement signifies that there be a genuine case or controversy involving two or more litigants on opposite sides of a genuine legal issue characterized by a true clash of interests. In the absence of these fundamental requirements, there can be no resort to the federal constitutional courts. With its decision in *Hayburn's Case*[29] in 1792, the Supreme Court wasted little time in officially apprising the fledgling Republic and its citizenry of this significant judicial fact of life—one that applies to all claimants. In *Hayburn*, the Court held unanimously that it could not legally carry out a congressional statute that it deemed not

---

[26]*Law*—broadly speaking—represents the rules of conduct that pertain to a given political order of society, rules that are backed by the organized force of the community. As it has evolved through the centuries, law has been made either by the political representatives of the people or by jurists. The former type of law is generally known as *statutory law*, the latter as *common law*. The crucial distinction between them is that between codified, written (*statutory*) law and unwritten (*common*) law based on custom and tradition.

[27]*Equity* is a supplement to the common law. It begins where the law ends, taking the form of a judicial decree (not a judgment of "yes" or "no").

[28]See p. 8 of this text.

[29]2 Dallas 409. See the opinions of Associate Justices John Blair and James Wilson.

"judicial in nature," although the justices did readily explain to a displeased Congress how its intent could be effectuated: by having President Washington's cabinet, rather than the judiciary, pass on disputed pension claims of invalid war veterans.

Having spelled out the basic jurisdictional case or controversy requirement, the judiciary article then explains the various kinds of jurisdiction available to the courts. Broadly speaking, these may be grouped under two major headings: one, according to the nature or character of the *subject matter* of the case; the other, according to the nature or character of the *parties* to the suit. Under the first category, the courts are empowered to adjudicate cases and controversies in law and equity arising under (1) the Constitution, a federal law, or a treaty; or (2) admiralty and maritime laws. Under the second category, a considerably larger and more complex one, the courts may adjudicate cases and controversies in law and equity if: (1) the United States is party to the suit; (2) one of the fifty states is a party to the suit (unless, in accordance with the injunctions of the Eleventh Amendment, the suit was commenced or prosecuted *against* a state by *any* individual or even a foreign country); (3) the cases are between citizens of *different* states (known as "diversity of citizenship" cases); (4) they affect *foreign* ambassadors and other duly accredited representatives of a foreign land; and (5) they arise between citizens of the *same* state because of a dispute involving land grants claimed under title of two or more states.

These seven grants or mandates of power do not necessarily signify their execution exclusively by the federal constitutional courts. Congress has implied authority to delegate or assign certain aspects of them to the several states of the Union, either on a *concurrent* or even an *exclusive* basis. An example of this is the congressional requirement that a civil diversity of citizenship suit—a suit between two or more citizens of different states—must encompass at least $10,000 in value in order to qualify for original federal constitutional court jurisdiction. If it falls below that figure, it must go to the state tribunals. Even when it *does* meet the stated amount, Congress has seen fit to permit *concurrent* state and federal jurisdiction at the parties' discretion. This does not, however, remove the superior claim to federal jurisdiction should the parties disagree.

Also, Congress has deemed it advisable to distribute areas of federal jurisdiction among the several courts, a commendably orderly arrangement that began with the creation of the judicial system itself in the Judiciary Act of 1789. Almost all federal cases of original jurisdiction (other than those involving two or more states as litigants, where the Supreme Court retains *original* jurisdiction) are assigned to the United States District Courts, whereas *appellate* jurisdiction from practically all district court adjudications lies with the United States Courts of Appeals. Moreover, there are certain areas where the sovereignty of the federal and state systems overlaps. In more areas, such as in cases dealing with theft involving flight in interstate commerce or in cases concerning embezzlement or robbery of federally insured banks, *both* federal and state jurisdiction may exist. As of mid-1986, the United States Supreme Court had resolutely declined to view the inherent possibilities of prosecution and punishment by *both* federal and state governments as constituting a violation of the "double jeopardy" safeguards of the Fifth Amendment or those of "due process of law" under the Fourteenth, regardless of which sovereignty might have commenced the action, and regardless of whether the case resulted in an initial acquittal.[30] But, by and large, the federal government makes it a practice not to try a case where there has already been a state prosecution for "substantially the same act or acts"—a policy that was judicially confirmed by the Court in a *per curiam* 6:3 decision in 1977 that may contain the seeds for a possible reversal of its erstwhile federalist stance on the issue.[31] (Table 1–1 outlines the jurisdiction of the three federal constitutional courts under discussion.)

United States District Courts. The ninety-four United States district courts, staffed by about 576 judges (1985), are the basic trial courts of the federal judiciary. In that role they are the busiest of the three court levels. From some points of view the work of a trial court is both more interesting and more creative than that in the two appellate tiers. The battle of opposing platoons of counsel—unfortunately and frequently viewed as a legal game by some practitioners as well as laypersons—takes place here. And it is here that we find the trial jury, that intriguing, albeit controversial, institution of citizen participation in the judicial process. Thus it is not surprising that some district judges, for example, U.S. District Court Judge Charles E. Wyzanski, Jr., have refused the honor of promotion to one of the two higher levels of the federal judiciary in favor of continued presence at the

---

[30]*Bartkus* v. *Illinois*, 359 U.S. 121 (1959) and *Abbate* v. *United States*, 359 U.S. 187 (1979). But *cf. Rinaldi* v. *United States*, 434 U.S. 22 (1977).

[31]*Rinaldi* v. *United States, loc. cit.* The issue reached the Court again in 1986.

TABLE 1–1 The Jurisdiction of the Three Major Federal Constitutional Courts of the United States (Courts Created under Article III of the Constitution)

Supreme Court of the United States, 9 judges, has:

Original jurisdiction in actions or controversies:

*1. Between the United States and a state.
  2. Between two or more states.
*3. Involving foreign ambassadors, other foreign public ministers, and foreign consuls or their "domestics or domestic servants, not inconsistent with the law of nations."
*4. *Commenced by a state against* citizens of another state or against aliens, *or against* a foreign country. (Note: if these actions are *commenced by the citizen or alien against a state,* or by a foreign country *against* a state, the suit must *begin in state court,* according to the provisions of Amendment Eleven.)

Appellate jurisdiction from:

  1. All lower federal *constitutional* courts; most, but not all, federal *legislative* courts; and the *territorial* courts.
  2. The highest state courts when a "substantial federal question" is involved.

Thirteen *United States (Circuit) Courts of Appeals,*[32] 168 judges (not counting "senior," i.e., retired) have:

Appellate jurisdiction *only* from:

  1. U.S. district courts.
  2. U.S. territorial courts, the U.S. Tax Court, the U.S. Claims Court, and some District of Columbia courts.
  3. The U.S. Court of International Trade.
  4. The U.S. Independent Regulatory Commissions.
  5. Certain federal administrative agencies and departments (for review, but also for *enforcement* of certain of their actions and orders).

Ninety-four *United States District Courts,* approximately 576 judges (not counting "senior" i.e., retired) have:

---

[32]The huge Fifth Circuit (Deep South) was halved in late 1980, thereby increasing from 11 to 12 the number of United States Courts of Appeals. October 1982 saw the creation of a 13th, the U.S. Court of Appeals for the Federal Circuit, which merged the appellate jurisdiction of the U.S. Court of Claims and the U.S. Court of Customs and Patent Appeals and granted additional jurisdiction when the United States is a defendant.

Original jurisdiction *only*† over:

1. All crimes against the United States.
2. All civil actions arising under the Constitution, laws, or treaties of the United States, wherein the matter in controversy exceeds $10,000 (unless the U.S. Supreme Court has jurisdiction as outlined above).
*3. Cases involving citizens of different states or citizens and aliens, provided the value of the controversy is in excess of $10,000.
4. Admiralty, maritime, and prize cases.
*5. Review and *enforcement* of orders and actions of certain federal administrative agencies and departments.
6. All such other cases as Congress may validly prescribe by law.††

Jurisdiction not exclusive—that is, while cases, according to Article III of the Constitution, are to originate here, legal arrangements may be made to have them handled by a different level court. For example, Congress has the power to give the federal district courts *concurrent original jurisdiction* over cases affecting foreign ambassadors and *some* cases in which a state is a party to the suit. See *United States* v. *Ravara,* 2 Dallas 297 (1793); *Bors* v. *Preston,* 111 U.S. 252 (1884); and *Ames* v. *Kansas,* 111 U.S. 449 (1884). And in 1964, the Supreme Court declined to review a Ninth Circuit Court decision that federal district courts have jurisdiction over suits *by the United States against a state.* (*California* v. *United States,* 379 U.S. 817.)

†A case can be made for the contention that these courts also have a measure of *appellate* jurisdiction, involving certain actions tried before U.S. Commissioners (one of whom is authorized for each federal district).

††As Congress did in 1984, for example, when it restructured the bankruptcy courts. Among the changes was the assignment of jurisdiction over Title II of the U.S. Code to the U.S. District Courts. (The 232 bankruptcy judges are distributed over the 94 district courts; they are *not* included in the above total number of judges.)

combatants' level. In recent years some 600,000 civil, criminal, and bankruptcy cases have been decided annually by the district courts.[33] No wonder that delays averaging from four to fifty months (1986) have plagued courts and litigants at this level, where almost all federal civil and criminal cases necessarily commence.

---

[33]In 1980 they received 168,789 civil, 28,921 criminal, and 360,960 bankruptcy cases—which are handled at the district court level by the 232 bankruptcy judges—for a total of 558,670. (Bankruptcy actions are routine, however, the judge normally accepts the findings of special "referees.") See *Annual Report(s) of the Administrative Office of the United States Courts.* The number of *civil* lawsuits filed annually in the federal courts increased from 59,284 in 1960 to 168,789 in 1980.

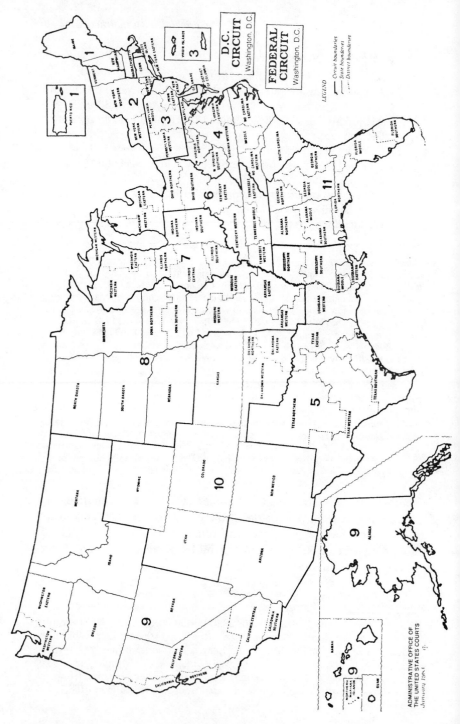

D.C. CIRCUIT
Washington, D.C.

FEDERAL CIRCUIT
Washington, D.C.

1

3
VIRGIN ISLANDS

1
PUERTO RICO

2

3

4

11

6

7

8

5

10

9

9
ALASKA

9
HAWAII

9
NORTHERN MARIANA ISLANDS

GUAM

ADMINISTRATIVE OFFICE OF
THE UNITED STATES COURTS
January 1983

18

It is also at the district level that the federal government brings suit to prosecute violations of federal laws. Typical examples of this would be tampering with the United States mail, contempt of Congress, and conspiracy to violate the Internal Revenue Code. United States district courts function in one or more delineated districts in each of the fifty states, the District of Columbia, Guam, Puerto Rico, the Virgin Islands, and the Mariana Islands, and have one or more judges. New York State, for example, has four districts (Western, Northern, Southern, and Eastern). The Southern District, encompassing Manhattan, the Bronx, and adjacent counties to the north, had the largest number of judges (twenty-seven) in a single district in 1986. Wyoming, on the other hand, had just two judges for its single district. (Figure 1–1 shows the various locations of the district courts and of the twelve geographically designated of the thirteen courts of appeals.)

United States Courts of Appeals. The thirteen United States courts of appeals are essentially *appellate* courts; they stand directly above the United States district courts in the federal constitutional judicial hierarchy. (They are also referred to as "circuit courts"—a vestige of the days when individual justices, including those of the Supreme Court, would literally "ride circuit" in pursuit of their judicial tasks, and as a reference to the thirteen judicial "circuits" into which the United States is divided for purposes of these tribunals.) As Table 1–1 indicates, the circuit courts also have certain statutory authority regarding review and enforcement of numerous federal administrative agencies. Appeals from the highest state courts bypass both district and circuit courts, assuming that appellants have properly exhausted all remedies at the state level below, and go directly to the United States Supreme Court, which has all but complete discretion

---

← **FIGURE 1–1** The United States Courts of Appeals and the United States District Courts (opposite)

Large numerals indicate various Courts of Appeals; heavy lines represent the jurisdictional boundaries of each circuit; broken lines represent jurisdictional boundaries of district courts in states having more than one district.

*D.C. indicates the "twelfth" circuit court, situated in the District of Columbia and titled "United States Circuit Court for the District of Columbia." A thirteenth circuit court, the "United States Court of Appeals for the Federal Circuit," was established as of October 1, 1982. It has no geographical area designation such as the other twelve do. See fn. 32. *Note:* In 1978 Congress added the Northern Mariana Islands as the 95th U.S. District Court, but it dropped the Canal Zone in 1982.

Source: Administrative Office of the United States Courts (1983).

to accept or reject a petition for review. There are also some instances in which it is possible to bypass the level of the court of appeals and go directly to the Supreme Court from a distrct court.[34]

Nonetheless, the usual appellate path of the judicial process begins in the courts of appeals. About 7,000 cases annually reach that level from the several district courts and other subordinate tribunals. A well-known example is the famous case of *Dennis* v. *United States*,[35] in which Eugene Dennis and his ten fellow leaders of the United States Communist Party appealed their lower-court convictions to the Court of Appeals for the Second Circuit. Unsuccessful in their appeal there, the eleven then appealed to the last tribunal, the United States Supreme Court, which sustained their conviction by a 6:2 vote.[36]

The thirteen circuits illustrated in Figure 1–1 (there were nine when the courts of appeals were established in 1891) together with the districts that lie in each circuit, have a total of 168 judges (1986). Sitting *en banc*, customarily groups of three judges hear cases, although there may be as many as fifteen judges. There is a chief judge for each Court of Appeals. Like the district court judges below but unlike the Supreme Court justices above, he or she may not become chief judge if over the age of sixty-four and must relinquish that chief judgeship upon having served seven years, while permitted to remain as an otherwise full-fledged member of the tribunal. Each of the thirteen circuits is theoretically "headed" by a justice of the United States Supreme Court, a throwback to the original days of "circuit riding"; the junior members in service of the Court are usually, although not always, assigned the four "extra" circuits. The role of the Supreme Court justices assigned to the various circuits is today little more than a token in view of the demands of time, but it does become a real one in instances such as petitions for extraordinary procedures in appeals

---

[34]Three, to be exact: (1) in decisions by special three-judge United States district courts, which are convened in certain statutorily provided cases, frequently involving questions of unconstitutionality; (2) where a direct appeal is statutorily authorized to the Supreme Court from a limited number of ordinary district court cases; and (3) upon a showing that a case is "of such imperative public importance...as to require immediate settlement"—e.g., the 1952 steel seizure case (*Youngstown Sheet and Tube Co.* v. *Sawyer*, 343 U.S. 579); the *Amchitka* nuclear test case of 1971 (*Committee for Nuclear Responsibility* v. *Schlesinger*, 404 U.S. 917); and the dramatic 1974 Nixon tapes case (*United States* v. *Nixon*, 417 U.S. 683). Congress has debated reducing that access.

[35]183 F. 2d (1950).

[36]341 U.S. 494 (1951).

and pleas for stays of execution. Thus Justice Charles Evans Whittaker was involved in the procedural "speed-up" in the *Little Rock Case*,[37] Justice William O. Douglas in the delays in the case of the convicted spies, Ethel and Julius Rosenberg, and again Justice Douglas as well as Justice Thurgood Marshall in the Cambodia bombing controversy.[38]

In the normal course of events, appeals from the United States district courts are duly heard and adjudicated finally at the bar of the circuit courts of appeals. Here no new *factual* evidence may be presented, as the record in the courts below constitute the basis for judgment. In some instances, of course, it is possible to appeal cases from these lower federal tribunals to the ultimate appellate tribunal, the United States Supreme Court.

The Supreme Court of the United States

There is no gainsaying the importance and the majesty of this most powerful of courts, not only in the United States, but in the entire free world. In the United States there is no appeal from the Supreme Court's "No," other than an appeal to the public and/or its representatives in Congress. Congress has the power and ability, within the limits of the Constitution and the realities of the political process, to reverse the Court by remedial legislation[39] or, joining with the states, by constitutional amendment.[40] But these are difficult and uncertain pathways, at least in the *short* run. In the *long* run, however, change is not only possible, but may well get a hand from the Court itself. Moreover, as a great student of the Constitution, Edward S. Corwin, was fond of putting it: "[T]he run must not be too long a run either!"[41]

---

[37]*Cooper* v. *Aaron*, 358 U.S. 1 (1958).

[38]*Rosenberg* v. *United States*, 346 U.S. 273 (1953) and *Holtzman* v. *Schlesinger*, 414 U.S. 1304 (1973).

[39]E.g., certain provisions of the Omnibus Crime Control and Safe Streets Act of 1968 and the Organized Crime Control Act of 1970.

[40]E.g., the enactment of the Twenty-sixth Amendment, ratified in record time in 1971, which enfranchised eighteen-year-olds at the *state* level—after the Court had struck down that portion of the Voting Rights Act of 1970 (*Oregon* v. *Mitchell*, 400 U.S. 112). (The Court, in that same opinion, had upheld their enfranchisement at the *federal* level.)

[41]*Court Over Constitution* (Princeton, N.J.: Princeton University Press, 1938), p. 127.

In the long run, the Supreme Court of the United States is "the child of its time." It does, indeed, possess considerable educational power but, as Alexis de Tocqueville observed five generations ago, ultimately "it is the power of public opinion." Decisions running counter to the broad consensus simply do not last in the *long* run. Still, the Court must be, and often has been, the leader of public opinion, not merely its register—as was true, in considerable degree, of the Warren Court. Finally, as Justice Robert H. Jackson observed so well in 1955, "The people have seemed to feel that the Supreme Court, whatever its defects, is still the most detached, dispassionate, and trustworthy custodian that our system affords for the translation of abstract into constitutional commands."[42] And so, in the final analysis, as they did so notably in *United States* v. *Nixon* in the troubled days of 1974,[43] the people ultimately turn to it for constitutional resolution and sustenance.

The public looks to the Court to be its guide, no matter how major or minor the constitutional or statutory issue involved. Thus there appeared in a prominent spot in *The New York Times* in the summer of 1959 the following breathless advertisement:

> *Starts Friday at the Little Carnegie*
> By Decision of
> The United States Supreme Court:
> D. H. Lawrence's
> controversial masterpiece
> *Lady Chatterley's Lover*
> The motion picture
> version of the most talked
> about book of the year.[44]

—*or*, to cite a different kind of adjudication:

> *Leo F. Koch, biology teacher at the University of Illinois, was denied today a Supreme Court hearing on his protest against dismissal for advocating [premarital] sexual intercourse among students.*[45]

---

[42]*The Supreme Court in the American System of Government* (Cambridge: Harvard University Press, 1955), p. 23.

[43]417 U.S. 683.

[44]*The New York Times*, July 5, 1959, referring to the decision in *Kingsley Corporation* v. *Regents of the University of New York*, 360 U.S. 684 (1959).

[45]*The New York Times*, January 14, 1964, *Koch* v. *Board of Trustees of the University of Illinois*, 375 U.S. 989 (1964).

—*or*, to point to a delicate problem of societal morals:

> *The principle that sustains compulsory vaccination is broad enough to cover cutting Fallopian tubes.... Three generations of imbeciles are enough.*[46]

—*or*, to adjudicate the most pressing social issue of our time:

> *We conclude that in the field of public education the doctrine of "separate but equal" has no place. Separate educational facilities are inherently unequal.*[47]

—*or*, to embark upon the most sensitive of matters of conscience:

> *It is neither sacrilegious nor antireligious to say that each separate government in this country should stay out of the business of writing or sanctioning official prayers and leave that purely religious function to the people themselves and to those the people choose to look to for religious guidance.*[48]

—*or*, this front-page headline appearing in newspapers all over the land on January 16, 1968:

> *Supreme Court Authorizes Pennsylvania and New York Central Railroads to Carry out Merger.*[49]

—*or*, the upholding of the publication of the 7,000-page series of secret government documents dealing with the origins of the United States involvement in the Indochina war, evoking this 1971 front-page headline:

> *Supreme Court, 6–3, Upholds Newspapers on Publication of the Pentagon Report; Times Resumes Its Series, Halted 15 Days.*[50]

---

[46]Justice Holmes, delivering the majority opinion in *Buck* v. *Bell*, 247 U.S. 200 (1927).

[47]Chief Justice Earl Warren, for the unanimous Court in *Brown* v. *Board of Education of Topeka, Kansas*, 347 U.S. 483 (1954).

[48]Justice Black, delivering the majority opinion in *Engel* v. *Vitale*, 370 U.S. 421 (1962).

[49]E.g., *The Philadelphia Inquirer* and *The New York Times*, referring to the *Penn-Central Merger* and *N & W Inclusion* cases, decided on January 15, 1968.

[50]*The New York Times*, July 1, 1972, p. 1, referring to the "Pentagon Papers" cases: *The New York Times* v. *United States* and *United States* v. *The Washington Post*, 403 U.S. 713 (1971).

—*or*, the attempted identification *cum* resolution of one of the most contentious, most emotional issues of the century—abortion:

> *A state criminal abortion statute...that excepts from criminality only a* life saving *procedure on behalf of the mother, without regard to pregnancy stage and without recognition of the other interests involved, is violative of the Due Process Clause of the Fourteenth Amendment.*[51]

—*or*, the front-page *New York Times* headline, "OK" for the hotly contested right to land the supersonic *Concorde* airliner at Kennedy International Airport:

> *Supreme Court Lifts Kennedy Ban on SST; Jet Due In Tomorrow.*[52]

—*or*, *Time* magazine's comment on the startling 1980 announcement *cum* holding:

> *Court allows patenting of new manufactured forms of life, which should spawn even more laboratory activity in a field whose* [sic] *boundaries can only be imagined.*[53]

—*or*, the Court's 9–0 stamp of approval on the United States–Iranian agreement for the release of American hostages:

> *Iran Hostage-Release Bargain is Upheld by Supreme Court.*[54]

—*or*, the Court's ringing 7:2 declaration of unconstitutionality of the then fifty-year-old congressional resort to the "one-or-two-house legislative veto" over executive action:

> *Court Limits Congress's Veto: U.S. Ruling Restricts Legislative Power Over Executive.*[55]

---

[51]Justice Harry Blackmun, rendering the 7:2 majority opinion in *Roe* v. *Wade*, 410 U.S. 113 (1973).

[52]*Port Authority of New York and New Jersey* v. *British Airways Board*, 434 U.S. 899 (1977).

[53]*Diamand* v. *Chakrabarty*, 447 U.S. 303. (An excellent example of statutory construction, the vote was the closest possible, 5:4.)

[54]*Dames and Moore* v. *Regan*, 453 U.S. 654, as reported on the front page of *The Washington Post*, July 3, 1981.

[55]*Immigration and Naturalization Service* v. *Chadha*, 462 U.S. 919 (1983), June 2, 1983.

These decisions represent a tiny sample of the far-reaching decisions by the tribunal, decisions which are the law of the land and which, in the absence of proper and permissible remedial action, must be obeyed. In the admonition of Justice Felix Frankfurter:

> *Even this court has the last say only for a time. Being composed of fallible men, it may err. But revision of its errors must be by orderly process of law.*
>
> *The court may be asked to reconsider its decisions, and this has been done successfully again and again throughout our history. Or, what this court has deemed its duty to decide may be changed by legislation, as it often has been, and, on occasion, by constitutional amendment.*[56]

There is no doubt, however, that the Court has a duty to decide, a duty to pass judgment in issues that properly come before it. For, to quote again from Justice Frankfurter, "...in the end, judgment cannot be escaped—the judgment of this court."[57] It is simply a fact of life that in the United States all social and political issues sooner or later seem to become judicial.

JURISDICTION

The highest tribunal, composed of nine justices,[58]—who are appointed by the President with the advice and consent of the Senate—possesses both *original* and *appellate* jurisdiction. However, it exercises the former only rarely, in part because of the scarcity of that type of case; in part because of its own and Congress's desire to share its power with the lower federal judiciary; and in part because of the strictures of the Eleventh Amendment. Indeed, it has had occasion to adjudicate cases in its original jurisdiction only about 150 times. An example of the Court's refusal to hear such a case is Massachusetts's challenge in 1970 to the constitutionality of the Indochina war.[59] In

---

[56]Concurring opinion, *Cooper* v. *Aaron*, 358 U.S. 1 (1958), quoting himself in *United States* v. *United Mine Workers*, 330 U.S. 258 (1947).

[57]Concurring opinion, *Sweezy* v. *New Hampshire, by Wyman, Attorney-General*, 354 U.S. 234 (1957), at 266–67.

[58]There have been as many as ten (1863) and as few as five (1801) justices on the bench, since the number of members of the Court, unlike the creation of the body itself, is subject to statutory discretion, *provided* the various constitutional safeguards (discussed earlier in the chapter) are observed.

[59]*Massachusetts* v. *Laird*, 400 U.S. 886.

theory there are four areas of original jurisdiction at the bar of the highest tribunal (see Table 1-1); but because of the grants of concurrent jurisdiction to other courts, the Supreme Court now exercises its original jurisdiction *exclusively* only in instances involving two or more states. One illustration is the hotly contested, long drawn-out water dispute between California and Arizona, which came to the Supreme Court as a matter of jurisdictional fact and right. After lengthy litigation involving rearguments and rehearings, and the employment by the Court of the special services of a fact-finding "master," the Court ruled 7:1 in favor of Arizona (Chief Justice Warren, an ex-governor of California, abstaining).[60] Another case of original jurisdiction, in a totally different area of concern, was Delaware's unsuccessful attempt to have the Court declare unconstitutional the electoral college.[61] Other cases were river boundary disputes between Louisiana and Texas and between Ohio and Kentucky.[62]

Appellate Jurisdiction

By far the primary task of the Supreme Court is in the realm of *appellate* jurisdiction. Here the Court serves as final arbiter on the construction of the Constitution and, within the confines of the taught tradition of the law and adherence to precedent (duly modified by its judicial prerogative to change its mind), it provides us with an authoritative and uniform interpretation of the law of the land. As Table 1-2 shows, appellate cases reach the Supreme Court from both the constitutional and the legislative lower federal courts and the highest state courts. There are three principal avenues, called *writs*, by which matters for appellate jurisdiction reach the Court: (1) by *certification;* (2) on what lawyers term *appeal*, that is, a writ issued as a matter of right; and (3) on *certiorari*, that is, a writ granted by the Court as a matter of discretion.[63]

Certification. This may be disposed of quickly for it is seldom used. Essentially an "inquiry" of or a request to a higher court by a lower one, certification presumably reaches "any question of law in

---

[60]*Arizona* v. *California,*373 U.S. 546 (1963).

[61]*Delaware et al.* v. *New York et al.*, 385 U.S. 895 (1966).

[62]*Texas* v. *Louisiana*, 410 U.S. 702 (1973) and *Ohio* v. *Kentucky*, 444 U.S. 335 (1980).

[63]The old *writ of error* was discontinued in 1928; its place has been taken by the writ of appeal. Another way for cases to reach the Court is by "extraordinary writ," such as *habeas corpus* or *quo warranto*.

any civil or criminal case in which instructions are desired" by a lower court, customarily a Court of Appeals or the Court of Claims. One of the very infrequent modern examples of its use was that by the Fifth Circuit Court of Appeals in 1963, which "certified" the question of whether its criminal contempt citation of Mississippi's Governor Ross R. Barnett and Lieutenant Governor Paul B. Johnson, Jr., necessitated a trial by jury. The Court of Appeals was evenly divided on the delicate question, 4:4, and it eagerly turned to the Supreme Court[64] to decide the ticklish matter arising out of the federally enforced admission of James H. Meredith to the (until then) entirely segregated University of Mississippi at Oxford. (The Supreme Court ultimately held 5:4 that the Constitution's jury trial requirements do not apply to contempt cases, but it indicated that any non-jury *criminal* sentence imposed must be limited to one akin to a "petty offense."[65])

Writ of Appeal. This is theoretically granted to a duly qualified applicant, known as the *appellant*, as a matter of statutorily granted *right*, with the answering party known as the *appellee* or *respondent*. But in 1928 the Court was given the important discretionary tool of evaluating the appeal as to whether the otherwise validly raised issue is of a "substantial" federal nature; hence, if it deems the issue to lack such substantiality, it may refuse to entertain the petition. Fully 50 to 60 percent of all writs of appeal fall victim to the rule and related jurisdictional loopholes, thus reducing to approximately 15 percent the share of writs of appeal among all cases and controversies presented to the Supreme Court. Table 1–2 outlines in detail the eight types of cases that may come to it on appeal, but the two most common instances are: (1) when a state court of last resort has ruled *in favor of a state law or a provision of a state constitution against a substantial challenge that it conflicts* with a provision of the *federal* Constitution, a *federal* law, or a *federal* treaty; (2) when a United States district court or, more likely today, one of the special three-judge district courts (which includes at least one judge from a United States court of appeals) has granted or denied an injunction in any proceeding required to be heard by such tribunal.

---

[64]375 U.S. 805 (1963).

[65]*United States* v. *Barnett*, 376 U.S. 681 (1964). One year later the Court of Appeals cleared the two because of "changed circumstances and conditions." (Ibid., 346 F. 2d 99.)

TABLE 1–2 United States Supreme Court Review

Cases normally reach the U.S. Supreme Court for purposes of review *(as distinct from original jurisdiction) in one of three principal ways:*

1. on APPEAL, i.e., as a matter of right;
2. on a writ of CERTIORARI, as a matter of Court discretion;
3. by CERTIFICATION. (The old writ of ERROR, a common law process strongly akin to (1) above, was statutorily discontinued in the federal courts in 1928. It brought the entire record of a case proceeding in a lower court before the Supreme Court for its consideration for alleged "errors of law" committed below.)

Note: Title 28 of the United States Code, formulated as a result of congressional legislation, governs the types of review available to an appellant. (See Secs. 1254 and 1257).

I. *Cases reaching the U.S. Supreme Court on* APPEAL (i.e., the Court reviews because it *must*).

   A. *From the state court of last resort* having statutory jurisdiction in any particular case (usually, but not always, the *highest state court,* which normally, but not always, is the state supreme court):

      1. When a state court has declared a federal law or a federal treaty, or provisions thereof, unconstitutional.

      2. When a state court has *upheld* a state law or a provision of the state constitution *against* the challenge that it *conflicts* with the federal Constitution, a federal law, a federal treaty, or any provision thereof.

   B. *From the U.S. (Circuit) Courts of Appeals:*

      1. When a state law or a provision of a state constitution has been *invalidated* because of a conflict with a federal law, a federal treaty, or a provision of the federal Constitution.

      2. When a federal law has been held *unconstitutional, provided* the United States, or one of its agencies, officers, or employees is a party to the suit.

   C. *From the U.S. District Courts:*

      1. When a federal statute has been held *unconstitutional, provided* the United States, or one of its agencies, officers, or employees is a party to the suit.

      2. When the United States is a party to a *civil* suit under the federal interstate-commerce, communication, or anti-trust laws.

3. When a *special three-judge district court* (which must include at least one circuit judge) has granted or denied an in-
terlocutory or permanent injunction in any proceeding
required to be heard by such a court. (These three-judge
courts sit only in suits brought to *restrain, on grounds of unconstitutionality, enforcement, operation, or execution of
federal or state statutes dealing with apportionment or
reapportionment of legislative districts,* and similarly, in instances in which such a court is required by specific acts of
Congress — e.g., the Civil Rights Act of 1964 and the Voting
Rights Act of 1965, as amended, and the Presidential Election Campaign Fund Act of 1974).

D. *From "any* [other] *court of the United States"* (comprising *constitutional, legislative,* and *territorial courts*) — and specifically
including special courts not found under A, B, and C above.
1. When a federal statute has been held *unconstitutional* in
any *civil* action, suit, or proceeding, *provided* the United
States, or one of its agencies, officers, or employees is a
party to it. (But in a 5:4 District of Columbia case decision in
1977, the Supreme Court ruled that it has no automatic
duty to review any decision in a local court striking down a
local law written by Congress; that there is, in other words,
no automatic right to appeal to the Supreme Court when
District of Columbia local courts strike down an act of Congress that applies only in the District itself [*Key* v. *Doyle,*
434 U.S. 59].)

II. *Cases reaching the U.S. Supreme Court on a writ of* CERTIORARI (i.e.,
because a minimum of *four* Supreme Court justices have agreed to a
review). Writs of *certiorari* are granted or denied at the *discretion of the
Court* — subject always to the latent power of Congress to define and
limit the *appellate* power of a Court.

A. *From the state court of last resort having statutory jurisdiction*
in any particular case (usually, but not always, the *highest state
court,* which normally, but not always, is the state supreme
court).
1. In all cases, *other than* those for which the remedy is
APPEAL (see I, A, 1 and 2 above), in which a *"substantial
federal question"* has been properly raised. (The Court itself
determines just what constitutes such a question.)

B. *From U.S. (circuit) courts of appeals* (and, in all pertinent cases,

(continued)

TABLE 1-2 Continued

from other lower courts of the United States, such as legislative courts.)
1. When a decision involves the *application or interpretation* of a federal law, a federal treaty, the federal Constitution, or provisions thereof.
2. Where the U.S. Court of Appeals has *upheld* a state law or a provision of a state constitution *against* the challenge that it conflicts with a federal law, a federal treaty, the federal Constitution, or provisions thereof.

An illustration of the first instance is the case of *Torcaso* v. *Watkins*,[66] which came to the Supreme Court upon Roy Torcaso's successful plea for review on appeal from his losing cause at the bar of the highest court of the State of Maryland, the Court of Appeals. At issue was a provision of the Maryland Constitution that compelled all state officeholders to declare their belief in God as a condition to public employment. Torcaso, a nonbeliever, refused to take the required oath, and challenged the pertinent provision as a violation of his religious freedom under the due process of law clause of the Fourteenth Amendment, as comprehended by the freedom of religion provisions of the First Amendment of the United States Constitution. The Supreme Court unanimously upheld Torcaso's challenge on appeal and struck down as unconstitutional the pertinent Maryland provision as a "religious test for public office." An example of the second instance of relatively frequent Supreme Court review on appeal was the 1964 decision in *Schiro* v. *Bynum*[67] in which it unanimously and summarily affirmed a three-judge district court decision striking down a Louisiana law requiring segregation at sports events and entertainments open to the general public. The constitutional issue thus adjudicated here was the meaning of the equal protection of the law clause of the Fourteenth Amendment.

Far more often than not, a petition for a writ of appeal is rejected by the highest tribunal of the land for "want of a substantial federal question." Examples are legion, ranging from the Court's refusal to hear the contention of the Stover family of Rye, New York, that it had a constitutional right of free expression to hang six clotheslines of laun-

---

[66]367 U.S. 488 (1961).
[67]375 U.S. 395.

dry in its yard as a protest against taxes,[68] to that of the due process claim of Pasquale Albanese of Newtown, Connecticut, who challenged a Connecticut law that allows a person injured by a drunk to sue the person who sold the drink.[69] In a potentially highly significant development, Congress moved in 1979 to *withdraw* much of the Court's obligatory appeal "by right" jurisdiction and substitute review by *certiorari*, but it still had not finally acted by summer of 1986.

Writ of Certiorari. This is the most frequently granted writ in the Supreme Court. A Latin term, translatable as "made more certain" or "better informed," it signifies the willingness of the Court to review the case, but not necessarily hear oral argument. Strictly a discretionary writ, it is granted when *a minimum of four justices* agree that "there are special and important reasons" (a requirement of the Court's own famous Rule 19 of the Court's Revised Rules of 1967) that warrant an order to the court below to "send up" the record for review. But more than 90 percent of all petitions for writs of certiorari are denied, and normally dismissed with only the terse order "petition for writ of certiorari denied." On occasion, however, that order will carry a note that one or more of the justices—but less than four—believe that certiorari should have been granted; these justices are usually identified.[70]

An intriguing and ever-contentious question is just what denial of a writ of certiorari means. It is clear enough what it means to the disappointed litigant: he or she lost. But the justices disagree among themselves on the matter at issue. For example, Justice Jackson viewed "uncert-worthiness" as a tacit agreement by a quorum of the justices that a decision below is good enough to stand, and that "the fatal sentence that in real life writes finis to many cases cannot in legal theory be a complete blank."[71] On the other hand, Justice Frankfurter

---

[68]*Stover* v. *New York*, 375 U.S. 42 (1963). A local ordinance proscribed such displays.

[69]*Albanese* v. *Gilleo*, 350 U.S. 845 (1955).

[70]E.g., Justices Douglas and Stewart, dissenting from the Court's 1967 refusal to grant the writ in *Mora* v. *McNamara* (389 U.S. 934)—a Viet Nam war legality case; and Douglas, this time joined by Brennan, did so again in another Viet Nam war legality case, one that invoked Congressional appropriations of funds (*Sarnoff* v. *Shultz*, 409 U.S. 929 [1972]). The two had similarly lost a year earlier in *Orlando* v. *Laird*, 404 U.S. 869.

[71]*Brown* v. *Allen*, 344 U.S. 443 (1953), at 543, concurring opinion. Elsewhere (at 540) he had uttered the often-quoted statement, "We are not final because we are infallible, but we are infallible only because we are final."

always insisted during his almost quarter of a century on the Court that no significance attaches to the denial of certiorari, that it "in no wise" implies Supreme Court approval of the decision below. On numerous occasions he stoutly defended his contention that all the denial means is that for reasons seldom, if ever, disclosed, four justices evidently do not believe that the case ought to be reviewed, that a denial is thus simply an avoidance of adjudication on the merits of the case.[72] Of course, it is possible, but highly improbable, to obtain a reconsideration or a rehearing by the Court.

A few examples of acceptance and rejection will indicate the diversity of petitions for certiorari (see Table 1–2 for the overall jurisdictional field). In recent years, among the more famous cases to come before the Court on certiorari from a lower federal court was the *Steel Seizure Case*,[73] which involved questions of separation of power. Another case from a state court of last resort was the successful claim of police brutality in violation of Fourteenth Amendment due process of law guarantees of one Rochin, a California citizen.[74] An instance of rejection from the state level is the unsuccessful due process plea by one Hirshhorn in opposition to a New York statute that makes it illegal for a man to masquerade as a woman in public.[75] Another denial of certiorari concerned a narcotics violation by one Beck. His conviction was based in part on the testimony of an alleged accomplice, who had initially pleaded guilty but later, after Beck had appealed his sentence, was permitted to change his plea and had the charge dismissed. Beck unsuccessfully raised Fifth Amendment due process violation claims—it was a federal case; Justices Black and Douglas dissented from the Court's denial of certiorari for they wanted the high court to review the claims.[76] Another is the denial of a law professor's claim that the *Rutgers Law Review's* rejection of his manuscript for a proposed article constituted state action denying him the equal protection of the laws under the Fourteenth Amendment! (He alleged that irrelevant personal bias had dictated the refusal.)[77]

---

[72]*Sheppard* v. *Ohio*, 352 U.S. 910 (1956), *certiorari* denied. (However the Court took up the case a decade later—ultimately resulting in Dr. Sheppard's victory, *Sheppard* v. *Maxwell*, 384 U.S. 333.)

[73]*Youngstown Sheet and Tube Co.* v. *Sawyer*, 343 U.S. 579 (1952).

[74]*Rochin* v. *California*, 342 U.S. 165 (1952).

[75]*Hirshhorn* v. *New York*, 386 U.S. 984 (1967).

[76]*Beck* v. *United States*, 375 U.S. 972 (1964).

[77]*Avins* v. *Rutgers*, 390 U.S. 920 (1968).

Supreme Court Workload

That the Supreme Court of the United States is a busy tribunal is axiomatic. Its case load has been growing steadily, despite the much needed and desired wide *discretionary* powers of review bestowed upon it by the so-called Judges Bill of 1925. Whether or not formal oral arguments are granted and written opinions are issued, merely to say "no" requires considerable time and energy. One of the least understood, yet most important aspects of the Court's work is that *every justice participates in each and every action of the Court,* no matter what its disposition may ultimately be. The Supreme Court is a collegial body, but it is not only a joint group of equi-powerful individuals. It is also a group of nine individual jurists who are joined together for the purpose of arriving at decisions and judgments growing out of their own judico-philosophical perspectives, perspectives that frequently do not permit agreement and thus result in concurring or even dissenting opinions. The chief justice is *primus inter pares* (first among equals), but his *primus* is confined largely to administrative aspects of the Court's work as well as the perhaps more crucial but undefinable one of "setting the tone."

Without burdening the reader with excessive statistics (these are readily available in the Annual Report(s) of the Administrative Office of the United States Courts), the 1984–1985 term of the Supreme Court saw 5,006 cases on its dockets (the Original, Appellate, and Miscellaneous), with 4,269 disposed of; the balance of 737 was carried over to the 1985–1986 term. Of those disposed of, 266 were decided on the merits; only 175 of these with full *written opinions*, the rest *per curiam* or by *memorandum order*—the latter featuring a terse order, such as "affirmed," "dismissed," or "reversed and remanded." The remainder of the large number of cases of which the Court disposed represents denials of review and assorted other dispositions. Again, it must be stressed that even a denial of certiorari calls for study and a position by each and every justice. Law clerks, those bright young law school products of whom each justice may now (1986) be assigned up to four, and the chief justice five, can be helpful indeed, but they cannot and do not act for their justices in any sense of the term. They are hardly the judicial Rasputins they are sometimes pictured to be by certain critics of the Court. It is the justice himself who must and does decide in his responsible and authoritative role, and in a capacity that, in the memorable characterization of Justice Frankfurter, calls for the combined ability and wisdom of a philosopher, historian, and prophet—to which abilities Justice William J. Brennan, Jr., wistfully added, "inordinate patience."[78] His predecessor and colleague Justice Holmes used to suggest that, to succeed, a justice would have to be a combination of Justinian, Jesus Christ, and John Marshall!

THE INSTITUTIONAL SETTING

Unless it is convoked into special session—as was done during the Little Rock, Arkansas, 1957–1958 high-school desegregation crisis[79]— the United States Supreme Court is in formal session thirty-six weeks annually, normally from the first or second Monday in October until the end of June. Occasionally it meets somewhat longer, as it did to adjudicate the *Pentagon Papers*[80] case and the *Nixon Tapes*[81] case at the end of its 1973–1974 term, and the armed forces registration case, *Rostker* v. *Goldberg*, at the conclusion of its 1980–1981 term.[82] (But there is more than enough "homework" to keep the jurists occupied on a year-round basis!) Since its construction in 1935, the home of the Court has been the magnificent Corinthian-columned, white-marbled structure at 1 First Street, S.E., Washington, D.C. 20543, fully guarded around the clock by a special Supreme Court police force. The beautiful, imposing structure was patterned after the Temple of Diana at Ephesus (one of the seven wonders of the ancient world) and the noble words "Equal Justice Under Law" are carved above the majestic entrance, which is enhanced by great bronze doors.

The Court convenes in a large and resplendent forty-four-foot, high-ceilinged courtroom, seating 300 people. Its nine justices are clad in black robes—those judicial vestments Judge Jerome Frank always wanted to see banished[83]—and are seated behind a raised bench (for 181 years a simple straight one, but since 1972 shaped in the form of a half-hexagon, or shallow "L"). When the Court is in session, the chief justice is the first to enter through the purplish-red draperies behind the bench, followed by the eight associate justices in order of seniority. The Court and the audience remain standing until the marshal has completed his traditional introduction: "Oyez, Oyez, Oyez! All persons having business before the Honorable, the Supreme

---

[78]Comment to the author, Philadelphia, Pa., May 24, 1962.

[79]*Cooper* v. *Aaron*, 358 U.S. 1 (1958).

[80]*The New York Times* v. *United States* and *United States* v. *The Washington Post*, 403 U.S. 713 (1971).

[81]*United States* v. *Nixon*, 417 U.S. 683 (1974).

[82]453 U.S. 57 (1981).

[83]See his amusing "The Cult of the Robe," in his *Courts on Trial: Myth and Reality in American Justice* (Princeton, N.J.: Princeton University Press, 1959), Ch. 18.

FIGURE 1–2 The Supreme Court*

```
                 8  6  4        2 | 1 | 3        5  7  9
   [10]                                                       [11]
                             [      12      ]
```

1. Chief Justice Burger

2. Justice Brennan	3. Justice White
4. Justice Marshall	5. Justice Blackmun
6. Justice Powell	7. Justice Rehnquist
8. Justice Stevens	9. Justice O'Connor
10. Clerk of the Court	11. Marshal of the Court

12. Counsel

*In mid-June 1986, Chief Justice Burger announced his retirement as of the end of the Court's term. President Reagan nominated Associate Justice Rehnquist to succeed Burger in the Center Chair and designated U.S. Court of Appeals Judge Antonin Scalia as Rehnquist's successor. As these pages went to press in August 1986, hearings on the nominations were in process.

Court of the United States, are admonished to draw near and give their attention, for the Court is now sitting. God save the United States and this Honorable Court"—a remark that has been the butt of a number of tasteless jokes. The seats of the nine justices are arranged according to length of continuous service on the bench: the chief justice in the center, flanked by the senior associate justice on his right, the second-ranking on his left, and continuing alternately in declining order of seniority (see Figure 1–2).

Oral Argument

The assembled Court hears oral argument normally for the first three (but occasionally on four) days in two weeks of each month, in those few cases—approximately 150–175 annually—that it has agreed to hear in this formal and impressive setting. (The other two weeks are spent behind closed doors considering cases and writing opinions.) For the oral arguments, forty copies of the printed briefs—with one set going to each justice—must have been filed with the Clerk of the Court well in advance, in accordance with prescribed format. Bona fide paupers, however, may file handwritten or typewritten briefs.[84] An important illustration of such an *in forma pauper-*

---

[84]A brief may also be submitted, with Court-permission, by a "friend of the Court." This is known as a brief *amicus curiae*, a burgeoning phenomenon, especially in civil rights cases.

is action is the handwritten, pencilled letter that Clarence Earl Gideon used to petition the Court for a *writ of habeas corpus*—resulting in the momentous overruling of *Betts* v. *Brady*[85] in the landmark decision of *Gideon* v. *Wainwright*.[86] (The latter "incorporated" the Sixth Amendment right to counsel in all criminal cases via the due process of law clause of the Fourteenth Amendment.) Briefs generally cite the facts, issues, questions presented, actions of lower courts, and all necessary legal arguments, together with the statutes and citations of cases on which they rely.

Oral argument[87] is heard on designated days from 10:00 A.M. to noon and from 1:00 until 3:00 P.M.[88] Infinitely more than the "perfunctory windowdressing," as it has been viewed as by some, it is both a fascinating and extremely significant aspect of the Court's public function, and it is a treat for those fortunates who have succeeded in obtaining one of the 300 available seats. (The media is allotted between 19 and 33 seats, 79 to 93 seats are reserved for the justices' families and members of the Bar, and the remaining 188 are available to the public, largely on a "first-come-first served" basis.) Despite the carefully drawn briefs, there is at least a chance that, in supplementing the printed briefs by oral emphasis and in the give-and-take of the questioning by the justices, one or more members may take a different view of the case than the one he or she might have formed upon initially reading the briefs.[89] Indeed, Justice Douglas publicly stated repeatedly that "oral arguments win or lose the case."[90] This is probably too drastic a view, for we have more than one pronouncement on

---

[85]316 U.S. 455 (1942).

[86]372 U.S. 335 (1963). See Anthony Lewis's exciting account of the story of this significant case in his *Gideon's Trumpet* (New York: Random House, 1964). Observed Gideon later: "I didn't start out to do anything for anybody but myself, but the decision has done a helluva lot of good." (*Time*, December 17, 1965, p. 39.) He died six years later, a significant figure in the annals of criminal justice.

[87]The Court does *not* have to hear oral argument, of course, in order to decide a case. Thus, in 1978, without hearing it, and basing their judgment on the legal papers submitted (a procedure used infrequently) the justices ruled that reducing the benefits of welfare recipients who move from the United States to Puerto Rico is *not* a violation of their constitutional rights (*Califano* v. *Torres*, 435 U.S. 1).

[88]Until 1970 there was only one-half hour for lunch; but Chief Justice Burger, cheered on by the press corps, determined that to be inhuman and altered it!

[89]See John Marshall Harlan, "What Part Does Oral Argument Play in the Conduct of an Appeal?" 41 *Cornell Law Quarterly* 6 (1955).

[90]*The Philadelphia Inquirer*, April 9, 1963, p. 3, and *The* (Charlottesville, Va.) *Daily Progress*, October 7, 1972, p. 2.

record in which justices made clear that the loser's argument was better than the winner's—for example, the Court's high compliment publicly paid to the then chief counsel for the A.F.L.–C.I.O., Arthur Goldberg, on the losing end of the Taft-Hartley Act injunction test case of *United Steel Workers of America* v. *United States*[91]—but there is no doubt that an oral argument may indeed prove to be both persuasive and decisive.

The lawyers who present their cases during oral argument are usually limited to one-half hour each for appellant and appellee, sometimes to an hour in those instances deemed by the Court to require a longer presentation. There are, however, notable exceptions, such as the desegregation-implementation case of 1955 when fourteen hours were allowed![92] Opposing counsel, all of whom must at some time have been admitted to practice before the Supreme Court, use a special lectern from which they address the justices "on high," fully expecting, and rarely disappointed in that expectation, to be frequently interrupted with searching questions for which no "time credit" is given. Attached to the lectern are two lights, the first of which gives a white warning signal five minutes prior to time expiration; when a red light flashes, counsel must stop instantly, unless the chief justice permits counsel to continue. Edwin McElwain, at one time Chief Justice Charles Evans Hughes's law clerk, relates that the formidable chief justice once stopped a distinguished New York attorney in the middle of the word "if"; and that, on another occasion, when asked by the same attorney how much of his time remained, Hughes, white beard shaking, replied sternly, "Fourteen seconds, Mr. Counsel."[93]

The "government's lawyer" at the bar of the Supreme Court is not the Attorney General or his deputy, but the number three person in the Department of Justice, the Solicitor-General. In charge of all the federal government's litigation before the Court, litigation that comprises roughly one-half of its entire workload, the Solicitor-General has often been a distinguished faculty member of a prestigious law school—for example, Professor Archibald E. Cox (1961–1965) of

---

[91]361 U.S. 49 (1959).

[92]*Brown* v. *Board of Education of Topeka*, 349 U.S. 294 (1955). But the record is held by the sixteen hours allotted to the water controversy case of *Arizona* v. *California* (fn. 60).

[93]"The Business of the Supreme Court as Conducted by Chief Justice Hughes," 63 *Harvard Law Review* 6 (1949).

Harvard, his Dean, Erwin N. Griswold (1967–1973), Professor Robert M. Bork of Yale (1973–1977), and Dean Rex E. Lee of Brigham Young University (1981–1985).

The Conference

The highly important weekly Friday Conference of the justices takes place usually from 9:30 or 10:00 A.M. to 5:30 or 6:00 P.M., around a large mahogany table behind securely locked doors. (Increasingly, the Friday Conference is being supplemented by post-3:00 P.M. Wednesday meetings and others.) Since 1910, when a "leak" was attributed to one of them, not even the pages have been present. No official record of the discussions in Conference is kept; messages from clerks are received at the door by the most junior associate justice present. We know little of what happens in Conference save what we have learned from memoirs of the justices and from their biographers. Yet it is entirely proper that such secrecy should exist—the Court cannot in good conscience open its deliberations to the glare of publicity, nor can it hold press conferences. The Court still suffers from, and has never forgotten, the one truly disastrous leak that occurred in its history (although allegedly there have been a half dozen or so others): In the *Dred Scott* case,[94] not only did the pro-slavery Justice John Catron—aided and abetted by his colleague, Robert C. Grier—evidently inform President-elect James Buchanan of the probable "line-up" (7:2) of the Court in that crucial decision one month prior to its official announcement; but also segments of the Northern press published the dissent of Justice Benjamin R. Curtis. The secrecy of the Court's work—its "Purple Curtain"—is an indispensable aspect of its labors and its posture.

In Conference, the justices, under the leadership of the chief justice, discuss the several cases they have recently heard in oral argument, as well as all pending motions and applications for review. An average Conference agenda covers about seventy-five items. Each member of the Court is advised in advance which cases will be discussed, and each member notes his or her tentative stand on his or her copy of the agenda. Here, too, applications for writs of certiorari are disposed of, either with verve and controlled dispatch, as used to be so characteristic of Chief Justice Hughes's regime, or with much deliberation and discussion—which was the practiced preference of Chief Justice Stone. No one can say with finality, however, which of

---

[94]*Dred Scott* v. *Sandford*, 19 Howard 393 (1857).

these two approaches is "better" or more "just." The nine justices, who have shaken hands with each other upon entering, are seated around a large, rectangular conference table. The chief justice gives his own view first in each case, followed by that of the other justices, all of whom are prepared to "recite," in descending order of seniority. When the time comes to take a *tentative* vote on the case, however, the voting commences with the *junior* justice, the somewhat debatable rationale being that he or she will thus speak up free from the influence of his or her more experienced brethren.[95] Each justice records all votes in a hinged, lockable red-leather docket book, and the Court is now set for the next stage of its tasks—writing the opinions.

Diverse Opinions

First, cases must be assigned. Here the chief justice must call upon all of his powers of diplomacy, strategy, and persuasion to achieve written decisions that will be: (1) understandable; (2) understood by the public; (3) persuasive; (4) eloquent; (5) "right"; and (6) leave as few ruffled feathers as possible among the justices. Gone are the days when, partly to achieve the above aims as he saw them, Chief Justice Marshall wrote most of the opinions himself, and, more often than not, for a unanimous Court! He believed that the Court's power and prestige would be enhanced if it were to speak with but a single voice. "Justices must write down their reasons for a decision," as Dean Rostow of the Yale Law School observed, "because they are partners with us, the citizens, in an agreed procedure for reaching responsible decisions."[96] Prior to Marshall's time, decisions customarily, although not always, were rendered *seriatim*[97]—that is, each author writing *and* delivering his opinion separately—a practice still prevalent with the Law Lords of Britain's House of Lords, and one that Thomas Jefferson, as president, wanted to institutionalize to counteract the powerful influence of his political enemy, John Marshall. Today, in

---

[95]According to one seasoned Court observer's account, the justices now also *vote* in descending order of seniority, and his account is now the prevailing view (Warren Weaver, *The New York Times*, February 6, 1975, p. 31m). For a controversial, largely undocumented account, see Bob Woodward and Scott Armstrong, *The Brethren: Inside the Supreme Court* (New York: Simon and Schuster, 1979).

[96]Eugene V. Rostow, *The Sovereign Prerogative: The Supreme Court and the Quest for Law* (New Haven, Conn.: Yale University Press, 1962), p. 89.

[97]A well-known illustration is the group of seriatim opinions by Justices Chase, Paterson, and Iredell in the early 1796 case of *Hylton* v. *United States*, 3 Dallas 171.

all cases heard on the merits, formal written opinions are rendered, save for those decided by memorandum orders, and those few in which a tie vote has resulted because of the absence or voluntary disqualification of one of the justices. (A tie vote has the effect of upholding the decision below.)[98] Except in cases of serious illness, the bench may confidently be expected to be at full strength for practically all of its decisions. On occasion a judicial turnover, resulting from death or retirement, may cause the new member to abstain because he or she had not been present at the oral argument, as e.g., Justice Byron R. White did in the *New York Prayer* case.[99] Moreover, unlike members of the legislature, the justices are extremely sensitive about even the faintest possibility of a conflict of interest, and, as Justice Rehnquist did in *United States* v. *Nixon*,[100] will abstain from participation rather than cause so much as a question of it. This principle did not greatly trouble Chief Justice Marshall in his day, as he was directly and personally involved in *Marbury* v. *Madison*![101] "When in doubt, do not sit" is now a firm policy of the members of the Court. Justice Clark even *resigned* from the Court when his son, Ramsey, became U.S. Attorney General in 1967.

The sole opinion-writing problem when the Court is unanimous is the selection of the author, who is always chosen by the chief justice in those instances.[102] Depending on the public significance of the decision and on the nature of the subject matter, the chief may assign himself to write the opinion, as Chief Justice Earl Warren did in the unanimous decision of the contentious and significant *Segregation Cases of 1954*,[103] and as Chief Justice Warren Burger did in the *Nixon*

[98]E.g., *Bailey* v. *Richardson*, 341 U.S. 918 (1951)—4:4, a loyalty-security case; *Grove Press* v. *Maryland State Board of Censors*, 401 U.S. 480 (1941)—4:4, upholding Maryland's ban on the showing of the movie "I Am Curious Yellow" in 1971; and *Bradley* v. *State Board of Education of the Commonwealth of Virginia*, 411 U.S. 913 (1973)—4:4, upholding Virginia's refusal to order cross-county busing.

[99]*Engel* v. *Vitale*, 370 U.S. 421 (1962).

[100]417 U.S. 683 (1974). Prior to his appointment to the Court, Rehnquist had been an Assistant Attorney General in the Nixon Administration.

[101]1 Cranch 137 (1803).

[102]A special situation was the Court's unique multiple authorship in the seminal desegregation enforcement case of *Cooper* v. *Aaron*, 358 U.S. 1 (1958), when *all* justices, beginning with Chief Justice Warren, and then listing the eight associate justices in descending order of seniority, "oversigned" its unanimous opinion (see p. 128, fn. 145).

[103]*Brown* v. *Board of Education of Topeka*, 347 U.S. 483.

Tapes case of 1974.[104] But when the chief justice is on the minority side
in a case, the assignment for the writing of the majority opinion will
ordinarily be made by the senior associate justice on *that* side. For example, Justice Frankfurter assigned Justice Tom C. Clark to write the
majority opinion for the 5:4 Court in a dual case involving the power
of congressional investigating committees.[105] The chief justice and/or
the senior associate justice will also always take into account the philosophical "bent" of an assignee in cases that may be expected to evoke
considerable public agitation. Thus Chief Justice Stone assigned one
of the Court's leading "liberals,"[106] Justice Black, to write the majority (6:3) opinion in the highly controversial *Japanese Relocation*
case.[107] Similarly, Chief Justice Warren assigned one of the Court's
leading "conservatives," and a deeply religious man, Justice Clark, to
write the hotly denounced opinion (8:1) outlawing the reading of the
Bible and the recitation of the Lord's Prayer in public schools.[108] This
does not, of course, always balm the wound or lessen the public outcry, but there is at least a chance that it might do so, and it is unquestionably sound judicial strategy.

Concurring Opinions. The Supreme Court may be expected to
be unanimous in about one-quarter to one-third of its decisions. The
others are decided chiefly by an absolute majority or by a mere plurality; the latter occurs when no absolute majority is attainable for the
Court's decision but when a particular plurality commanded more
votes than any other combination. A less-than-happy syndrome,
"plurality" opinions have been resorted to with increasing frequency
of late. The Warren Court provided forty plurality opinions between
1953 and 1969 and the Burger Court rendered eighty-eight between
1969 and 1981. Both "concurring" and "dissenting" opinions are frequent, and their length sometimes exceeds that of the majority or plurality opinion. A *concurring opinion* is one which, while concurring
in the *result*, does not agree with the reasoning or the line of logic that
brought the decision about. A concurring opinion does count as a vote

---

[104]417 U.S. 683.

[105]*Wilkinson and Braden* v. *United States*, 365 U.S. 399 and 431 (1961).

[106]A *caveat* is in order regarding these labels, and this author, for one, does not approve of them, especially not in so complex a setting as the Supreme Court.

[107]*Korematsu* v. *United States*, 323 U.S. 214 (1944).

[108]*School District of Abington Township* v. *Schempp* and *Murray* v. *Curlett*, 374
U.S. 203 (1963).

on the side of the majority. Thus Justice Clark agreed with the (6:2) decision in *Baker* v. *Carr*,[109] in which the Court took the momentous step of holding that alleged illegal or "invidiously discriminating" districting and redistricting by state legislatures was a federally justiciable controversy, but he disagreed with aspects of the rationale employed by the majority. (In that same case, Justice Frankfurter wrote a sixty-eight-page *dissenting* opinion, in which Justice John Marshall Harlan joined.) There are those who are quite critical of concurring opinions, while approving of dissenting opinions, for they believe that a concurring opinion is essentially meaningless: that it represents verbiage that has no effect upon the vote in the case, and that it is hence both confusing and unnecessary, and would more profitably be confined to footnotes to the majority opinion. Still, it is a demonstrable fact that many a concurring opinion has left an important mark on the course of constitutional law; for example, Justice Clark's in the *Steel Seizure* case (in which he pointed the finger at the President's refusal to utilize available statutes) and Justin Harlan's in *Estes* v. *Texas* (in which he limited the Court's holding to "notorious" cases).[110] Some concurring opinons read like dissenting ones—and, indeed, that is sometimes their genesis; for example, Justice Brandeis's concurring opinion in *Whitney* v. *California* and Chief Justice Burger's in *Roe* v. *Wade*.[111]

Dissenting Opinions. These opinions are not normally subject to the same criticism, although on occasion criticism may well be appropriate. The dissenting opinion by Justice Clark in the coerced confession case of *Rogers* v. *Richmond*,[112] in which Justice Potter Stewart joined, is a case in point. While in disagreement with certain technical aspects, that dissenting opinion was actually far more of a concurrence with the majority than a bona fide dissenting opinion on the claim of coercion. Another rather unhelpful practice is a simple *dissent* without any explanation, which leaves the observer guessing as to the motives of the jurist—an intriguing, sometimes nasty, but hardly very professional sport! The bare announcement in the landmark case

---

[109]369 U.S. 186 (1962).

[110]343 U.S. 579 (1952) and 381 U.S. 532 (1965), respectively. The Court qualified Harlan's *Estes* opinion in its 1981 decision in *Chandler* v. *Florida*, 449 U.S. 560.

[111]274 U.S. 357 (1927) and 410 U.S. 113 (1973), respectively.

[112]365 U.S. 534 (1961).

of *Palko* v. *Connecticut*,[113] "Mr. Justice [Pierce] Butler dissents," is meaningless other than that it counts as a vote on the negative side of the decision. But whatever one's personal appraisal of the merits of a particular dissenting opinion, rendering such an opinion is a practice that is frequent, and generally desirable, as a beacon of a profoundly held conviction. Hence, it may well strengthen rather than weaken a particular issue, although there is no doubt that it may be an exasperating practice in the eyes of the public and, indeed, that it may have a tendency to muddy the judicio-political waters. Be that as it may, there is no gainsaying the memorable evaluation of the dissenting opinion by Charles Evans Hughes, then writing as an ex-associate justice of the Supreme Court and soon to be its eleventh chief justice:

> A *dissent[ing opinion] in a court of last resort is an appeal to the brooding spirit of the law, to the intelligence of a future day, when a later decision may possibly correct the error into which the dissenting judge believes the court to have been betrayed.*[114]

Although Hughes rarely either dissented or wrote dissenting opinions, and next to John Marshall, and perhaps Earl Warren, was unquestionably the most dominant "chief" to sit on the Court, he often expressed the point of view that there is no reason to expect more unanimity on difficult problems of law than in the "higher reaches" of physics, philosophy, or theology.

Proving Roscoe Pound's wise observation that ". . . dissenting opinions may be the symptom of life in the law of time,"[115] many a memorable dissenting opinion has gone on to become, in due course, the voice of the majority of the Court or even its unanimous voice. Examples are legion; two opinions by Justice Holmes, one of the great dissenters,[116] serve amply to illustrate this significant phenomenon. In

---

[113]302 U.S. 319 (1937).

[114]*The Supreme Court of the United States* (New York: Columbia University Press, 1928), p. 68.

[115]"Preface," in *Justice Musmanno Dissents* (Indianapolis: Bobbs-Merrill Co., 1956). See also Justice Brennan's Hastings College of Law Lecture, "In Defense of Dissents," November 18, 1985.

[116]Actually he wrote only 72 dissenting opinions, ranking him eleventh in dissents; the "champion" so far (as of summer 1986) is Justice Douglas with 586 written dissenting opinions.

his angry and anguished dissenting opinion in *Hammer* v. *Dagen-hart*[117] (the child labor case), he vainly cried out[118] against the 5:4 majority's declaration of unconstitutionality of the Keating-Owen Child Labor Law of 1916 on grounds of its illegal interference with the powers reserved to the states under the Tenth Amendment under the guise of the congressional power over interstate commerce. This decision was unanimously and specifically overruled by the Hughes Court in *United States* v. *Darby*[119] in 1941. And there is Holmes's earlier, perhaps even better-known, dissenting opinion in the New York bakeshop case, *Lochner* v. *New York.*[120] In the face of the majority's position that New York state's attempt to limit by statute the hours of bakeshop employees to ten per day and sixty per week was an unconstitutional infraction of the liberty-of-contract phrase of the due process of law clause of Amendment Fourteen, he declaimed with icy majesty and scorn: "The Fourteenth Amendment does not enact Mr. Herbert Spencer's *Social Statics.*" Holmes was ninety-three years old and no longer on the Court when *Lochner's* fate was sealed with the upholding of New York's Milk Control Law in 1934, in the narrowly decided (5:4) *Nebbia* v. *New York.*[121] He was delighted!

No discussion of how dissenting opinions, no matter how lonely, may become majority opinions would be complete without mention of the historic, lone dissenting opinion by Justice Marshall Harlan from the 8:1 Court decision upholding the "separate but equal" concept in *Plessy* v. *Ferguson*[122] in 1896. His solitary and moving exhortation, "[O]ur Constitution is color-blind, and neither knows nor tolerates classes among citizens," had to wait fifty-eight years to become the unanimous opinion of the Court in *Brown* v. *Board of Education of Topeka.*[123]

Creating Opinions. With every justice participating at each and every stage of every opinion, the actual drafting of opinions is a laborious and time-consuming task, more often than not steeped in

---

[117]247 U.S. 251 (1918).

[118]"It is not for this Court to pronounce when prohibition is necessary to regulation if it ever may be necessary—to say that it is permissible as against strong drink, but not as against the product of ruined lives" (Ibid., at 280).

[119]312 U.S. 100.

[120]198 U.S. 45 (1905).

[121]291 U.S. 502.

[122]163 U.S. 537.

[123]347 U.S. 483 (1954).

compromise. Aided by their clerks in research tasks, and by the private Supreme Court Library with its staff of fourteen, the justices, in general, and those who have been assigned opinions, in particular, go about this crucial stage of their work with deliberate diligence. Opinions are drafted and proof copies—printed behind locked doors by the Court's own private professional printers in the basement—are circulated among the members until such time as give-and-take (and not a little "bargaining") may produce an acceptable end result. Justice Brennan reported that once, after he was assigned the writing of an opinion by Chief Justice Warren, he had to compose *ten* printed drafts before one proved to be acceptable as the opinion of the Court.[124] But the same justice, on another occasion, told the world in a separate memorandum that he attached to an opinion he had written for a closely divided Court: "It cannot be suggested in cases where the author is the mere instrument of the Court he must forego expression of his own conviction."[125] On the other hand, the judicial game of persuasion *cum* bargaining may be blunt and direct, as is evidenced by a memorandum sent by the usually gentle Chief Justice Stone to the not always professionally gentle Justice Frankfurter:

> *If you wish to write [the opinion] placing the case on the ground which I think tenable and desirable, I shall cheerfully join you. If not, I will add a few observations for myself.*[126]

And Justice James F. Byrnes's price to his "chief" (Stone) in 1941 for refraining from dissenting in the important *California Migration Case, Edwards* v. *California,*[127] was to be permitted to write the Court's unanimous opinion in favor of Fred Edwards—but on grounds of the interstate commerce, rather than the "privileges and immunities" clause. This caused four justices to join in a concurring opinion stating a preference for the latter ground, yet it did not render the tribunal any the less unanimous in votes. In short, it is clear that although the published opinions of the Court are ostensibly the prod-

---

[124]"Inside View of the High Court," *The New York Times Magazine*, October 6, 1963, p. 102.

[125]*Abbate* v. *United States*, 359 U.S. 187 (1959), at 196. Similar illustrations of this practice are Justice Jackson in *Wheeling Steel Corporation* v. *Glander*, 337 U.S. 562 (1949), at 576, Justice Cardozo in *Helvering* v. *Davis*, 301 U.S. 619 (1937), at 639, and Chief Justice Burger in the *Pentagon Papers* case, 403 U.S. 713 (1971).

[126]Cited by Alpheus T. Mason, *Harlan Fisk Stone: Pillar of the Law* (New York: The Viking Press, 1956), p. 501.

[127]314 U.S. 160.

uct of one person, they are, in effect, that of many minds (as is so ably detailed in Richard Kluger's *Simple Justice*).[128] Whoever is charged with the writing of an opinion more often than not is obliged to add to, delete, modify, or even throw out the original draft in order to retain and/or secure the acquiescence of the necessary number of colleagues.

Because each member of the Supreme Court of the United States takes part in each and every stage of the consideration of a case, it should not be surprising, then, to find certain ambiguities or even contradictions in a given opinion. This fact of judicial life lends itself to the favorite parlor game of many vocal Court critics (notably the legal fraternity who ought to know better)—sticking pins and throwing darts into the end product with, of course, the delightful advantage of 20/20 hindsight.

Opinion Days. On those days during each month when the Court is in session, it formally and publicly announces its written opinions from the collegial bench. They are then duly recorded and immortalized in the series of official volumes known as the *United States Reports*.[129] (*Per curiam* opinions and the routine memorandum orders are not announced publicly on these Opinion Days, but are made a part of the permanent record in the *Reports*.) In ascending order of seniority, the various authors of the full opinions may read them, paraphrase them, summarize them, excerpt them, or simply state them as a matter of fact. The method of presentation is left entirely to the discretion of the justices concerned, although there is some pressure for brevity. Hence a listener ought to be prepared for anything from a brief announcement or ten-minute synopsis to a word-by-word lecture, as it were, running perhaps into an hour or more, although the latter is uncommon. On occasion, extemporaneous outbursts accompany the reading of a particular opinion; this may result in a warm or not-so-warm exchange between author and commentator. Thus Justice Douglas did not hesitate to charge that the

---

[128]*Simple Justice: The History of Brown* v. *Board of Education and Black America's Struggle for Equality* (New York: Alfred A. Knopf, 1976), especially Chapter 25.

[129]The *Reports* and their forerunners (the latter kept by official court reporters under their names) are bound back to 1790. There are also three *unofficial* publications of opinions: *The Lawyers' Edition; The Supreme Court Reporter;* and *United States Law Week.* (The *Reports*, however, constitute the *sole* official ones.)

fifty-two-page *Arizona* v. *California*[130] majority opinion, written by his usually close collaborator on the Court, Justice Black, sounded "more like a Congressional committee report than a judicial opinion"—a comment he did not write in his dissenting opinion. Douglas added with biting sarcasm:

> *The advantage of a long opinion such as the one Justice Black has filed is that it is very difficult to see how it failed to reach the right result, because one gets lost in words.*[131]

Ratio Decidendi and Obiter Dictum. It is important to distinguish between the *ratio decidendi* and the *obiter dictum* of an opinion. The former becomes *res judicata*, that is, the settled point of law of the case. It is the legal rule to be complied with and adhered to in perpetuity, unless altered or abolished by judicial, legislative, or amendment processes. The *obiter dictum*, on the other hand, is actually a gratuitous statement, one that expresses a belief, a warning, an exhortation, a viewpoint, or simply a sentiment, not essential to the holding in the case but somehow, however vaguely, related thereto. *Obiter dicta* or *dicta*, as they are simply called, are present frequently and may suggest possible future developments. Chief Justice Marshall, many of whose famous opinions were replete with *dicta*, was a past master. One controversial *dictum* was raised in a set of fairly recent cases:[132] Justice Arthur J. Goldberg, joined by Justices Douglas and Brennan, suggested that the imposition of the death penalty for rape might well constitute the kind of "cruel and unusual punishment" proscribed by the Eighth Amendment to the United States Constitution (a question not raised by either petitioner in the briefs). But the *ratio decidendi* of that opinion, in which the six other justices joined, was that the doomed petitioners' due process claims did *not* warrant Supreme Court review—at least not then.[133]

---

[130]373 U.S. 546 (1963).

[131]*The New York Times,* June 4, 1963, p. 22.

[132]*Snider* v. *Cunningham* and *Rudolf* v. *Alabama,* 375 U.S. 889 (1963).

[133]But note *Furman* v. *Georgia,* 408 U.S. 238 (1972) and subsequent developments in the capital punishment realm, capped by *Gregg* v. *Georgia,* 428 U.S. 153 (1976), affirming its constitutionality under carefully guarded conditions. (See p. 137, *infra.*) For additional developments see *Roberts* v. *Louisiana* I (1976) and II (1977), 428 U.S. 325 and 431 U.S. 633, respectively, and *Eddings* v. *Oklahoma,* 455 U.S. 104 (1982). By late June 1986, sixty-one people had been executed (following the above *Gregg* decision).

Compliance and Noncompliance. Once decided and announced, the Supreme Court's decision is presumably the law of the land, and it should, consequently, automatically find ready compliance by the jurisdictions below. Normally, this is the case; indeed, *it must be* if our system of government under law means anything at all. However, compliance is by no means always automatic, and even when it seems to take place, evasions of the spirit of the decision by "reinterpretation" in the lower courts are not uncommon. Aside from the rather rare outright *defiance* of a Supreme Court order by courts below, noncompliance or snail-like compliance usually takes place because of one of several reasons or peculiarities inherent in our judicial process. One is that even given the Court's unmistakably sweeping general order in a decision—such as its pronouncement against state-imposed or state-prescribed prayers in the public schools in *Engel* v. *Vitale*[134]—the decision is in fact applicable solely to the case or controversy *in that particular case* (in *Engel* v. *Vitale* the State of New York). The fact that the majority opinion by Justice Black made clear that no such limitation was either intended or implied was thus "legally" ignored by certain jurisdictions in a host of states, for example, New Jersey and Pennsylvania, despite rulings by the two attorneys general involved that the case did apply to *all* such practices throughout the United States. Yet a 1969 survey by *The New York Times* demonstrated that 13 percent of the nation's schools—and fully 50 percent of those in the South—continued to employ some type of devotional readings.[135] Similar noncompliance, in the absence of new suits specifically brought to cover additional jurisdictions, occurred after the Court's decision in 1948 barring the practice of "released time" in public school buildings.[136] The most obvious illustration of all is the regionwide initial noncompliance and, in some cases, outright defiance of the Court's decision in the public school segregation cases of 1954 and 1955[137] and their progeny (not to mention the ingeniously and ingenuously propounded state and local legislative and executive circumventions).

Another tenet of the judicial process that invites noncompliance in certain instances is that the United States Supreme Court has no

[134]370 U.S. 421 (1962).

[135]March 26, 1969, p. 1.

[136]*McCollum* v. *Board of Education of Champagne*, 333 U.S. 203.

[137]*Brown* v. *Board of Education of Topeka*, 347 U.S. 483 (1954) and 349 U.S. 294 (1955).

power to make a *final determination* of any cases in which it reviews judgment of *state* courts. All it can do is to decide the *federal issue* involved and *remand* the case to the state court below, usually its highest appellate court, for a final adjudication "not inconsistent with this opinion." Since the state courts may then raise new issues on remand, it is not terribly difficult, if the desire exists, thus to alter "legally," or even evade, the substantive intent of a United States Supreme Court decision. A notorious illustration is the case of Virgil Hawkins, a Florida black, who had been denied admission to the University of Florida Law School in 1949 because of his race. After lengthy legal stratagems and delays, commencing in 1950, and assorted maneuvers on all levels of the Florida State judiciary over a period of almost ten years, Hawkins was finally *ordered* admitted by the United States Supreme Court after the Florida Supreme Court continued to stall in the most patent manner; yet Hawkins never was in fact able to enter. Instead, he received his law degree at the New England School of Law in 1965. Eleven years later, now seventy years old, he was at last admitted to the Florida bar.[138]

It would be a disservice, however, to leave the impression that the Court's decisions are regularly and predictably evaded or defied. The vast majority are complied with promptly and properly—even when they are highly unpopular and contentious. This fact of judicial life is clearly illustrated by such emotional and far-reaching matters of public policy as legislative apportionment and the granting of counsel in *all* criminal cases, as a result of the Supreme Court decisions in *Baker* v. *Carr*[139] and *Reynolds* v. *Sims*,[140] and *Gideon* v. *Wainwright*[141] and *Argersinger* v. *Hamlin*,[142] respectively. These decisions prompted meaningful compliance in most instances. Thus, as a result of *Baker*,

---

[138]*Florida* ex rel *Hawkins* v. *Board of Control*, 347 U.S. 471 (1954); 350 U.S. 413 (1956); 355 U.S. 839 (1957). For an account of the Hawkins dilemma, see Walter F. Murphy and C. Herman Pritchett, *Courts, Judges, and Politics* (New York: Random House, 1961), pp. 606–618. See also the grisly history of the case of *Williams* v. *Georgia*, 349 U.S. 375 (1955); *Williams* v. *State*, 88 S.E. 2d 376 (1955); and *Williams* v. *Georgia*, 350 U.S. 950 (1956), *certiorari* denied. For a partial account of Williams's travail, see Murphy and Pritchett, *loc. cit.*, 3rd ed. (1979), pp. 390–393. See also 12 *Florida State University Law Review* 1 (Spring 1984).

[139]369 U.S. 186 (1962).
[140]377 U.S. 533 (1964).
[141]372 U.S. 335 (1963).
[142]407 U.S. 25 (1972).

by the end of 1966—a mere four years later—forty-one states had reapportioned one or more houses of their legislatures.[143] And this is as it should be. Informed, serious, constructive criticism of the Court is both desirable and necessary; defiance of the ultimate tribunal, however, must be barred—which does not, of course, mean that it will not be attempted.

---

[143]24 *Congressional Quarterly Weekly Report* 2055. The 97th Congress (1981–82) had an average deviation from the ideal district size of less than one-half of 1 percent, whereas in the 88th (1963) it was 17 percent!

2

Courts and Public Policy:

Personnel, Judicial Review, and Activism vs. Restraint

The Court's general role of judicial review, of constitutional and statutory interpretation, will now be addressed, as well as the men and women who staff it and the lower courts. To better understand the role of the judiciary in policy making, several aspects of the judicial process must first be analyzed. Some of these may well have already become more or less apparent to the reader as a result of the preceding discussions of the characteristics of our courts, in general, and the United States Supreme Court, in particular, as institutions at once governmental, human, and political. Nonetheless, they need additional amplification, and our consideration of them will thus naturally commence with a glance at the individuals who comprise the judiciary.

Judges and Justices

SELECTION AND TENURE

The process of staffing the courts is neither mysterious nor particularly Machiavellian, folklore to the contrary. Essentially, there are just two ways of "getting on the bench": by *election* or *appointment* (although, as explained below, there do exist combinations of the two in a good many states). *All* federal jurists are appointed; but state jurists may be either elected or appointed, depending upon a state's constitutional or statutory provisions.

Election. The several states of the fledgling Union turned to the elective method largely as a result of the post–Constitution Convention trend to "democratize" government. Election was either by ballot by the electorate, or, less frequently, by the legislature. Election remains a widely practiced, if hardly universally applauded,[1] approach to court staffing throughout the states for at least *some* members of the judiciary, their terms varying greatly in length from four years to life (Rhode Island).[2] The basic requirement is to obtain one's political party's nomination and then hope for the best in the general election. However, *real* contests are more often the exception than the rule, and active "politicking" by judicial candidates, especially incumbents, is usually, albeit certainly not always, regarded as improper. Moreover, there are some instances in which certain judicial nominees may run on bipartisan (New York) or even nonpartisan (Washington) tickets for at least some judicial posts; and in several states the "sitting judge" principle is in vogue, whereby both political parties at least theoretically are pledged to support the incumbent, no matter what his or her political affiliation may be.

Appointment. In the states, appointment of at least some jurists for terms of varying length is usually by gubernatorial selection plus senatorial confirmation; but there are also judicial appointments by commissions, legislatures, and courts. On the federal level, however, every prospective judge and justice (a title reserved there to members of the Supreme Court) is nominated by the president and submitted to the Senate for approval by simply majority vote. At levels below the

---

[1]Chief Justice Roger J. Traynor of the California Supreme Court told a judicial conference in the fall of 1970 that the "greatest single improvement that could be made in the administration of this country would be to get rid of the popular election of judges" (*The New York Times*, October 5, 1970, p. 34). At that time fully 82 percent of the judges on local and state courts were elected. (Ibid.) That figure has dropped somewhat since, but a majority is still elected.

[2]On this point, and on court staffing generally, see my work *The Judicial Process: An Introductory Analysis of the Courts of the United States, England, and France*, 5th ed. (New York: Oxford University Press, 1986), Ch. II. On Supreme Court staffing, see my work *Justices and Presidents: A Political History of Appointments to the Supreme Court*, 2d. ed. (New York: Oxford University Press, 1985). See also the works of John R. Schmidhauser, cited in fn. 38.

Supreme Court, judicial selection by the chief executive is customarily delegated to the attorney general and his deputy, although President Carter instituted the practice of an initial nomination by citizen-staffed commissions comprised of lay as well as professional persons for all U.S. circuit court of appeals vacancies.[3] This arrangement was terminated by President Reagan in May 1981. Carter had also success-fully persuaded a number of senators to create similar bodies for U.S. district court vacancies.[4] Of course, when it comes to the choice of a new Supreme Court justice, the selection process turns into a much more personal one for the president. But no matter which level of the federal judiciary may be involved, at least three significant facts of political life must be understood and considered in order to obtain a realistic picture of that selection process.

The *first* fact is that it is not practically possible for the chief exec-utive to designate a member of the federal bench and see him or her confirmed, without at least the grudging approval of the United States senators from the nominee's home state. Indeed, some powerful senators of the president's political party will insist not only on the right of approval of his choice, but on the right to have particular can-didates of their own appointed. This law of politics applies most acutely, but not exclusively, to the judges of the United States district bench. In the case of the Supreme Court nominees, however, the law of politics governs more as a matter of courtesy than necessity, for it is generally agreed that Supreme Court justices ought to be regarded as the president's personal choices—despite twenty-seven significant il-lustrations to the contrary, such as the Senate's rejection of Cleve-land's nominations of William B. Hornblower and Wheeler H. Peckham; Grant's choices of Ebenezer R. Hoar and George R. Williams; the 1930 rejection by 39:41 of Hoover's selection of U.S. Court of Appeals Judge John J. Parker; the 1968 filibuster against

---

[3]Established by an executive order in February 1977, as amended in May 1978, the U.S. Circuit Judge Nominating Commission consisted of thirteen "subcommis-sions," one for each circuit, with two each for the large 5th and 9th, comprising circa eleven members each who, by the terms of the Presidential Order, not only had to contain both lawyers and non-lawyers, but also had to include both men and women and members of minority groups.

[4]When he left office in January 1981, Carter had persuaded senators from thirty states to do so, but the results remained inconclusive. Other senators categorically refused to comply—for example, Senator Lloyd Bentsen (D.-Tex,), who announced: "I am the merit commission for Texas" (*The Washington Post*, Nov. 15, 1978, p. 4A). Similar postures were taken by such Democratic colleagues as Adlai E. Stevenson, III (Ill.), Paul Sarbanes (Md.), and Thomas F. Eagleton (Mo.).

Johnson's attempted promotion of Abe Fortas to chief justice;[5] the Senate's 45:55 rejection of the Nixon nomination of Clement F. Haynsworth, Jr.; and that of G. Harrold Carswell, 45:51, in 1969 and 1970, respectively. The reasons for these rejections varied, but they comprised political opposition to the appointing president; the candidate's personal involvement with a delicate political problem; "senatorial courtesy";[6] the questionable ability of the nominee; his political "unreliability";[7] his ethics; or "getting" at the Court itself—that is, the 1968 anti-Fortas filibuster, which was really directed against the Warren Court's judicial posture.

The *second* important factor in the selection process is the significant role played by the fourteen-member[8] Committee on Federal Judiciary of the American Bar Association. Its functions began to receive maximum attention and presidential cooperation during the Truman administration. Although some observers question the wisdom of

---

[5]When an attempt to invoke closure failed 45:43 that fall, Fortas asked the president to withdraw his nomination. (In 1969 he resigned from the bench.)

[6]The term signifies a firmly accepted custom, dating back to the First Congress and George Washington, whereby the president is expected, as a matter of political patronage practice and courtesy, to consult with the nominee's home state senator(s) prior to his designation—provided the senator is a member of the president's political party. Failing to respect this custom, the president will usually see the invocation of "senatorial courtesy" under which the aggrieved senator's colleagues will, on his call for the nominee's defeat, support him as a matter of fraternal courtesy. The magic words, uttered by the president's senatorial adversary, are that the nominee is "personally obnoxious!" Until Senator "Ted" Kennedy (D.-Mass.), upon taking over as the Chairman of the Senate Committee on the Judiciary in 1979, announced that he would no longer recognize or respect it, the "blue-slip" system had been a time-honored interesting and important byproduct of "senatorial courtesy." The system was formally restored by Senator Strom Thurmond (R.-S.C.) in 1981, but he has not attempted to enforce it meaningfully. Once the president formally nominates someone, the Committee sends the home state senators a blue slip, asking his or her "opinion and information concerning the nomination." That blue slip is only returned if the senator approves; if not returned, it signifies disapproval, which, in the case of a senator from the president's own party, is regarded as a veto, in which the Committee will normally automatically concur.

[7]See the detailed article by Henry J. Abraham and Edward M. Goldberg, "A Note on the Appointment of Justices of the Supreme Court of the United States," 46 *American Bar Association Journal* 147 (February 1960).

[8]One member from each of the twelve geographical federal judicial circuits, one chairman, and one extra member for the large 9th district, none from the nongeographical 13th. Commissioners serve for three years, with one possible renewal.

delegating to a private group—which is not without certain specific professional and perhaps personal interests and biases—the right to evaluate all federal judicial personnel prior to the nomination stage, the Committee has developed into a respected and powerful element of the nominating process. Its procedure is to investigate all prospective nominees below Supreme Court level[9] over a six- to eight-week period, and then to "rate" them for the attention of the Attorney General in one of four categories: "EWQ" (Exceptionally Well Qualified); "WQ" (Well Qualified); "Q" (Qualified); or "NQ" (Not Qualified). It should be noted here, however, that the lowest ranking is not necessarily a reflection on the nominee's character or ability. For instance, as a matter of policy the A.B.A.'s Committee will not normally approve anyone who has reached the age of sixty-four and no one above sixty unless ratable at least "WQ." It is loath to recommend lawyers without trial experience; and it generally insists on fifteen years of experience in "the rough and tumble of legal practice."[10] To cite one year of the Committee's activities, in 1962 President Kennedy nominated and saw appointed 100 federal judges; of these, the Committee had rated 16 "EWQ," 45 "WQ," 31 "Q," and 8 "NQ." That the names of 8 "NQ" judges were nevertheless forwarded to and approved by the Senate is proof of the political pressures that prey upon the chief executives—especially at the start of a new administration that represents a change in party. Still, a number of other "NQ" ratees were never nominated by President Kennedy, a testimonial to the important role of the A.B.A.'s influential Committee. *No* "NQ"s at all were approved between 1965 and 1975, when President Ford succeeded in pushing through the Senator Lowell P. Weicker (R.-Conn.) nomination of the state's ex-Governor, Thomas J. Meskill, a fellow Republican, to the

---

[9]Since a late 1971 confrontation between the Committee and President Nixon and his Attorney General, John N. Mitchell, the latter submitted his recommendation for the Nixon Administration's last two Supreme Court nominations directly to the president, thus bypassing the A.B.A. Committee until the nominee's name had become public—but the Committee issued its evaluations anyway. President Ford restored the *status quo ante* as soon as the first opportunity (the John Paul Stevens nomination in 1975) arose. "—— the A.B.A.," exploded Nixon in ordering a cessation of the practice (as reported by James Goodman, "The Politics of Federal Judges," *Juris Doctor*, June 1977, p. 26).

[10]Committee member Robert L. Trescher to author, December 9, 1971. For many years it used a "Not Qualified by Reason of Age" category (variously applied at age sixty or sixty-four and up), but it discontinued that classification as of January 1, 1981.

U.S. Court of Appeals—notwithstanding the A.B.A.'s unanimous "NQ" rating of the nominee.[11] President Carter sent up 6 "NQ"s, of whom 3 were confirmed. As of this writing (mid-1986) President Reagan had forwarded only one "NQ," but the nominee died prior to Senate action.

The *third* factor is a rather subtle but increasingly demonstrable one:[12] the role, difficult to assess but clearly present, that incumbent and retired members of the tribunal—especially at the highest level in the person of the Chief Justice of the United States—play in suggesting nominees to the president. We know, for example, that Chief Justice Taft was not at all reluctant in expressing his thoughts to presidents Harding, Coolidge, and Hoover—"bombarding" the chief executives with suggestions is a more apt description; that his successor, Hughes, followed a similar course of action with Hoover and F.D.R.; that Associate Justice Stone went so far as to write to President Hoover that he would be willing to resign and relinquish his seat if it would take that sacrifice to propel the president into nominating Justice Cardozo to the Supreme Court; that President Kennedy apparently consulted with Chief Justice Warren and Justice Frankfurter in 1962 regarding Arthur J. Goldberg, Frankfurter's successor to the bench; that President Johnson consulted Warren concerning his successor as chief justice; and that Justice Rehnquist urged President Reagan to nominate Sandra Day O'Connor in 1981.

"Mixed" Appointment and Election.   In order to combat the chief criticism of the elective and appointive methods, yet still retain the virtues of these methods, different versions of a compromise plan have evolved in a third of the states,[13] with California and Missouri as the pioneers.

The *California Plan*, adopted by referendum vote in 1934, extends to some,[14] but not all, of California's judges. Under it, the gover-

---

[11]For an account of the event, see Jerry Landauer, "How Not to Pick a Judge," *The Wall Street Journal*, April 10, 1975, p. 4.

[12]See Henry J. Abraham and Bruce Allen Murphy, "The Influence of Sitting and Retired Justices on Presidential Supreme Court Nominations," 3 *Hastings Constitutional Law Review* 1 (Winter 1976).

[13]Variants existed in 1986 in Arizona, Alaska, Colorado, Florida, Georgia, Hawaii, Idaho, Illinois, Indiana, Iowa, Kansas, Maryland, Montana, Nebraska, New York, Oklahoma, South Dakota, Tennessee, Utah, Vermont, and Wyoming.

[14]Those of the Supreme Court and the district courts of appeals.

nor nominates one prospective jurist to a Commission on Judicial Appointments, composed of the chief justice of the State Supreme Court, the presiding judge of the pertinent District Court of Appeals, and the attorney general. If the Commission accepts the governor's nominee—and so far only once (in 1940) has a commission rejected one—he or she is declared appointed until the next general election at which he or she must face the electorate for the full twelve-year term of office. The candidate runs unopposed on a ballot that simply asks the question "Shall [name] be elected to the office for the term prescribed by law?"

The *Missouri Plan* uses a somewhat different method. Here, nonpartisan nominating boards, known as appellate commissions and operating on different court levels,[15] select *three* candidates for every vacant judgeship, from whom the governor appoints *one* until the next general election but no less than for one year. Thereafter, as in California, the incumbent faces the electorate for a full twelve-year term, running unopposed on a nonpartisan ballot containing the question "Shall Judge [name] of the [name] Court be retained in office?"[16] Members of the nonsalaried appellate commissions are designated for staggered six-year terms of office; they may hold neither public nor political party office. A typical commission, such as that for the Missouri Supreme Court and the lower appellate courts, consists of the chief justice of the former as chairperson; three lawyers selected by the state bar (one from each of the three courts of appeals); and

---

[15]Supreme Court; district courts of appeals; circuit courts; other lower courts.

[16]Not suprisingly, the response is almost inevitably affirmative. Thus during the first three decades of its life—from 1940 through 1970—of 179 judicial contests conducted, the Missouri electorate rejected *but one* candidate—and he received 46.4 percent affirmative votes. (He happened to be a circuit court judge prominently identified with the then-discredited Pendergast political machine.) (See Richard A. Watson, "Judging the Judges," 53 *Judicature* 289, February 1970). In 1976 only 3 of 353 judges on retention ballots throughout the nation were rejected. (See William Jenkins, Jr., "Who Wins When No One Loses?" 61 *Judicature* 2, August 1977, pp. 79–86.) But California Governor Edmund G. Brown, Jr.'s controversial appointment of Rose Elizabeth Bird as chief justice in 1977 survived the 1978 retention test by a mere 51.7 percent of the votes cast. Of 486 facing retention elections in 1978 only 13 were rejected (1 appellate and 12 trial judges). Altogether, in the first forty-six years of existence of the retention election plan, only 33 failed to be re-elected. See Susan B. Carbon, "Judicial Retention Elections: Are They Serving Their Intended Purpose?" 64 *Judicature* 51 (November 1980), pp. 213; 221–33. As of mid-1986 *no* Californian running for retention had been rejected, but Chief Justice Bird faced a bitter battle that November.

three citizen laypersons, appointed by the governor from the three appellate districts.

On the whole, these mixed systems have proved to be both popular and successful in the jurisdictions where they have been tried, for they combine the democratic notion of accountability to the electorate with an appealing method of selecting prospective judicial personnel that is based upon a type of separation of powers. Still, a question arises as to how much effort will be engendered by a sitting judge to establish a "popular" record for the benefit of the electorate. Perhaps there is really no effective substitute for the responsibility and accountability that are found, at least in theory, in the appointive method, provided it is backed by long tenure. As it stands, "on balance our judicial system still represents primarily a compromise between representativeness and neutral competence."[17]

Tenure of Office and Emoluments. On the state level tenure is either of substantial length or for "good behavior"—that is, life. On the federal level, "good behavior" tenure is constitutionally mandated for all constitutional court judges; legislative court jurists may be given term appointments, and often are, but there has been an increasing tendency for Congress to accord them life tenure as well. Retirement provisions are different for the state and federal governments. Under the federal plan, adopted in 1937, federal judges may (but are not required to)[18] retire on full pay at age seventy if they have served ten years on the federal bench, and at age sixty-five after fifteen years of such service.[19]

Removal of *state* judges used to be possible only by impeachment and conviction; now in some states they are removable by joint gubernatorial-legislative action (New Hampshire); in some by legislative resolution (Utah); in some by recall by popular vote (Arizona); in

---

[17]Herbert Kaufman, *Politics and Policies in State and Local Government* (Englewood Cliffs, N.J.: Prentice-Hall, 1963), p. 60.

[18]However, except in a two-judge district, chief judges of the federal district and appellate courts must relinquish that status upon reaching the age of seventy, although they may continue on the bench.

[19]These requirements are waived in the presence of physical disability, where retirement pay is computed on the basis of length of service. Widows and dependents receive an annual sum equivalent to 37.5 percent of the judge's average salary. See p. 10 of this text for judicial salary scales.

most by judicial commissions (California); and in others by special tribunals such as the Commission on Judicial Conduct in New York.[20]

On the *federal* level, however, judges (other than magistrates and bankruptcy judges) are involuntarily removable only via impeachment by a simple majority vote of the House of Representatives and conviction thereafter by the Senate by a two-thirds vote of the members present and voting, there being a quorum on the floor. Except for the members of the Supreme Court, federal judges are, however, subject to disciplinary procedures short of removal by the judicial councils of the twelve judicial circuits as a result of a 1980 congressional statute. Of the thirteen impeachment proceedings formally initiated by the House to date, ten were directed against federal judges;[21] nine other judges resigned before formal charges could be lodged against them. Of the nine impeachment trials involving federal judges, five resulted in acquittals,[22] four in removals.[23] Among the former was the sole one involving a justice of the Supreme Court, Associate Justice Samuel Chase, who was acquitted by a four-vote margin in 1805, with Vice-President Aaron Burr presiding over the Senate proceedings and with Chief Justice Marshall as an important defense witness.

QUALIFICATIONS AND NOMINATIONS

Judicial Qualifications. On the whole, the only statutory requirement for judicial nomination present in the *states* for most courts

---

[20]In 1963 its predecessor, the Court on the Judiciary, ousted two state judges for "unethical judicial conduct"; also one each in 1970, 1973, and 1975. The Louisiana Supreme Court by a 6:1 vote ordered a state court judge ousted in 1970 for his involvement and arrest in a vice raid at a motel stag party. Wisconsin's Supreme Court suspended for three years a state judge for sundry violations of the Judicial Code of Ethics, including "gross personal misconduct with six women... with offensive sexual overtones."

[21]The other three were against Senator William Blount of Tennessee in 1789; President Andrew Johnson in 1868; and Secretary of War William Belknap in 1876. Only nine of the ten impeachments of federal judges went to trial; the one directed against Judge Mark D. Helahay became academic when he resigned before the trial could commence. (He had been impeached by voice vote.)

[22]Samuel Chase (1805); James H. Peck (1830); Charles Swayne (1905); George W. English (1926); and Harold Louderback (1933).

[23]John Pickering (19:7 in 1804); West W. Humphreys (38:0 in 1862); Robert W. Archbald (*viva voce* in 1913); and Halsted L. Ritter (56:28 in 1936).

is a law degree (or, as was still possible in a few states in 1986, the completion of three or four years of reading law plus a stiff examination); for others not even an LLB. or J.D. is required for certain magistrate positions. No statutory or constitutional requirement *whatsoever* exists on the *federal level*, but there is unquestionably an unwritten law concerning the need for a law degree: no nonlawyer stands even the slightest chance of nomination, no matter how learned he or she may be otherwise (although Justice Black, among others, often suggested that at least one nonlawyer serve on the Supreme Court of the United States).

The matter of *judicial experience* is in a different category: considerable lip service is paid to it, and some chief executives have insisted upon it for certain levels (e.g., President Eisenhower for his nominees to the Supreme Court after Earl Warren); but its absence has by no means been a block to nomination even to the United States Supreme Court. Of the 101 men and the 1 woman who had served on that tribunal between 1789 and early 1986, only 22 had had ten years or more on any lower court levels at the times of their appointments. The last one with that much experience prior to Chief Justice Burger's appointment in 1969 was Justice Cardozo, who had served for eighteen years on New York benches when President Hoover nominated him to succeed Justice Holmes in 1932. Some 43 justices had had none at all. Yet among these are some of the most revered and illustrious names in America's judicial annals: 5 of the 15 chief justices—Taney, S. P. Chase, Waite, Fuller, and Warren[24]—and such associate justices as Story, Miller, Bradley, Brandeis, Sutherland, Roberts, Frankfurter, and Robert Jackson. In the oft-quoted words of Justice Frankfurter, neither judicial experience nor geographic considerations nor political affiliation should play the slightest role in the considerations leading to appointment to even the highest bench in the land; such selection should be "wholly on the basis of functional fitness." To him, the essential qualities of a Supreme Court justice were but three: those of the philosopher, historian, and prophet (to which, as already noted, Justice Brennan added a fourth: "inordinate patience"). To seal further his basic contention, Frankfurter once told an attentive audience of lawyers and law students:

---

[24]Actually, one could easily list John Marshall as well, for his sole judicial experience was a three-year stint on the very minor local Richmond City (Virgina) Hustings Court, from 1785–1788.

> *One is entitled to say without qualification that the correlation be-*
> *tween prior judicial experience and fitness for the Supreme Court is*
> *zero. The significance of the greatest among the Justices who had*
> *such experience, Holmes and Cardozo, derived not from that judi-*
> *cial experience but from the fact that they were Holmes and*
> *Cardozo. They were thinkers, and more particularly, legal philoso-*
> *phers.*[25]

Nonetheless, the issue of judicial experience is never quite dormant, and there is no doubt that at least some consideration is given to it, depending upon the stance of the nominating authority. Individual members of Congress call sporadically for some statutory requirement—usually providing for upwards of five years of service on a lower court bench[26]—but no such legislation has ever been passed. And it is not likely to be, given continued opposition by the bar, the executive, and the judiciary itself.

Motivations behind Presidential Nominations. A favorite indoor sport of the practitioners of the law and politics, as well as the public at large, is to speculate upon the reasons why an individual is nominated by a chief executive to serve on a tribunal. This becomes a particularly intriguing guessing game at the level of the Supreme Court of the United States, whose appointees obviously are more prominent than those at lower levels.

Presidential motivations in selecting a future justice of the Supreme Court are both complex and multiple, and vary with each president. There is, however, a fairly reliable quintet of factors that is present in most presidential choices to the august tribunal (and, for that matter, to the lower federal benches). In no particular order, they are the nominee's:

1. objective professional merit (including judicial experience);
2. political "availability";
3. ideological "appropriateness";
4. personal "attractiveness" to the president;
5. geographical, religious, racial, sexual, and other socio-political background.

---

[25]"The Supreme Court in the Mirror of Justices," 105 *University of Pennsylvania Law Review* 781 (1957).

[26]In 1978–1979, for example, thirteen such measures were introduced in Congress.

Not all of these considerations necessarily play a role in each selection, but a majority of them unquestionably does; one of them is usually upper-most in significance; and probably all are given at least some thought by the president and his advisers.

Thus, the *merit* factor proved to be decisive in President Hoover's reluctant designation of Justice Cardozo, but the other four factors also played key roles, affirmatively or negatively. Hoover did not really wish to nominate Cardozo, although he recognized clearly the judicial greatness and personal integrity of this dedicated, experienced, principled, learned, and brilliant New York jurist—a bachelor, a Democrat, and a Sephardic Jew. Public and private demands for Cardozo's nomination to succeed to the Holmes seat on the Court were clear and persistent; and they were spearheaded by such important figures as Idaho's influential and powerful Republican Senator William E. Borah—not commonly known for his love of easterners—and by Justice Stone, who offered to relinquish his seat in favor of Cardozo when Hoover raised the argument that the Court already had two New Yorkers on the bench (Stone and Chief Justice Hughes). When Hoover suggested possible "religious and sectarian" repercussions—sitting Justice Brandeis also was Jewish—Borah told the president that "anyone who raises the question of race [sic] is unfit to advise you concerning so important a matter."[27] Amidst universal public applause, Hoover then surrendered, and the Senate unanimously confirmed Cardozo within moments after his nomination reached the floor.

Political "availability" includes both the official party allegiance of the designee and his or her acceptability—or at least the nominee's "non-obnoxiousness"—to his or her home state senators, provided these are of the president's own political party. By and large, an old political maxim governs here; namely, that "there are just as many good *Republican* [or *Democratic*, as the case may be] lawyers—so why appoint someone from the enemy camp?"[28] There have been deviations from this concept, and there are always a few "sops" thrown to the opposition, but there is no mistaking the pattern. To illustrate: President Wilson appointed 73 Democrats and 1 Republican as feder-

---

[27]Claudius O. Johnson, *Borah of Idaho* (New York: Longman's Green and Co., 1936), p. 452.

[28]"Think Republican," Chairman C. B. Rogers Morton of the Republican National Committee urged President Nixon in his consideration of possible successors to Chief Justice Warren and Justice Fortas (*The New York Times*, May 17, 1969, p. 1).

al jurists; Harding, Coolidge, and Hoover a total of 198 Republicans and 20 Democrats; F.D.R., 194 Democrats and 8 Republicans; Truman, 128 Democrats and 13 Republicans; Eisenhower, 178 Republicans and 11 Democrats; Kennedy, 105 Democrats, 10 Republicans, 1 Independent, and 1 member of the New York Liberal Party; Johnson, 155 Democrats and 12 Republicans; Nixon, 205 Republicans, 16 Democrats, and 2 Independents; and Carter, provided by the Omnibus Judgeships Act of 1978 with the opportunity to appoint 117 new district and 35 new circuit judges, *in addition* to some 140 attrition replacements—an opportunity unequalled in the country's history—selected a mere 9 non-Democrats. Thus the pattern is clear. It is true that 13 Supreme Court justices of opposite party allegiance have been appointed,[29] yet ready explanations governed each instance.[30] The overall percentage of same-as-president's-party appointments has ranged from a low of 82.2 (Taft) to 98.6 (Wilson).

Ideological "appropriateness" played a role in most of the above thirteen cases. This concept is also known as a nominee's "real politics"—that is, what is surmised to be, on the basis of an educated guess, the candidate's actual personal philosophy, regardless of formal party adherence, a philosophy that the appointing authority presumes, with fingers crossed, will express itself on the bench. As President Theodore Roosevelt put it succinctly in a well-known statement to Henry Cabot Lodge (R.-Mass.) concerning the "appropriateness" of Horace H. Lurton, ". . . the *nominal* politics of the man has nothing to do with his actions on the bench. His *real* politics are all important. . . ." And he then proceeded to outline how "right" he was on sundry public questions.[31] But more than once a chief executive's hopes and advance analysis have proved to be erroneous. The case of Madison's appointment of Joseph Story, Theodore Roosevelt's of Holmes, Wilson's of James C. McReynolds, and Eisenhower's of Earl

---

[29]Nelson-D (Tyler-W.); Field-D. (Lincoln-R.); H. E. Jackson-D (B. Harrison-R.); Lurton-D., promotion of E. D. White-D., and J. R. Lamar-D. (Taft-R.); Butler-D. (Harding-R.); Brandeis-R. (Wilson-D); Cardozo-D. (Hoover-R.); promotion of Stone-R. (F.D.R.-D.); Burton-R. (Truman-D.); Brennan-D. (Eisenhower-R.); and Powell-D. (Nixon-R.). Some would add the Frankfurter appointment (Ind.) by F.D.R.

[30]See my books *The Judicial Process*, pp. 68–74, and *Justices and Presidents*, Ch. IV, especially pp. 65–67, for elaboration.

[31]Henry Cabot Lodge, *Selections from the Correspondence of Theodore Roosevelt and Henry Cabot Lodge*, 1884–1918 (New York: Charles Scribner's Sons, 1925), Vol II, p. 228.

Warren and William J. Brennan, Jr. are obvious illustrations of the point.

Consequently, it is not easy to "pack" the Court—although many have tried. Perhaps the most famous case was President Franklin D. Roosevelt's abortive effort in 1937; but the first to "pack" was in fact President Washington, who insisted on a set of seven criteria[32] for his nominees. "You shoot an arrow into a far-distant future when you appoint a Justice," aptly commented Alexander M. Bickel, "and not the man himself can tell you what he will think about some of the problems that he will face."[33] In characteristic language and with candor, President Truman observed that "packing the Supreme Court can't be done, because I've tried it and it won't work. . . . Whenever you put a man on the Supreme Court he ceases to be your friend. I am sure of that."[34]

A nominee's *personal "attractiveness" to the president* may play a decisive role in a president's decision to select an individual, regardless of the other factors at issue. Close personal friendship thus unquestionably accounted in large measure for the Supreme Court nomination of Messrs. Vinson, Clark, and Minton by President Truman, that of Byron R. White by President Kennedy, and that of Abe Fortas by President Johnson.

The last among the five outstanding factors embraces the American "melting-pot"—or "not-so-melting pot"—considerations of *religion, geography*, and now, insistently and increasingly, *race* and *sex*. They are usually present—either negatively or positively. The case of Justice Cardozo illustrates the first: neither the presence of two other New Yorkers nor that of his co-religionist Brandeis was permitted to stand in the way, although President Hoover saw them as genuine and overriding barriers. In the "positive" sense, President Eisenhower's designations of Charles Evan Whittaker of Illinois and Potter Stewart of Ohio reflected his concern with the absence of the Midwest on the Court. And the fact that thirty-one states had sent justices to the Supreme Court as of its 1985–1986 term would appear to bear out the regional factor consideration. The same is true for religion: that William J. Brennan was from New Jersey (key state) and a Roman

---

[32](1) Advocacy of federalism; (2) a "fighting participant" in the Revolution; (3) "fitness"; (4) judicial experience; (5) "proper" geography; (6) "love of our country"; and (7) active political participation in "life of state or nation."

[33]*The New York Times*, May 23, 1969, p. 24.

[34]*The Philadelphia Bulletin*, April 29, 1959, p. 1 (reporting the president's lecture at Columbia University on the preceding day).

Catholic (a religion then not "represented" on the Court) was surely not lost on President Eisenhower and his advisers when Brennan was nominated to the Supreme Court during the presidential election year of 1956. Although President Truman ignored the "religious" factor when he appointed Tom C. Clark to succeed Justice Murphy in 1949, and President Nixon did likewise with his appointment of Harry A. Blackmun to replace Justice Fortas, it has become an accepted axiom of American politics that there should be a Jew and a Roman Catholic on the highest bench at all times. As of the 1982–1983 term, six Roman Catholics[35] and five Jews[36] had served on the Court; the other ninety-one have been Protestants.[37] The pressure to establish a niche for another minority group, the blacks, culminated in 1967 with President Johnson's appointment of Thurgood Marshall—the great-grandson of a slave and the son of a Pullman steward. And a "woman's seat" was all but institutionalized with the appointment of Sandra Day O'Connor in late 1981. (It was not until 1979 that every state had at least one woman judge.)

The Typical Justice of the Supreme Court of the United States. A composite of the typical jurist on the highest bench of the land, reflecting the various aspects and factors of the selection process as well as statistical facts of the past, would look as follows at the time of accession to the Court:

> *A 50–55-year-old male; white; generally Protestant; of Anglo-Saxon stock (all except fifteen to date); upper-middle to high social status; reared in a non-rural but not necessarily urban environment; member of an economically comfortable, civic-minded, politically active family; with B.A. and LLB. or J.D. degrees (one-third of these from "Ivy League" institutions); experienced in some public or civic office.*[38]

---

[35]Taney, E. D. White, McKenna, Butler, Murphy, and Brennan.

[36]Brandeis, Cardozo, Frankfurter, Goldberg, and Fortas. (President Fillmore had offered an appointment to Judah P. Benjamin of Louisiana in 1853—sixty-three years before Brandeis became the first Jew to sit on the Supreme Court—but Benjamin preferred to be in the U.S. Senate.)

[37]Episcopalian, 26; Presbyterian 17; Unitarian, 6; Baptist, 5; Congregationalist, 3; Methodist, 4; Disciples of Christ, 2; Quaker, 1; Unspecified Protestant, 25.

[38]For an interesting study in this connection, see John R. Schmidhauser, *The Supreme Court: Its Politics, Personalities and Procedures* (New York: Holt, Rinehart and Winston, 1960), Ch. 3, *passim* and his *Judges and Justices: The Federal Appel-*

We shall now examine the jurist's role in the Court's ultimate power of judicial review.

Judicial Review

GENESIS

Judicial Review Defined. The power of judicial review is the most awesome and potentially the most effective power in the hands of the judiciary of the United States, in general, and the Supreme Court, in particular. Peculiar to countries that, like the United States, operate under a federal system, it is a power at once controversial and misunderstood, maligned and applauded. Any definition would have to state at least the following:

> *Judicial review is the ultimate power of any court to declare unconstitutional and hence unenforceable: (1) any law; (2) any official action based upon a law; and (3) any other action by a public official that it deems to be in conflict with the Constitution.*

A court also practices judicial review, of course, when it *upholds* a law or action. What a court does accordingly is to apply the *superior* of two laws—here, the United States Constitution—against a statute, some action or activity by a public official, or even a segment of a state Constitution. But a Court does not do this lightly or frequently; it does so only after careful, minute analysis, reflection, and weighing of alternatives, in line with the canons of the taught tradition of the law, against a backdrop of judicial self-restraint. Every court of record in the United States, no matter how high or low, possesses this fascinating power, this "principled process of enunciating and applying enduring values of our society."[39] Our concern here is with the exercise of this power by the federal Supreme Court.

Judicial review is a power not lightly or frequently exercised, and whenever the Court can find its way clear to do so, it avoids the drastic remedy of meeting the constitutional issue—for meeting it may

---

late Judiciary (Boston: Little, Brown and Co., 1979), Chs. 2 and 3, *passim.* See also my *Justices and Presidents*, Ch. IV, "Why They Get There: Qualifications and Rationalizations," *passim.*

[39]Alexander M. Bickel, *The Least Dangerous Branch* (Indianapolis: Bobbs-Merrill Co., 1962), p. 58.

well mean the exercise of the ultimate "no-saying" power. The Court would much rather handle a delicate problem by statutory interpretation than by going to the constitutional jugular, especially since it is often possible thus to achieve similar results. Such Supreme Court decisions as those dealing with the loyalty-security field[40] and the range and extent of the Smith Act of 1940[41] are obvious cases in point. Others are legion. Conscious of its conservative role as the theoretically weakest of the triumvirate of governmental branches, and aware of public sensitivity in the fields at issue, the Court has chosen a course of action in all those instances that comes close to having the proverbial cake (judicial judgment) and eating it too (acting as a restraining and explanatory agency, yet avoiding nullification).

Some Examples.   The Court, of course, does from time to time exercise judicial review in its ultimate sense; as of early 1986, it had done so since its first session some 1,000 times in the instance of *state* legislation and state constitutional provisions (over 900 of these came after 1870), and 135 times in the case of *federal* enactments.[42] An example of the exercise vis-à-vis state legislation is the declaration of unconstitutionality of an Arizona statute that made it unlawful to operate within the state a railroad train consisting of more than fourteen passenger or seventy freight cars, because the law was held to place an undue burden on interstate commerce.[43] One dealing with a section of a state constitution is the voiding of a provision of the Maryland Constitution that compelled all officeholders to declare their belief in God as a condition of employment, because such a requirement was held to constitute a "religious test for public office," thus invading the individual's right of freedom of religion.[44] On the federal level, involving an *act of Congress*, a section of the Food and Drug Act concerned with the procedure of factory inspection was struck down as unconstitutionally vague under the "due process of law" clause of the Fifth Amendment.[45] A famous example of judicial review over an *ultra vires action of an official of the United States* was the Supreme Court's

---

[40]For example, *Cole* v. *Young*, 351 U.S. 536 (1956) and *Schneider* v. *Smith*, 390 U.S. 17 (1968).

[41]For example, *Yates et al.* v. *United States*, 354 U.S. 298 (1957); *Scales* v. *United States*, 367 U.S. 203 (1961); and *Noto* v. *United States*, 367 U.S. 290 (1961).

[42]For a table of these through late 1985, see my *The Judicial Process*, pp. 293–301.

[43]*Southern Pacific Co.* v. *Arizona*, 325 U.S. 761 (1945).

[44]*Torcaso* v. *Watkins*, 367 U.S. 488 (1961).

[45]*United States* v. *Cardiff*, 344 U.S. 174 (1952).

ringing "no" to President Truman when he seized the steel mills in
1951. The "no" was based on the chief executive's alleged usurpation
of legislative power.[46] A more recent example was the Court's unanimous order to President Nixon in July 1974 to surrender certain of the
notorious "Watergate Tapes."[47] And a far-reaching "no" to Congress
came in 1983 with the Court's 7:2 declaration of unconstitutionality
of the one- and/or two-house congressional (or legislative) veto, a
practice then imbedded in 212 laws enacted since 1932.[48]

The most contentious of these various modes of judicial review
has always been the striking down by the Court of an act of Congress
or a portion thereof. (Respecting the principle of "separability," the
Court will try hard to save as much of a law's framework as is constitutionally feasible in a given case.[49]) It is in saying "no" to the legislature that the issue of majoritarian rule would appear to be most
clearly and perceptibly joined—for there the highest echelon of the judicial branch, in the ultimate authority of nine *appointed* individuals,
says to a majority of the highest echelon of *elected* and, presumably,
representative legislative branch, that it has violated the basic law of
the land. In other words, it is here that one branch of government becomes *the* authoritative interpreter of the Constitution, the protesta-
tions of another "equal" branch of the government to the contrary
notwithstanding.

The Arbiter.   Obviously, there must be an arbiter! Theoretically
it is both plausible and attractive—to some, but certainly not to all,
citizens of the Republic—to contend that in a bona fide democracy
what the majority wants the majority should get, giving due regard to
the rights of the minority—as spelled out in the basic document that
governs the body politic. Certainly, or so the argument goes, majoritarian government becomes a hollow shell indeed, if a duly elected,
legally constituted body of the people's representatives is denied the
right and the ability to respond to people's majoritarian wishes, as

[46]*Youngstown Sheet and Tube Co.* v. *Sawyer*, 343 U.S. 579 (1952).

[47]*United States* v. *Nixon*, 417 U.S. 683.

[48]*Immigration and Naturalization Service* v. *Chadha*, 462 U.S. 919.

[49]The series of decisions declaring portions of the Uniform Code of Military Justice
Act of 1950 unconstitutional are cases in point: e.g., *United States* ex rel. *Toth* v.
Quarles, 350 U.S. 11 (1955); *Reid* v. *Covert* and *Kinsella* v. *Krueger*, 354 U.S. 1
(1957); *Kinsella* v. *United States* ex rel. *Singleton*, 361 U.S. 234 (1960); *Grisham* v.
Hagan and *McElroy* v. *United States*, 361 U.S. 278 (1960).

expressed by their representatives assembled in Congress. Why should an undemocratically constituted body of nine elitists, who are not responsible to the people via the ballot box, be accorded the overriding power to strike down what the people want? Is not Congress, and is not the executive branch of government, equally capable of judging and interpreting the constitutionality of a proposed measure or course of action? Are they not equally devoted to the principle of government under law? It may be quite all right, so the argument continues, for the judiciary to "interpret" and to "adjudicate," but *not* to strike down as unconstitutional anything that a majority has enacted within the confines of the law and the Constitution. This, in substance, was Thomas Jefferson's argument once he had turned against judicial review. (He had been a supporter of that power until the judiciary began to sanction the hated Alien and Sedition Acts of 1789 rather than declare them unconstitutional.)

The answer to this argument is obvious *and* complicated. It is obvious because our Founding Fathers never intended our governmental organization and base to be a *pure* democracy. They were afraid of the excesses of democracy, as they saw it, and they constituted the basic document with safeguards against any potential "tyranny of the majority." This was done not only vis-à-vis the relationship between the individual and the government, but also vis-à-vis the relationship of the various governmental branches. Thus was born a *federal* system of government, with not only a division of powers between it and the states, but a central government in which the three main branches were separated, yet still checked and balanced by one another. And the new format was spelled out in a written document—the Constitution of the United States of America. Far from wanting to see a governmental form like the pure democracy of Athenian days, or even a fusion of powers like that of our British cousins, the Founding Fathers thus determined that majorities must be checked and observed at almost every turn. Who would be more qualified than the judiciary to be both legitimator and arbiter, to render a final judgment regarding infractions of the basic law? Hence the Founding Fathers widely recognized the idea of judicial review as the surest tool for the arbiter, and although they failed to spell out the power, it is clear that they agreed with the Father of the Constitution, James Madison, who wrote that the

> [*J*]*udiciary is truly the only defensive armor of the Federal Government, or rather for the Constitution and laws of the United States.*

> *Strip it of that armor and the door is wide open for nullification, anarchy, and convulsion.* [50]

As the years went by, however, and despite the Marshallian stroke of judicial statemanship and statecraft in *Marbury* v. *Madison*[51] (see below), doubts about the extent of the role of the legitimator and arbiter have never completely been laid to rest, even in the minds of some of the most famous jurists, especially since the Court has at times patently engaged in prescriptive policy making.[52] Thus both Justice Holmes and Judge Learned Hand, two towering figures in American jurisprudence, although recognizing the need for a federal legitimator and arbiter, consistently wondered whether it would be absolutely essential at the level of the operation of the national government. They were convinced that a legitimator and, assuredly, an arbiter were indeed needed to have the last word in disputes involving the mechanism of the federal *system*, that is, in disputes between the central government and the states, for they recognized that the Union could not survive otherwise in the image of its creation. *But* they did not believe that the "Republic would come to an end" if the courts were deprived of the power of judicial review regarding other legislation passed by Congress.

This position, however laudable in terms of judicial self-restraint, ignores that role of the judiciary, in general, and of the Supreme Court, in particular, which casts it as the guardian of our individual liberties—a role that has occupied it increasingly during the course of this turbulent century. As such it has become the greatest institutional safeguard for the individual and the small group. Here, in saying "no" to government—both national and state—it has become the last bulwark against majoritarian excesses. In being willing to stand up and be counted, in refusing to be cowed by criticism and opprobrium, the Supreme Court has acted as a "moral goad" to the other two branches. Unlike the legislative and executive wings, the judiciary does not count constituents; is neither engaged nor interested in a popularity contest; and is far from that arena that so frequently has seen the other two, and notably the legislature, close to what Judge

---

[50]As quoted by Charles Warren in *The Supreme Court in United States History* (Boston: Little, Brown, 1937), Vol. I, p. 740.

[51]Cranch 137 (1803).

[52]E.g., *Swann* v. *Charlotte-Mecklenburg Board of Education*, discussed on pp. 183–184 of this text; *Roe* v. *Wade* and other "privacy" decisions, outlined on p. 105 of this text; and *Steelworkers* v. *Weber*, explained on pp. 193–194 of this text.

Learned Hand himself viewed as "the pressure of public hysteria, public panic, and public greed." And even if a transfer of the judicial guardianship to other institutions of government were theoretically desirable, which few thoughtful citizens believe, it would be politically impossible. What sane citizen of the United States would wish to have the ultimate exercise of his or her individual liberties, including the provisions of the Bill of Rights, be at the mercy of partisan political bodies?

Historical Justification? The other prong of the basic argument is far more complicated, for even if we accept the Court's necessary role as arbiter and legitimator—as most Americans do, depending somewhat upon whose ox is being gored—what of the historical justification of the practice? This query has been a constant one ever since *Marbury* v. *Madison*—and even prior to that historic decision—because the Founding Fathers *did not* spell out the power of judicial review in so many words, and its presence today results from a combination of historical experience, judicial interpretation, and rather obvious necessity.

Little would be gained by a lengthy rehashing of the historical argument and evidence. It is a fact that the Constitution makes no *specific* reference to judicial review. It is also a fact that the Founding Fathers clearly envisaged it; that it was debated at length in the Constitutional Convention in Philadelphia in 1787; that the most authoritative historical research available on the point, that by Charles Beard,[53] indicates that between twenty-five and thirty-two of the fifty-five delegates to the Constitutional Convention, including three-fourths of the Convention's leaders, generally favored judicial review; that such significant framers as Madison, Hamilton, and Gouverneur Morris went publicly on record as so holding; and that, indeed, the supremacy clause of Article VI of the Constitution and Article III, Section 2, of the basic document strongly imply the power at issue. It is fair to conclude that the debate over the *legitimacy* of judicial review has been settled by history.[54]

Marbury v. Madison. We cannot pass on to consider some of the ramifications of judicial review in the judicial and governmental pro-

---

[53]*The Supreme Court and the Constitution*, rev. ed. (Englewood Cliffs, N.J.: Prentice-Hall, 1962).

[54]See the perceptive article by John P. Roche, "Judicial Self-Restraint," 49 *The American Political Science Review* (September 1955).

cess without pausing to glance at its judicial "birth," as it were—with Chief Justice Marshall in the role of midwife—in the hallowed case of *Marbury* v. *Madison*.[55] It is a case that has been aptly called "the rib of the Constitution,"[56] and which Justice Frankfurter characterized as "indispensable" to the "character of a written constitution."[57] Marshall, who had been a delegate to the Ratifying Convention of Virginia, a one-term congressman from that state, John Adams's Secretary of State, and a brilliant lawyer, understood the Constitution and the needs of his land. He was determined to mold them as he deemed wise and appropriate. His chance came in what, with the possible exception of his decision in *McCulloch* v. *Maryland*[58] some sixteen years later, is the most significant decision on constitutional law ever rendered by the Court. That he should have disqualified himself from sitting in the case; that it could readily have been disposed of without meeting the constitutional issue; and that the construction itself was unnecessarily tortuous—none of these considerations now matters in the face of Marshall's momentous holding that "an act repugnant to the Constitution is void" and that it lies with the courts to determine the question of validity.

The background of *Marbury* v. *Madison* is sufficiently well known to obviate any lengthy discussion.[59] Briefly, John Adams, second president of the United States, had been defeated for re-election in 1800 by his arch political rival, Thomas Jefferson. In order to salvage at least something for his thoroughly trounced Federalist Party, Adams, in 1801, with the aid of an obliging lame-duck Federalist Congress, caused to have two statutes adopted—the Circuit Court and the District of Columbia Acts—that enabled him to nominate, and have his Senate confirm, fifty-nine federal judges—including his own secretary of state, John Marshall—and thus "pack" the judicial branch with "safe and loyal" Federalists. Presumably they would see

---

[55]1 Cranch 137 (1803).

[56]Glendon A. Schubert, *Constitutional Politics* (New York: Holt, Rinehart and Winston, 1960), p. 178.

[57]"John Marshall and the Judicial Function" in *Government Under Law* (Cambridge: Harvard University Press, 1956), p. 8.

[58]4 Wheaton, 316 (1819).

[59]For a full and penetrating treatment, see Supreme Court Justice Harold H. Burton's article, "The Cornerstone of Constitutional Law: The Extraordinary Case of Marbury v. Madison," 36 *American Bar Association Journal* 805 (October 1950). For a more historical piece, see John A. Garraty, "The Case of the Missing Commissions," in *Quarrels That Have Shaped the Constitution* (New York: Harper & Row, 1964).

to it that any excesses of the incoming Republican "radicals" and "Jacobins" would be held to a minimum. Prophetically, it became Marshall's job, as the outgoing secretary of state, to deliver the commissions of these last-minute appointees, often called the Adams "Midnight Judges." But because of the pressure of time and last-minute preparations for the inauguration—when he would have to swear in his cordially disliked distant cousin as chief executive of the United States—Marshall failed to deliver seventeen of the judicial commissions, literally leaving them on the desk of his successor, James Madison. When Jefferson and Madison found these undelivered commissions, the new president exclaimed: "The nominations crowded in by Mr. Adams after he knew he was not appointing for himself I treat as mere nullities."[60] And, according to one account, the commissions were "disposed of with the other waste paper and rubbish of the office."[61]

Among the disappointed appointees were William Marbury and three colleagues,[62] who had been duly nominated and confirmed as justices of the peace for the District of Columbia. They hired Adams's Attorney General, Charles Lee, to take their case to court. Lee saw his best chance in Section 13 of the Judiciary Act of 1789, the basic statute that had organized the federal judiciary. This gave to the Supreme Court the authority to issue *writs of mandamus* (Latin for "we command"), writs commanding a public officer to perform his or her official, ministerial, nondiscretionary duty. In 1803,[63] the case of *Marbury* v. *Madison* thus reached the original docket jurisdiction of the highest court of the land, with Chief Justice John Marshall presiding. Marshall promptly issued an order to Madison to show cause why the requested writ should not be issued against him—an order that was ignored by the secretary of state. The stage was now set for the momentous opinion and decision.

Marshall, shrewd and wise, recognized that he was confronted with a Hobson's choice: if he were to *grant* the writ of mandamus in the face of almost certain disobedience by Madison (acting upon Jefferson's instructions), the fledgling Supreme Court would be powerless to do anything about enforcing its order; yet if he were to *refuse*

---

[60]Charles Warren, *The Supreme Court in United States History*, rev. ed. (Boston: Little, Brown, 1937), Vol. I, p. 201.

[61]Charles S. Hyneman, *The Supreme Court on Trial* (New York: Atherton Press, 1963), p. 75.

[62]Denis Ramsey, William Harper, and Robert Townshend Hooe.

[63]Congress's angry Jeffersonian majority had cancelled the Court's 1802 term!

to grant the writ, Jefferson would triumph. Facing that unenviable choice squarely, Marshall ingeniously managed to have his cake and eat it too. In what his biographer, Senator Albert J. Beveridge of Indiana, described as "a coup as bold in design and daring as that by which the Constitution had been framed,"[64] Marshall—conscious of and delighting in what was indubitably an emotion-charged, fascinating political situation—*declared Section 13 of the Judiciary Act unconstitutional.* It was unconstitutional, he wrote for his unanimous Court,[65] because Congress had given to the Supreme Court a power which it could not legally receive: for that power represented a *statutory* addition to the Court's *original* jurisdiction—a jurisdiction that could be altered *only by constitutional amendment* (as indeed it had been by the Eleventh Amendment in 1798, following the case of *Chisholm* v. *Georgia*[66] of 1793). "An act repugnant to the Constitution is void," crowed the chief justice, explaining that it is

> *emphatically* the province and duty of the judicial department to say what the law is. *Those who apply the rule to particular cases, must of necessity expound and interpret that rule...A law repugnant to the Constitution is void;...courts as well as other departments are bound by that instrument.*[67]

True, said Marshall, Marbury and his friends were clearly entitled to their commissions, and he denounced Jefferson and Madison from the bench in scathing terms. Proceeding with *dicta* that consumed twenty of the twenty-seven pages of the case, he announced that not only did the legal right to the commission exist, but that Lee had been correct in assuming that the laws of the country afforded a remedy. Unfortunately, that remedy was unconstitutional.

And thus judicial review was born formally as the potent power we know today, although it had actually already been applied in five minor instances prior to *Marbury*, in effect as early as 1792 and 1794.[68] But Marshall had now given it the dignity of both full dress

---

[64] *The Life of John Marshall* (Boston: Houghton Mifflin Co., 1919), Vols. I and III, pp. 323 and 142, respectively.

[65] Associate Justices Paterson, S. Chase, and Washington (Moore and Cushing not sitting in the case).

[66] 2 Dallas 419.

[67] *Marbury* v. *Madison*, 1 Cranch (1803). (Italics supplied.)

[68] See *Hayburn's Case*, 2 Dallas 409 (1792); *United States* v. *Yale Todd*, decided in 1794, but not cited until it became a footnote fifty-seven years later in *United States* v. *Ferreira*, 13 Howard 40 (1851); *Ware* v. *Hylton*, 3 Dallas 199 (1796);

and full explanation. And he delighted in the knowledge that by his *coup de main*, blending apparent rather than real judicial self-abnegation with very real judicial branch's claim to equi-powerful partnership in the tripartite governmental system, he had attained a major goal of the democracy-distrusting Federalists.

Although Marshall evidently strained the judicial process by making *Marbury* v. *Madison* the catalyst for the pronunciamento of the judicial veto, there is not the slightest doubt that judicial review is crucial to the federal character of the governmental process in the United States, the principles of separation of powers, and those of limited government. Whatever his motives were—and they were at once noble and crafty—the great chief justice rendered a monumental service to the republic in expounding the doctrine. Far from being a usurpation, judicial review, a product of our common Western history and the "logical result of centuries of European thought and colonial experiences,"[69] has conclusively powerful claims to authenticity, buttressed by a strong line of precedents and convincing contemporary literature. That its exercise has inevitably become a "can of worms" is both understandable and fascinating, and very much a matter of line-drawing.

LINE-DRAWING AND JUDICIAL POLICY

Judging and Legislating

Even those who are philosophically opposed to the principle of judicial review grant that courts must possess the authority to interpret and to adjudicate, but that they must not "legislate." In that view they do not differ significantly from those who favor the principle of judicial review. The difficult problem—and it is one that is crucial to an understanding of the continuing controversy that has embroiled the judiciary, in general, and the Supreme Court, in particular—is where to draw the line between *"judging"* and *"legislating,"* especially since there is no agreement on these definitions.

In a sense, all judging is "legislating" and all legislating is "judging." What the basic indictment of the Court refers to, of

---

Clerke v. *Harwood*, 3 Dallas 342 (1797); and *Hylton* v. *United States*, 3 Dallas 171 (1796). In *Yale Todd* the Court had declared a federal pension claim law *unconstitutional*, but in all the other precedents here cited, it had *upheld* legislation that was challenged on constitutional grounds.

[69]Mauro Cappelletti, *Judicial Review in the Contemporary World* (Indianapolis: Bobbs-Merrill Co., 1971), p. 25.

course, is its alleged making of policy, its "law making," its prescriptive policy making, even given its ultimate power of judicial review—for these are presumably matters reserved to the legislature. In fact, there is little or no disagreement with this basic premise. The difficulties arise in what one views as proper adjudication and how one regards judicial decisions. What appears to be a bona fide exercise of judicial power to some will appear to others as an unjustifiable judicial assumption of legislative authority—of "law making" instead of "law finding."

In Chapter 4, we will discuss the Supreme Court's decision on the use of the twenty-two-word New York State-composed nondenominational prayer in the public schools, which the high tribunal ruled to be a violation of the principle of separation of church and state, and hence an unconstitutional infringement of the First Amendment.[70] Those who favored the decision regarded it as not only a proper but a necessary exercise of the judicial function. Those who opposed it, on the other hand, castigated the decision as unwarranted judicial legislation that denied the legislative majority the right to set public policy. When, after long years of refusing to hear the question of legislative districting on grounds that it was of a "political nature" and thus beyond its jurisdiction, the Court finally reversed itself in 1962 in *Baker* v. *Carr*[71] and declared the issue justiciable in line with the requirements of the Fourteenth Amendment (and later Article I of the main body of the Constitution),[72] there were those who agreed wholeheartedly, and those—including Justice Felix Frankfurter, who wrote a sixty-eight-page dissenting opinion in the case—who thought the Court had ventured into the sphere of legislating. And it goes without saying that similarly opposing views extended to the Court's dramatic post-*Gideon*[73] right-to-counsel extension cases of the 1960s;[74] greeted what is probably the most far-reaching social policy decision of the century, the unanimous desegregation case of *Brown* v. *Board of Education*;[75] and engulfed the Court's contentious holdings

---

[70]*Engel* v. *Vitale*, 370 U.S. 421 (1962).

[71]369 U.S. 186 (1962).

[72]*Wesberry* v. *Sanders*, 376 U.S. 1 (1964).

[73]*Gideon* v. *Wainwright*, 372 U.S. 335 (1963). See the discussion of that case in this text, pp. 130–132.

[74]372 U.S. 335 (1963); *Massiah* v. *United States*, 377 U.S. 201 (1964); *Escobedo* v. *Illinois*, 378 U.S. 478 (1964); especially *Miranda* v. *Arizona*, 384 U.S. 436 (1966); and *Orozco* v. *Texas*, 394 U.S. 324 (1969).

[75]347 U.S. 483 (1954).

in the emotion-charged *Abortion Cases* of 1973 and their subsequent extensions.[76]

Ox-Goring?   The *Brown* case raises the intriguing point that much of the criticism directed at the Court over the judging-legislating dichotomy is a direct reaction to the goring of personal oxen. The emotion-charged problems of racial desegregation and integration are tailor-made for such a charge. Thus the earlier counterparts of those most vehement in their attack on the Court for "outrageous judicial usurpation of legislative power" in 1954 had lauded the Court a century before when it decided the famous case of *Dred Scott v. Sandford*[77] "their" way. Conversely, the earlier counterparts of the backers of the 1954 *Brown* decision had been denunciatory of *Dred Scott* in 1857. A myriad of similar illustrations quickly come to mind to lend substance to the basic charge that much of the criticism of the Court is sheer sophistry and ax-grinding. One need only look to the avalanche of declarations of unconstitutionality of New Deal legislation by the pre-1937 Court on sundry constitutional grounds (thirteen of these coming between 1934 and 1936) when the majority of the justices, backed by the foes of the New Deal, insisted that all they did was "to lay the article of the Constitution which is invoked beside the statute which is challenged" and then decide "whether the latter squares with the former." In the thirteen cases just alluded to, the New Deal laws never seemed to "square" in the eyes of Justices Van Devanter, Sutherland, McReynolds, and Butler, and frequently not in those of Chief Justice Hughes and Justice Roberts. Yet they almost always did seem to "square" in the eyes of Justices Brandeis, Stone, and Cardozo.

Who had the better "eyes" and what does the verb "to square" mean? Considerable subjectivity attends the problem, primarily on

---

[76]*Roe* v. *Wade*, 410 U.S. 113 and *Doe* v. *Bolton*, 410 U.S. 179 (1973); *Planned Parenthood of Missouri* v. *Danforth*, 428 U.S. 52 (1976); *Beal* v. *Doe, Maher* v. *Doe*, and *Polker* v. *Doe*, 432 U.S. 438, 526, 519 (1977); *Caulotti* v. *Franklin*, 439 U.S. 379 (1979) and *Bellotti* v. *Baird*, 443 U.S. 622 (1979); *Harris* v. *McRae*, 448 U.S. 297 (1980); *H.L.* v. *Matheson*, 450 U.S. 398 (1981); the trio of 1983 *Abortion Cases*, 462 U.S. 416, 476, and 506, respectively, and the 1986 *Thornburgh* holding.

[77]19 Howard 393 (1857). The case featured nine opinions, Chief Justice Taney delivering the principal one, Justices Curtis and McLean dissenting. Taney's opinion for the Court held, a.o., that no Negro could be a citizen; that the Negro was a person of "an inferior order"; that he was a slave and thus his master's permanent property, no matter whether the latter took him to free or slave territory; and that the Missouri Compromise was unconstitutional.

the part of those whose own ox is being gored, but also on the part of the justices themselves. Still, any interpretation that dismisses the basic argument as one bottomed on purely personal values is guilty of considerable oversimplification of a highly vexatious and significant issue.

Judicial "Monks or Scientists"? One thing is clear: judges are judges, but they are also "men, not disembodied spirits." In the words of Justice Frankfurter, a principal apostle of judicial self-restraint, "as men, they respond to human situations. They do not reside in a vacuum." Justice McReynolds insisted characteristically that a jurist cannot and should not be "an amorphous dummy, unspotted by human emotions." As Chief Justice Warren wrote, "our judges are not monks or scientists, but participants in the living stream of our national life, steering the law between the dangers of rigidity on the one hand and formlessness on the other."[78] He thus echoed the realistic appraisal four decades earlier by Thomas Reed Powell, who had observed that "[j]udges have preferences for social policies as you and I. They form their judgments after the varying fashions in which you and I form ours. They have hands, organs, dimensions, senses, affections, passions. They are warmed by the same winter and summer and by the same ideas as a layman is."[79]

In interpreting our basic document, judges do, of course, "legislate," a fact of judicial life recognized "without hesitation" by Justice Holmes when he wrote that, indeed, jurists "do and must legislate." He, like his successors, Cardozo and Frankfurter, fully believed in judicial self-abnegation. But, he added—and it is a "but" crucial to the issue under discussion—they can legislate "only interstitially; they are confined from molar to molecular motions."[80] These motions are rigidly circumscribed by walls that are unseen by the layperson, walls built of the heritage of the taught tradition of the law. No one expressed this at once more pungently and beautifully than Justice Cardozo who, after acknowledging that "the great tides and currents which engulf the rest of men, do not turn aside in their course, and pass the judges idly by,"[81] wisely explained that a jurist

---

[78]"The Law and the Future," 52 *Fortune* 106 (November 1955).

[79]"The Logic and Rhetoric of Constitutional Law," 15 *Journal of Philosophy, Psychology, and Scientific Method* 656 (1918).

[80]*Southern Pacific Co.* v. *Jensen*, 244 U.S. 205 (1916), at 221.

[81]*The Nature of the Judicial Process* (New Haven: Yale University Press, 1921), p. 168.

is not to innovate at pleasure. He is not a knight-errant, roaming at will in pursuit of his own ideal of beauty or of goodness. He is to draw his inspiration from consecrated principles. He is not to yield to spasmodic sentiment, to vague and unregulated benevolence. He is to exercise a discretion informed by tradition, methodized by analogy, disciplined by system, and subordinated to "the primordial necessity of order in the social life."[82]

Guidelines of the Taught Tradition of the Law

The "consecrated principles" of which Justice Cardozo spoke are part and parcel of the taught tradition of the law, which guides and motivates the judges in their decisions. Many facets combine to bring this tradition and these principles of life, and although they are almost inevitably interpreted along somewhat divergent lines by different judges (of whom Justices Black and Frankfurter are excellent illustrations), they *are* ascertainable. There is that abiding sense of judicial integrity that comes with the robe; a consciousness of precedent; rules of procedure; recognition of the Court's threefold role as a governmental, political, and legal institution; the presumption of constitutionality of legislation; an awareness of membership in the body politic, of the responsibility of not being too far out of step with consensus—certainly not in the *long* run; the concept of equality before the law and at the bar of the Supreme Court. A few words of explanation for some of these guidelines, particularly those of a policy-procedure nature, are in order.

Adherence to Precedent. As a principle of judicial policy, adherence to precedent—the doctrine of *stare decisis et quieta non movere* ("let the decision stand and do not disturb the calm")—is both necessary and desirable. It is normally accepted as a rule of thumb unless there is clear reason for change. This, of course, requires a careful weighing of alternatives available, for it often comes down to a choice of precedents. Precedents abound, and not all precedents are of equal rank. Lord Coke lauded ". . . the known certaintie of the law [which] is the saftie of all. . . ." but he was neither adverse to overturning precedent nor to manufacturing one. Indeed, we must not expect what Chief Justice Hughes called "the icy stratosphere of certainty." According to Justice Brandeis, *stare decisis*

---

[82]Ibid., p. 141.

> *is usually the wise policy because in most matters it is more impor-*
> *tant that the applicable rule of law be settled than that it be settled*
> *right....This is commonly true even where the error is a matter of*
> *serious concern, provided correction can be had by legislation.* But
> in cases involving the Federal Constitution, where correction
> through legislation is practically impossible, this Court has often
> overruled its earlier decisions. *The Court bows to the lessons of expe-*
> *rience and the force of better reasoning, recognizing that the process*
> *of trial and error, so fruitful in the physical sciences is appropriate*
> *also in the judicial function.*[83]

And, in so doing, the Court both "judges" and "legislates." In the
wistful words of Justice Stewart, endeavoring to explain his change of
mind vis-à-vis precedent in an important labor case: "Wisdom too
often never comes, and so one ought not to reject it merely because it
comes late."[84]

Procedural Guidelines. Organized, predictable procedure is of
the essence to any judicial body, and particularly to the highest tribunal, for the vast majority of its work, and certainly its *raison d'être*, is
appellate. Hence:

1. A definite *"case"* or *"controversy"* at law or in equity between
bona fide adversaries under the Constitution, involving the protection
or enforcement of valuable legal rights, or the punishment, preven-
tion, or redress of wrongs directly concerning the party or parties
bringing suit, must exist before the Court will entertain its consideration.

2. As pointed out in considerable detail in Chapter 1, the Court must
have *jurisdiction* over the subject matter and/or the *parties* involved
in a case. And, of course, the issue must be *justiciable:* it must lie within the judiciary's power and authority to adjudicate it.

3. The party or parties bringing suit must have *standing.* This
requires proof that whoever brings suit is personally and substantially
injured by a statute or governmental action or is in substantial danger

---

[83]*Burnett* v. *Coronado Oil and Gas Co.,* 285 U.S. 293 (1932). (Italics added.)
[84]*Boys Market* v. *Retail Clerks' Union,* 398 U.S. 235 (1970), at 255. In fact, he
quoted Justice Frankfurter—one of the staunchest adherents to precedent, in
Henslee v. *Union Planters Bank,* 335 U.S. 595 (1949), at 600.

of such injury, and/or is a member of the class or group[85] to whom the action or statute applies.[86]

4. As was explained in Chapter 1, the federal constitutional judiciary may not render *advisory opinions.* This matter was settled as early as 1793, when Chief Justice Jay told President Washington that he would not answer certain questions put to him by the chief executive because the Court could not tender legal advice, its role being confined to decisions of cases that arose in the course of bona fide litigation.

5. The Court will not entertain generalities, which means that a petitioner must not only invoke a specific clause of the Constitution but that the matter to be litigated must comprise a specific *live* constitutional issue.

6. The Court will not pass on the constitutionality of a statute or official action at the behest of one who has *availed himself of its benefits,* but subsequently decided to challenge its legality.

7. Prior to making applications for review, *all remedies below must have been exhausted* in prescribed lower court procedure, scrupulously followed.

8. The federal question raised at the bar of the Court must be *substantial* rather than trivial, must be the pivotal point of the case, and must be a part of the plaintiff's case rather than a part of his opponent's defense.

9. Although it is axiomatic that "matters of law grow downward into roots of fact, and matters of fact reach upward, without a break, into matters of law,"[87] it is true as a matter of policy-procedure that

---

[85]See the perceptive article by Karen Orren, "Standing to Sue: Interest Group Conflict in the Federal Courts," 70 *The American Political Science Review* 723 (September 1976).

[86]"Class action" suits in federal courts have nearly doubled since 1970, and the Court moved to limit their facility drastically. See, for example, *Eisen* v. *Carlisle and Jacqueline,* 416 U.S. 979 (1974) and *Oppenheimer Fund* v. *Sanders,* 437 U.S. 340 (1978). See my *The Judicial Process,* pp. 370–74. But the Court has evinced a tendency to open other modes of access, such as its recent, highly permissive, interpretation of the Civil Rights Act of 1871 (e.g., its 1980 holding in *Maine* v. *Thiboutot,* 448 U.S. 1).

[87]John Dickinson, *Administrative Justice and the Supremacy of Law* (Cambridge: Harvard University Press, 1927), p. 55.

the Supreme Court, as an appellate tribunal, will not normally accept matters of *fact* rather than those of *law* for bases of review.

Presumption of Constitutionality of Legislation. Even if the challenge to a legislative enactment is entirely valid and proper, the Court—true to its role as a judicial rather than a law-making body —*will presume a law's constitutionality.* If the Court must meet the constitutional issue per se—something it will try hard to avoid in line with its dedication to uphold rather than destroy the will of the law-making majority—it will, as Chief Justice Hughes put it so cogently in 1937, at a critical moment in the Court's history, endeavor to

> *save and not to destroy. We have repeatedly held that as between two possible interpretations of a statute, by one of which it would be unconstitutional and the other valid, our plain duty is to adopt that which will save the act. Even to avoid a serious doubt the rule is the same.*[88]

It follows logically, then, that if a case or controversy can conceivably be decided upon *any other than on constitutional grounds*—such as by statutory construction, which constitutes the greatest single area of the Court's work, or if it can rest on an independent state ground—the Court will normally be more than eager to decide it thus. "The most important thing we do is *not* doing," said Justice Brandeis once in this connection, and the Court has thus saved itself many a battle with Congress.

In fact, it is here that the Court, to an important degree, can have its cake and eat it too, for statutory construction may well mean that the teeth of a law are being pulled even while the appearance *cum* illusion of its existence remains. For example, when the Court ruled in *Yates* v. *United States*[89] that the *theoretical* advocacy of the overthrow of the government by force and violence was not a violation of the Smith Act of 1940, it went to great lengths to point out that it had *not* overruled its landmark decision of six years earlier upholding that statute in *Dennis* v. *United States*,[90] but that it merely construed and interpreted its meaning. Thus the act per se still stood against First and Fifth Amendment challenges, but in construing the essential dif-

---

[88]*National Labor Relations Board* v. *Jones and Laughlin Steel Corporation*, 301 U.S. 1.

[89]354 U.S. 298 (1957).

[90]341 U.S. 494 (1951).

ference between "theoretical advocacy" and "advocacy in the realm of *action*," the Court had in effect amended the Smith Act and rendered convictions under it by the government far more difficult. Its author, veteran Congressman Howard Smith (D.-Va.), protested on the floor of the House that the Court had misconstrued congressional intent. Yet, with the exception of a relatively minor amendment involving the meaning and extent of the verb "organize," Congress failed to do anything to alter the Court's ruling. Any search for congressional "intent or purpose" inevitably becomes somewhat of an exercise in psychoanalysis. Nor, as Justice Cardozo once observed acidly, is "a great principle of constitutional law susceptible of comprehensive statement in an adjective."[91]

Be that as it may, the Court will not ordinarily impute illegal motives to the lawmakers. But it is inevitable that different interpretations will be put upon the Court's policy of deference to the legislature, especially when, as illustrated above, statutory construction all but accomplishes the decimation of law while holding aloft its shell. It is hence not surprising that even on the Court itself, those in the minority will frequently accuse the majority of ignoring the will of Congress by indulging in judicial legislating. A contemporary example is the dissenting opinion of Justice Clark in a 5:4 decision, in which the majority held that a resident Swiss alien, one George E. M. Fleuti, who had left the country "briefly and casually," did not, on his return, make an "entry" of the kind that under the congressional statute at issue in the case would subject him to deportation for "pre-entry misbehavior." With dripping sarcasm, Clark began his dissenting opinion as follows:

> *I dissent from the Court's judgment and opinion because "statutory construction" means to me that the Court can* construe *but not that it can* construct *them. The latter function is reserved to the Congress.*[92]

The words "construe" and "construct" were underlined. Naturally, the majority's interpretation or construction was and is always subject to change by Congress, which in effect can pass a law saying "We did not mean what you said we did; *here* is what we *really* meant." But although this is done from time to time it is the exception rather than the

[91]*Carter* v. *Carter Coal Co.*, 298 U.S. 238 (1936), at 327, dissenting opinion.
[92]*Rosenberg* v. *Fleuti*, 374 U.S. 449 (1963). Justice Clark was joined in this dissent by Justices Harlan, Stewart, and White.

rule. For Congress is normally quick to criticize but slow to act—which indubitably leads to the interpretation that the Court may well have been right in its judgment in the first place.

Judicial Limitations.　It is of the highest importance to recognize that, as a matter of fundamental policy, the Court brings a genuine sense of deference to the legislative will; but there are limits, and in some areas these limits are now reached earlier than in others. *Prior* to 1937 (to use the most obvious illustration of the point) that limit was reached by a majority of the Court rather quickly in the realm of substantive due process as applied to economic-proprietarian and social legislation growing out of the experimental programs of the New Nationalism, the New Freedom, and the New Deal. Yet infinite restraint was shown regarding governmental enactments or practices concerning the cultural freedoms in the Bill of Rights. Conversely, the *post-1937* Court majority has turned the tables dramatically and drastically: Since that time it has been almost impossible for government, state as well as federal, to do "wrong" in the realm of economic-proprietarian and social legislation—yet government is constantly in hot water with the Court regarding the Bill of Rights and the "due process" and "equal protection of the laws" clauses of the Fourteenth Amendment.

Although this judicial metamorphosis has occurred, the Supreme Court insists that it is not designed either to serve as a check against inept, unwise, emotional, narrowminded legislators—or against unwise, unfair, silly, poor, injudicious, stupid, even undemocratic legislation or executive-administrative action. The cardinal question for the Court is always and must always remain: "Is it legal? Is it constitutional? Can it stand?" It is not easy to stand aloof in the face of legislation and actions that offend the mind and heart—but with that, in the words of the judicial philosopher *par excellence* of our age, Justice Holmes, "we have no [official judicial] concern."[93] No one made the point more eloquently than Justice Frankfurter, when, writing in dissent, he warned:

> It is not easy to stand aloof and allow want of wisdom to prevail, to disregard one's own strongly held view of what is wise in the conduct of affairs. But it is not the business of this Court to pronounce policy. It must observe a fastidious regard for limitations on its own

---

[93]*Noble State Bank* v. *Haskell,* 219 U.S. 575 (1910).

> *power, and this precludes the Court's giving effect to its own notions*
> *of what is wise or politic. That self-restraint is of the essence in the*
> *observation of the judicial oath, for the Constitution has not*
> *authorized the justices to sit in judgment on the wisdom of what*
> *Congress and the executive branch do....* [94]

This, of course, is another way of reiterating the point made by
Chief Justice Waite more than eighty years earlier in the landmark
case of *Munn* v. *Illinois*,[95] where he wrote that for "protection against
abuses by legislatures the people must resort to the polls not the
courts." Or, to turn to the more contemporary statement by the second Justice Harlan, writing in his now famous dissent in *Reynolds* v.
Sims in 1964: "The Constitution is not a panacea for every blot upon
the public welfare; nor should this Court, ordained as a judicial body,
be thought of as a general haven for reform movements."[96]

Judicial Activism and Judicial Restraint

It is easy and appropriate to agree with the basic philosophy of judicial self-restraint, but it cannot settle the concurrent interpretive
problem of finding that area where the "Constitution expressly forbids." The Court cannot settle it by any ready and easy formula, for
no formula, other than the basic commitment to judicial self-
restraint, is either discernible or devisable; and not even the many and
energetic modern apostles of the scientific method and behaviorism
can help us draw such a line.

In essence, the matter comes back to individual interpretation by
the jurists concerned. In the final analysis, it is the Supreme Court
that must decide the ultimate constitutional question—and, as we
have seen again and again, it does so often only because the other two
branches, and notably the legislature, have failed or refused to perform their jobs and have passed the proverbial "buck" to the Court.
Now, the Court of course can continue that game, but there comes a
time when it will refuse to play and, rising to its responsibility as it
conceives of it, will tackle the issue, no matter how delicate, or how
violent the public response. Obvious examples are the controversies
involving desegregation, criminal justice, privacy, and legislative re-

---

[94]*Trop* v. *Dulles*, 356 U.S. 86 (1958).
[95]94 U.S. 113 (1876).
[96]377 U.S. 533, at 624.

districting. In accepting the challenge and in deciding the emotion-charged, difficult public issues and policies involved, the Court indeed did judge *and* legislate. Perhaps it did so because, as ex-Attorney General Francis Biddle often suggested, these comprise the areas of the "can't helps." But, above all, it did so because it *is* the guardian and interpreter of the Constitution; a Constitution, in Chief Justice Marshall's words, "intended to endure for ages to come, and consequently, to be adapted to the various *crises* of human affairs,"[97] a Constitution that, as Justice Holmes stated, must ever be alive to "the felt necessities of the time." Still, is that not an essentially *political* task?

Dichotomies. Not surprisingly, against this background various justices approach their tasks of judging and interpreting in such a way as to indicate radically different judicial philosophies. Vast oversimplification, and sometimes deliberate crass misinterpretation, has attended these manifestations of differences. Often lay and professional commentators on this basic problem have simply tried to explain it by classifying two "kinds" of justices on the bench: those they deem to be "liberals" and those they deem "conservative." Two less helpful, less accurate, and more confusing classifications can hardly be imagined! For just *who* is being so classified, and *why?* Broadly speaking, the tag "liberal" has been given to those justices on the post-1930 Court who have been willing to give a generous interpretation to the Bill of Rights and the Civil War Amendments, on the one hand, and have consistently upheld governmental legislation in the socioeconomic realm, on the other (e.g., Justices Holmes, Brandeis, Stone, Cardozo, Black, Douglas, Murphy, Rutledge, Warren, Brennan, Goldberg, Marshall, and Stevens). The label "conservative" has been awarded to those who have variously given less generous interpretations *either* in one *or* in both of these areas (e.g., Justices Van Devanter, McReynolds, Butler, Sutherland, Hughes, Roberts, Frankfurter, Reed, Jackson, Burton, Byrnes, Vinson, Minton, Clark, Whittaker, Harlan, Jr., Stewart, White, Burger, Powell, and Rehnquist). A more facile oversimplification is scarcely fathomable!

True, the "quads" (Van Devanter, Sutherland, McReynolds, and Butler) did predictably and consistently vote together to strike down a host of legislative socioeconomic experimentations that came before them—and they were often, but not always, joined by Hughes and

---

[97]*McCulloch* v. *Maryland*, 4 Wheaton 315 (1819), at 413.

Roberts. But it was Hughes and Roberts who exercised the 1937 "switch-in-time-that-saved-nine"—whatever their contentious motivations may have been in fact. Moreover, Van Devanter and Sutherland had a much more "liberal" outlook on the exercise of executive power, especially in foreign affairs, than did McReynolds and Butler, *and* the former two would often vote to support First and Fourteenth Amendment claims, whereas McReynolds and Butler rarely did. True also that Justices Frankfurter, Reed, Jackson, and Burton practiced considerably more judicial self-restraint in constitutional questions concerning the Bill of Rights than their brothers Black, Douglas, Murphy, and Rutledge, to use obvious examples. *But*, they were equally as "liberal" as the latter four when it came to the upholding of governmental legislation and regulation in the socioeconomic sphere.

To indicate further the folly of the tags "liberal" and "conservative," Justice Jackson's Bill of Rights record *before* he went to Nürnberg as Chief Prosecutor for the United States in the War Crimes Trials was decidedly more "liberal" in the First Amendment area than *after* his return. Justice Clark was generally regarded as a "conservative" on civil liberty questions by the critics, but he had a "liberal" record in the majority of First Amendment cases, other than those in the area of "national security." Clearly, the "liberal" versus "conservative" dichotomy is unhelpful, inaccurate, and confusing.

Judicial "Activism" versus "Restraint." More helpful classifications, if we must have them, are those jurists who are regarded as adhering to a judicial philosophy of "self-restraint"[98] versus those who are styled "activists." The former jurisprudence adheres, by and

---

[98]Professor Philip Kurland makes six basic assumptions for the doctrine of judicial self-restraint: "One is history and the obligation that constitutionalism imposes to adhere to the essential meaning put in the document by its framers. A second is the intrinsically undemocratic nature of the Supreme Court. A third is a corollary to the second, an abiding respect for the judgments of those branches of the government that are elected representatives of their constituents. A fourth is the recognition that judicial error at this level is more difficult of correction than other forms of judicial action. A fifth is respect for the judgments of earlier courts. But [sixth], the essential feature of judicial restraint that has gained most attention and aroused the greatest doubts probably because few men are themselves big enough to abide by its command—is the notion of rejection of personal preference." (Philip B. Kurland, *Mr. Justice Frankfurter and the Supreme Court* [Chicago: University of Chicago Press, 1971], p. 5.) For a conceptualism of "activism," see Bradley C. Canon, "Defining the Dimensions of Judicial Activism," 66 *Judicature* 6 (December–January, 1983).

large, to a "legal positivist" approach, the latter to that of a "legal realist."

In short, the "self-restrainers" will bend over backwards to permit the political branches of the government to act or not to act or to have the upper hand, even in areas of marginal constitutionality, provided that the action (or legislation) is not *really* a violation of the Constitution *as they see it.* The "activists," on the other hand, believe in a more affirmative, some would say aggressive, judicial policy, and are more ready to say "no," to governmental enactments and actions because they more quickly see a constitutional violation by the political branches. Moreover, unlike the "self-restrainers," the "activists" are inclined to "legislate," to "prescribe policy." This was the case, or so the charge goes, in the highly significant 1962 case of *Baker* v. *Carr,*[99] when the Supreme Court held the question of state apportionment and redistricting to be justiciable at the bar of the courts. In that 6:2 decision, the opinion was written by Justice Brennan ("activist"), joined by the chief justice ("activist"), and Justice Black ("carefully qualified activist"); but Justice Stewart ("moderate self-restrainer") concurred in a separate opinion, as did Justice Douglas ("advanced activist") and Justice Clark ("moderate self-restrainer"); while lengthy dissenting opinions were filed by Justices Frankfurter and Harlan (both principled "self-restrainers"). The position of the latter two is symptomatic of the basic cleavage in judicial philosophies: Frankfurter and Harlan insisted that the Court majority had usurped legislative functions; had entered the "political thicket"; had accepted a "political question" for review; and would thus find itself involved in a "mathematical quagmire."

Yet if the "line-up" in *Baker* v. *Carr* illustrates that Court's division on the question of involvement (Justice Whittaker did not participate in the case), it also illustrates the difficulty of labels. Moreover, *each* and every one of the above justices—and certainly not exempting Justice Douglas, the chief villain in the eyes of those who condemn "activism"—would deserve the label "self-restrainer" regarding governmental action in the socioeconomic sphere.

Categorizations. What it comes down to basically, then, is the position of the justices on the question of *when* the Court should enter the field to say "no." There is no question that Justices Black and Douglas, for example, generally said "no" long before Justices Frank-

---

[99]369 U.S. 186.

furter and Harlan did in the realm of most, but by no means all, provisions of the Bill of Rights. In that sense, we are thus confronted by two jurisprudential poles: Black and Douglas are characterized as "activists" (although they often split, Douglas the avowedly far more advanced, far more policy-prescriptive, except in the realms of speech and press[100] where Black was an avowed "absolutist"), and Frankfurter and Harlan, philosophical devotees of British majority rule and legislative supremacy, are "self-restrainters." Ironically, this gives the Black-Douglas group the same label as the Sutherland-Van Devanter-Butler-McReynolds group of the 1930s, since the latter practiced obvious "activism" in the economic realm. Yet in varying degrees they, especially McReynolds and Butler, were "self-restrainters" in civil liberties. It must be made crystal clear, however, that Black, for one, vehemently and eloquently rejected any and all "labelling" until the day he died in 1971, after more than thirty-four years of distinguished service on the Supreme Court.[101] Moreover, it is crucial to bear in mind Black's libertarian creed was operative only if he found *literal* (specifically expressed) warrant for it in the Constitution's verbiage.

Although it *is* possible to find these two broadly divergent philosophies of law on the bench, and although it *is* evident that the two poles are identifiable *in certain areas*—that they do exist, and that they are even predictable to an extent—any explanation that would label the Black-Douglas group as judging with its "heart" and the Frankfurter-Harlan group with its "head" is a gross oversimplification. In the final analysis it comes down to a basic difference of reading constitutional commands in the light of the judicial function (and there are remarkable differences *within* each group[102]). To conclude with the classic illustration of the First Amendment, Justice Black read as an *absolute* injunction against governmental action the words: "Congress shall make no law... abridging the freedom of speech, or of the press..." To Black and his followers this is indeed an absolute. "No to me means

---

[100]Yet even here Black was willing to proscribe *conduct*, as distinct from *expression*, whereas Douglas rarely, if ever, did. See, for example, the demonstration and/or "sit-in" cases of *Brown* v. *Louisiana*, 383 U.S. 131 (1966) and *Adderley* v. *Florida*, 385 U.S. 39 (1966). Two other dramatic splits between the two, with Douglas siding with the individual, were the "black armband" and "fuck the draft" cases of *Tinker* v. *Des Moines Independent Community School District*, 393 U.S. 503 (1969) and *Cohen* v. *California*, 403 U.S. 15 (1971), respectively. Harlan sided with Black in the former but with Douglas in the latter! Lines *are* elusive.

[101]See his *A Constitutional Faith* (New York: Alfred A. Knopf, 1968), pp. 15–22.

[102]See fn. 100.

no," as he said so often. Yet in the eyes of Justice Frankfurter—whom Yale Law Professor Fred Rodell called "the Emily Post of the Supreme Court"—and his followers, no matter how *unwise* a law in the area may be, it must stand in line with the canons of judicial self-restraint. As "F.F." put the matter in his concurring opinion in *Dennis* v. *United States,* upholding the Smith Act of 1940 against First and Fifth Amendment challenges:

> . . . *The demands of free speech in a democratic society as well as the interest in national security are better served by candid and informed weighing of the competing interests, within the confines of the judicial process, than by announcing dogmas too inflexible for the non-Euclidian problems to be solved. . . . [But] full responsibility for the choice cannot be given to the courts. Courts are not representative bodies. They are not designed to be a good reflex of a democratic society. Their judgment is best informed, and therefore most dependable, within narrow limits. Their essential quality is detachment, founded on independence.* [103]

Black agreed with much of the five last sentences and he wholeheartedly concurred insofar as the philosophy, stated so cogently by Frankfurter, applied to the socioeconomic realm. But he dissented vigorously from the "balancing" theme of the opening passages. To Black and his followers, freedom of expression—provided it is that and not proscribable "conduct"—(1) is not balanceable, for it is an *absolute;* and (2) the task of determining its constitutionality is peculiarly the province of the judicial branch whose responsibility it is to safeguard that matrix of all freedoms.

THE COURT AND PUBLIC POLICY

In spite of the above considerations, several important facts of judicial life point to a cardinal lesson of the Court's role in the legal, political, and governmental process: *The Court may have the last say, but potentially it has the last say only for a time.* The Supreme Court's only genuine power is the power to persuade; the purse and the sword are in other hands, as Alexander Hamilton put it so well in *The Federalist* #78.

The Court may be reversed in a variety of ways, and this has frequently been done. It may be reversed, totally or partly, *by legisla-*

---

[103]341 U.S. 494 (1951).

tive actions—as it was, for example, when Congress granted E. I. du
Pont de Nemours and Co., Inc., legislative relief[104] after the firm had
lost twice at the bar of the Supreme Court in an involved and expensive stock acquisition and holding matter,[105] and when it amended
Title VII of the Civil Rights Act of 1964 to clothe pregnancies with the
status of "disability" after the Court had ruled that the law did not
compel employers to provide "disability" benefits for pregnant workers.[106] It may *reverse itself by overruling* an earlier decision—as it did
when it unanimously upheld the wage-and-hour provisions of the
Fair Labor Standards Act of 1938 in *United States* v. *Darby* in 1941,
specifically overruling its earlier decision striking down 5:4 a similar
congressional enactment in 1918 in *Hammer* v. *Dagenhart*.[107] It may
alter an earlier decision by *distinguishing or modifying it,* thus in effect reversing itself, as it did so exasperatingly in the five *Covert-
Krueger* cases[108] between 1955 and 1960; here by no means solely, or
even predominantly, due to changes in membership on the Court, as
has been the natural course in many instances. And, finally, the
Court's judgment may be effectively reversed by the *passage of a constitutional amendment,* which was accomplished with the enactment
of Amendments Eleven, Thirteen, Fourteen, Fifteen, Sixteen, Nineteen, Twenty-four, and Twenty-six.[109] If not without some toil and
trouble, the Supreme Court may thus be overruled by other forces of
government, headed by Congress, or it may overrule itself. Most of its
decisions do "stick," but quite a few are altered or rendered moot.

In Step. There is no doubt that, generally speaking, the policy
of the Court—whose members, after all, are "children of their
times"—never departs drastically from the policy of the law-making

---

[104]Public Law 87-403, signed by President Kennedy on February 2, 1962, known
as the Williams-Bennett bill.

[105]*United States* v. *E. I. du Pont de Nemours and Co.*, 353 U.S. 586 (1957) and 366
U.S. 316 (1961).

[106]*General Electric Co.* v. *Gilbert*, 429 U.S. 125 (1978).

[107]312 U.S. 100 and 247 U.S. 251, respectively.

[108]*Kinsella* v. *Krueger*, 371 U.S. 470 and *Reid* v. *Covert*, U.S. 487 (June 11, 1956);
ditto, 352 U.S. 901 (November 5, 1956); ditto, 354 U.S. 1 (June 10, 1957); *Kinsella*
v. *Singleton*, 361 U.S. 234 and *Grisham* v. *Hagan*, 361 U.S. 278 (January 18,
1960).

[109]The Eleventh concerned the original jurisdiction of the Court; Thirteen, Fourteen, and Fifteen were the Civil War Amendments; Sixteen, the Income Tax;
Nineteen, Woman Suffrage; Twenty-four, the Poll Tax, and Twenty-six, the
eighteen-year-old vote in state and local as well as federal elections.

majority *in the long run*. Notable exceptions are decisions involving the Bill of Rights, especially Amendments One and Five, and the egalitarian and due process facets of the Fourteenth—exceptions clearly demonstrated during 1940–1949, 1954–1957, and again markedly and continuously since 1962, although less so in the criminal justice sector with the advent of the Burger Court of the early 1970s.

In the short run, the Court has often been out of step with the lawmaking majority, but it either succeeded in its short-run educational mission or it "came around" in the long run; and, in the appropriate words of Edward S. Corwin, "the run must not be too long a run, either!"

In the timeless observation of Alexis de Tocqueville of over a century ago, the justices do indeed possess enormous power, "but it is the power of public opinion"—although the Court must be a leader of it, not merely its register. The Supreme Court is quite conscious of the overall exhortation, well expressed by Francis Biddle, that "we must not get away too far from life, and should continually touch the earth for renewed vitality."[110] If the Court is to thrive, it must, in line with Professor Wallace Mendelson's admonition, "respect the social forces that determine elections and other major political settlements. No court can long withstand the morals of its era."[111] The Court is much better at saying what the government *may* or *may not* do than at prescribing what it *must* do and *how* it must go about doing it. Indeed, the Court should resolutely shun prescriptive policy making.

The Custodian. Nonetheless, the Supreme Court of the United States must play its role as educator, legitimator, and arbiter. It must remain true to its function as teacher in an eternal national constitutional seminar. No other branch can fill that role. It acts "as the instrument of national moral values that have not been able to find other governmental expressions"[112]—always assuming, of course, that it functions within its authorized sphere of constitutional and statutory application and interpretation. Thus, it defines values and pro-

---

[110]Biddle, in Jackson, *The Supreme Court in the American System of Government* (Cambridge, Mass.: Harvard University Press, 1965), p. 73.

[111]*Justices Black and Frankfurter: Conflict in the Court* (Chicago: University of Chicago Press, 1961), pp. 75–76. See also Robert A. Dahl, "The Supreme Court and Majority Control," in his *Pluralist Democracy in the United States: Conflict and Consent* (Chicago: Rand McNally & Co., 1967), pp. 154–170.

[112]Anthony Lewis, *The New York Times Magazine*, June 17, 1962, p. 38.

claims principles and, as our "sober second thought,"[113] is the natural forum in our society for the individual and for the small group. "The Court's essential function," wrote Chief Justice Warren tellingly in 1968, "is to act as the final arbiter of minority rights."[114]

The Supreme Court is simply the greatest institutional safeguard we possess. Despite the storms that have buffeted and whipped it, it has remained our national conscience as well as our institutional common sense. And, as Justice Robert H. Jackson told his countrymen in *The Supreme Court in the American System of Government*,[115] the small but superb book that became his epitaph:

> *The people have seemed to feel that the Supreme Court, whatever its defects, is still the most detached, dispassionate, and trustworthy custodian that our system affords for the translation of abstract into concrete constitutional commands.*[116]

As such, the Court continues to fulfill the fascinating, crucial, however delicate, role of heeding the "felt necessities of the time,"[117] while holding aloft the proud banner of constitutional fundamentals.

---

[113]Charles L. Black, Jr., *The People and the Court: Judicial Review in a Democracy* (New York: The Macmillan Co., 1960), p. 12.

[114]As quoted in *The Philadelphia Inquirer*, October 4, 1968, p. 2.

[115]The lectures comprising it were delivered at Harvard University by his son. See fn. 110.

[116]Ibid., p. 23.

[117]Oliver Wendell Holmes, Jr., *The Common Law* (Boston: Little, Brown and Co., 1881), p. 1.

3

Fundamental Freedoms:

Basic Considerations

Whatever one's individual views may be regarding either the wisdom or the appropriateness of the Court's role in our democratic society, one thing is clear: the Supreme Court of the United States is beyond question *the* great and ultimate defender of the basic freedoms of the American people. Rightly or wrongly, the Court, since the mid-1920s, has frequently stepped into the perceived vacuum created by the failure—or possibly default—of Congress and the executive branch to discharge certain responsibilities imposed or implied for those realms by the Constitution. On balance, there is simply no doubt that the Supreme Court has been the steadfast guardian of the people's liberties. Its continuing involvement with the basic or cultural freedoms—variously termed civil rights and civil liberties[1]—reflects the growing concern of the people, both as individuals and as

---

[1]Although some would object, the two terms are used interchangeably here. They are to be distinguished from all the other rights and freedoms individuals may enjoy under law because they are especially protected, in one manner or another, against violation *by governments* on all levels. (In Canada, the term civil *rights* refers exclusively to *private* relations—the legal relationship between person and person in private life.) See J.A. Corry and Henry J. Abraham, *Elements of Democratic Government*, 4th ed. (New York: Oxford University Press, 1964), pp. 234–239.

members of interest groups, with these freedoms and the concomitant rights and responsibilities that inevitably attend them.[2]

A Changed Emphasis

The development of judicial concern and action over civil rights, largely a post-1920 phenomenon, applies particularly to that area of the basic freedoms variously known as "cultural," "political," "human," or—awkwardly, but quite meaningfully—"noneconomic-proprietarian." This does not imply that there is no judicial concern with the economic-proprietarian sphere, but the vast majority of the civil rights of this century have been in other areas. They may be categorized chiefly, if somewhat loosely, into six delineations: (1) due process of law in the criminal justice sector; (2) political equality in suffrage and legislative apportionment; (3) egalitarian concerns in the realms of race, sex, age, national origin, and alienage; (4) freedom of religion and separation of church and state; and (5) freedom of expression.

Even a cursory glance at the Court's history shows that the economic-proprietarian sphere was very much in the focus of the Court's work *prior* to the arrival of the New Deal, and especially so during the chief justiceships of Melvin W. Fuller (1888–1910), Edward D. White (1910–1921), William Howard Taft (1921–1930), and Charles Evans Hughes, who became chief justice in 1930. But the Hughes Court's emphasis on the sacredness of the economic sphere in effect terminated with the legendary "switch-in-time-that-saved-nine" in 1937, four years prior to the chief justice's resignation in 1941. Both the beginning and the end of the period 1888–1937 witnessed the zenith of the Court's emphasis upon economic freedom. It was Fuller's Court (with fifteen declarations of unconstitutionality of *federal* legislation alone) that "rediscovered" the tool of substantive due process. The latter, concerning itself with a law's substance or content, had been arguably "created" by John Marshall with his freedom of contract decisions in the *Dartmouth College* and *Fletcher* cases[3]—in order to strike down myriad attempts (with isolated

---

[2]On these problems, see my *Freedom and the Court: Civil Rights and Liberties in the United States*, 4th ed. (New York: Oxford University Press, 1982), *passim*.

[3]*Dartmouth College* v. *Woodward*, 4 Wheaton 518 (1819) and *Fletcher* v. *Peck*, 6 Cranch 87 (1810). Ultimately, however, the parenthood of substantive due process was attributed to a New York state court decision in 1859 in *Wynehamer* v. *People* (see p. 109 and fn. 44 of this text).

exceptions[4]) by both federal and state legislatures to experiment with socioeconomic regulatory legislation, on the grounds that these experiments violated the all but absolute liberty of contract viewed as mandated by the due process of law clauses of the Fifth and Fourteenth Amendments.[5] And it was Hughes's Court, at the end of that fifty-year period, with fourteen *federal* declarations of unconstitutionality alone, which upheld the general legal philosophy of the Fuller Court while using a somewhat different rationale: that federal legislative experimentation in the economic-proprietarian spheres was *ultra vires*—that is, beyond its authority—since it allegedly invaded, if it did not usurp, areas of constitutional authority reserved to the several states under the Tenth Amendment.[6] With but a few latter-day exceptions,[7] when the states did try to legislate in the economic-proprietarian sphere, they found themselves slapped down by the Court in accordance with variants of the old substantive due process concept.[8]

But those days are clearly gone. Ever since the advent of the "New Deal Court" in 1937 (dating from Justice Willis Van Devanter's retirement in June of that year and his subsequent replacement by Justice Black,[9] President Roosevelt's first appointment[10]), the Court's preoc-

---

[4]E.g., *Holden* v. *Hardy*, 169 U.S. 366 (an eight-hour Utah law for copper miners and smelters in 1896) and *Muller* v. *Oregon*, 208 U.S. 412 (a 1903 Oregon ten-hour law for women in most industrial establishments—this being the famed *Brandeis Brief* case).

[5]See, among others, *Lochner* v. *New York*, 198 U.S. 45 (1905)—a state statute; *Adair* v. *United States*, 208 U.S. 161 (1908)—a federal statute. For a different point of view, see John E. Semouche, *Charting the Future: The Supreme Court Responds to a Changing Society, 1890–1920* (Westport, Conn.: Greenwood Press, 1978).

[6]See, among others, *United States* v. *Butler*, 297 U.S. 1 (1936) and *Carter* v. *Carter Coal Co.*, 298 U.S. 238 (1936).

[7]For example, *Nebbia* v. *New York*, 291 U.S. 502 (1934) and *Home Building and Loan Association* v. *Blaisdell*, 290 U.S. 398 (1934).

[8]For example, *New York State Ice Co.* v. *Liebmann*, 285 U.S. 262 (1932) and *Morehead* v. *New York* ex rel *Tipaldo*, 298 U.S. 587 (1936).

[9]As of Black's ascent, the New Deal could usually count on, in addition to Black's, the votes of Justices Cardozo, Brandeis, Stone and—after their 1937 "conversion"—Chief Justice Hughes and/or Justice Owen J. Roberts.

[10]Counting Black's appointment and his elevation of Justice Stone to the chief justiceship after Hughes's retirement, F.D.R. appointed nine justices: Stanley F. Reed, Felix Frankfurter, William O. Douglas, Frank Murphy, Robert H. Jackson, James F. Byrnes, and Wiley B. Rutledge. Only President George Washington had appointed more: ten (actually fourteen, but four declined to serve).

cupation with the basic freedoms has been with the "noneconomic," and in particular with the six areas categorized above. Thus in 1976 a total of 5,320 civil rights suits alone were brought against employers in federal court, a 1500 percent increase from 1970! Between its enactment in 1871 and 1920, only twenty-one cases were brought under the Civil Rights Act of 1871, which authorizes suits against "every person" who "under color of law" violates the civil rights of another. In 1976 alone, 17, 543 suits were filed under that old statute—a figure that has continued to increase apace. Federal civil rights suits filed by *state* prison inmates in *federal* courts soared from 5,000 in 1973 to 17,889 in 1983.[11] Thus the overwhelming majority of judicial vetoes imposed upon the states since the 1937 "switch-in-time-that-saved nine," and *all but* seven of such vetoes against the national government—a total of sixty-two by early 1986[12]—have been invoked be-

---

[11]See A. E. Dick Howard, "I'll See You in Court: The States and the Supreme Court." Monograph published by the National Governors' Association, Center for Public Policy Research, Williamsburg, Va., 1980, and *The Daily Progress*, Charlottesville, Va., April 14, 1984, p. 1.

[12](1) *Tot* v. *United States*, 319 U.S. 463 (1943); (2) *United States* v. *Lovett*, 328 U.S. 303 (1946); (3) *United States* v. *Cardiff*, 344 U.S. 174 (1952); (4) *Bolling* v. *Sharpe*, 347 U.S. 497 (1954); (5) *United States* ex rel *Toth* v. *Quarles*, 350 U.S. 11 (1955); (6)–(8) *Reid* v. *Covert* and *Kinsella* v. *Kruger*, later coupled with *Kinsella* v. *Singleton* and *Grisham* v. *Hagan* and *McElroy* v. *United States*, 354 U.S. 1 (1957); 361 U.S. 234 (1960); and 361 U.S. 278 and 361 U.S. 281, respectively; (9) *Trop* v. *Dulles*, 356 U.S. 86 (1958); (10) *Kennedy* v. *Mendoza-Martinez*, 372 U.S. 144 (1963); (11) *Rusk* v. *Cort*, 372 U.S. 144 (1963); (12) *Schneider* v. *Rusk*, 377 U.S. 1963 (1964); (13) *Aptheker* v. *Secretary*, 378 U.S. 500 (1964); (14) *Lamont* v. *Postmaster General* and *Fixa* v. *Heilberg*, 381 U.S. 301 (1965); (15) *United States* v. *Brown*, 381 U.S. 437 (1965); (16) *United States* v. *Romano*, 382 U.S. 136 (1965); (17) *Afroyim* v. *Rusk*, 387 U.S. 253 (1967); (18) *United States* v. *Robel*, 389 U.S. 258 (1967); (19)–(21) *Marchetti* v. *United States*, 390 U.S. 39 (1968) and *Grosso* v. *United States*, 390 U.S. 62 (1968) and *Haynes* v. *United States*, 390 U.S. 85 (1968); (22) *United States* v. *Jackson*, 390 U.S. 569 (1968); (23) *Washington* v. *Legrant*, 394 U.S. 618 (1969)—usually cited under *Shapiro* v. *Thompson*; (24)–(28) *Leary* v. *United States*, 395 U.S. 6 (1969); (29)*Turner* v. *United States*, 396 U.S. 398 (1970); (30) *Schacht* v. *United States*, 398 U.S. 58 (1970); (31) *Oregon* v. *Mitchell*, 400 U.S. 112 (1970); (32) and (33) *Blount* v. *Rizzi* and *United States* v. *The Book Bin*, 400 U.S. 410; (34) *Tilton* v. *Richardson*, 403 U.S. 672 (1971); (35) *Chief of Capitol Police* v. *Jeanette Rankin Brigade*, 409 U.S. 972 (1972); (36) *Richardson* v. *Davis* and *Richardson* v. *Griffin*, 409 U.S. 1069 (1972); (37) and (38) *U.S. Department of Agriculture* v. *Murry* and *U.S. Department of Agriculture* v. *Moreno*, 413 U.S. 508 and 413 U.S. 528 (1973), respectively; (39) and (40) *Frontiero* v. *Richardson*, 411 U.S. 677 (1973); (41) *Jiminez* v. *Weinberger*, 417 U.S. 628 (1974); (42) *Weinberger* v. *Wiesenfeld*, 420 U.S. 636 (1975); (43) and (44) *Buckley* v. *Valeo*, 424 U.S. 1 (1976); (45) and (46) *National League of Cities* v. *Usery*, 426

cause they infringed on personal liberties, other than economic, safeguarded under the federal Constitution.

The "Double Standard"

This raises an intriguing question or problem. Since the Court, as of a generation or so ago, has obviously been willing to strike a much stronger blow for basic freedoms and against governmental encroachment in the "cultural" or "noneconomic" realm, has it not, in fact, adopted a judicial "double standard"?[13] If so, how, if at all, is such a double standard justifiable? Briefly and oversimplified—for it is never possible completely to divorce the "economic" from the "noneconomic"—the double standard detected here gives all but *carte blanche* to legislative experimentation, state as well as federal, in the realm of economic-proprietarian activities; whereas it gives minute and repeated scrutiny to complaints in litigation alleging encroachment upon the cultural, basic freedoms sphere. In other words, an appellant's complaint that a state or federal wage-and-hour, child labor, or similar type of law infringes on substantive due process—a complaint that would have found an enthusiastic reception by the Fuller Court—would receive short shrift by today's Supreme Court. Indeed, it would probably not even be granted review.

This posture is generally justified by the highest tribunal (and, incidentally, by those below) on the grounds of judicial self-restraint. It

U.S. 833 (1976); (47) *Califano v. Goldfarb*, 430 U.S. 199 (1977); (48) *Califano v. Silbowitz*, 430 U.S. 934 (1977); (49) *Railroad Retirement Board* v. *Kalina*, 431 U.S. 909 (1977); (50) *Marshall* v. *Barlow*, 436 U.S. 307 (1978); (51) *Califano v. Westcott*, 443 U.S. 76 (1979); (52) and (53) *United States* v. *Will*, 449 U.S. 200 (1984); (54) *Common Cause* v. *Schmitt*, 455 U.S. 129 (1982); (55) *Railway Labor Exec. Assn.* v. *Gibbons*, 455 U.S. 757 (1982); (56) *Northern Pipeline Construction Co.* v. *Marathon Pipeline Co.*, 458 U.S. 50 (1982); (57) *United States* v. *Grace*, 461 U.S. 171 (1983); (58) *I.N.S.* v. *Chadha*, 462 U.S. 919 (1983); (59) *Bolger* v. *Young's Drugs*, 463 U.S. 60 (1983); (60) *F.C.C.* v. *League of Women's Voters of California*, 468 U.S. 364 (1984); (61) *Regan* v. *Time, Inc.*, 468 U.S. 641 (1984); and (62) *F.E.C.* v. *National Conservative Political Action Committee*, 53 LW 4293 (1985). For capsule commentaries of these cases through 1985, see my *The Judicial Process: An Introductory Analysis of the Courts of the United States, England, and France*, 5th ed. (New York: Oxford University Press, 1986), pp. 293–308.

[13]For a rigorous attack on that approach and a clarion call for a return to a "full preservation of property rights," see Bernard H. Siegan, *Economic Liberties and the Constitution* (Chicago: University of Chicago Press, 1980).

is based upon the contention that legislators must be given the benefit of the doubt in an area that is so peculiarly suited to their judgment as that of the economic-proprietarian sector. On the other hand, an appellant's complaint that state or federal legislation or executive-administrative practices in criminal law enforcement have violated an individual's due process of law, or that a state or federal statute or official practice has infringed on the constitutional rights of racial or religious minorities or women would almost certainly receive close judicial scrutiny. How, then, is such a double standard justifiable?

Any justification poses a fascinating moral dilemma, for in a sense it attributes political legitimacy to the people's representatives and other public servants in one area, while questioning their potency in the other. Basically, it is a double standard resolutely supported even by both Justice Holmes and Brandeis. These two great, long-term jurists, who had considerable faith in the legislative process, albeit for somewhat different reasons,[14] were quite willing to trust what might be termed judicial subjectivity and competence in the "preferred" area—and especially in that of the First Amendment's protections of religion, speech, press, assembly, and petition[15]—while denying or subordinating it in the economic-proprietarian, the social sphere. In somewhat different language, the governing theme here is that the Court must guard against mistaken self-abnegation, lest the basic freedoms of Americans "be eroded to the point where their restoration becomes impossible."[16]

JUSTIFICATION

In justifying the double standard, four specific reasons are commonly advanced, not necessarily in any order of significance. *First*, the Bill of Rights in our Constitution—which has now been *judicially* held to be largely, although not entirely, applicable to the several states via the Fourteenth Amendment's due process of law clause—is assuredly

---

[14]See the superb study of the Holmes-Brandeis tradition and its effect upon American democracy in Samuel J. Konefsky's *The Legacy of Holmes and Brandeis: A Study in the Influence of Ideas* (New York: The Macmillan Co., 1956).

[15]As Stone read Holmes, judges, "should not be too rigidly bound to the tenets of judicial self-restraint in cases involving civil liberties." (Asserted by Stone in a letter to Clinton Rossiter, April 12, 1941, and thus quoted by Alpheus T. Mason, *Harlan Fiske Stone: Pillar of the Law* (New York: The Viking Press, 1956), p. 516.)

[16]Loren P. Beth, "The Case for Judicial Protection of Civil Liberties," 17 *The Journal of Politics* 112 (February 1955).

explicit in its language. Thus its famed First Article commences with the ringing injunction that "Congress shall make *no law respecting* an establishment of religion, or *prohibiting* the free exercise thereof; or *abridging* the freedom of speech, or of the press. . . ."[17] In the firm judgment of Justice Black, for one, "no law" means just that:

> *It is my belief that there are "absolutes" in our Bill of Rights, and that they were put there on purpose by men who knew what words meant, and meant their prohibitions to be "absolutes." . . . The phrase "Congress shall make no law" is composed of plain words, easily understood. . . the language of this Amendment [is not] anything less than absolute.*[18]

One need not subscribe to this "absolutist" concept of Justice Black—which rests on somewhat dubious grounds, however generous and attractive the sentiment may be—to recognize the specificity and explicitness of the language of the Bill of Rights. That language finds no applicable counterpart in purely economic terms *anywhere* in the basic document. The socioeconomic realm is addressed in the much more vague, much more general, language of the "due process of law" clauses of the Fifth and Fourteenth Amendments and the latter's "equal protection of the laws" clause. (The generous Marshallian interpretation of the impairment of the obligation-of-contracts clause of the Constitution[19] retains little, if any, effective meaning today.)

Second, and closely allied to the first reason, is the contention that the Bill of Rights deals with the most basic of all of our freedoms, those upon which all the others rest. For what purpose are the rights of

---

[17]Italics added.

[18]Hugo L. Black, "The Bill of Rights," 35 *New York University Law Review* 867, 874 (April 1960). As he put the matter elsewhere: "I think that state regulation [of economic affairs] should be viewed quite differently than where it touches or involves freedom of speech, press, religion, assembly, or other specific safeguards of the Bill of Rights. It is the duty of this Court to be alert to see that these *constitutionally preferred rights* are not abridged." Dissenting opinion, *Morey* v. *Doud*, 354 U.S. 457 (1957), at 471. (Italics added.)

[19]Art. I, Sec. 10, Cl. 1. See, among others, his opinions in *Dartmouth College* v. *Woodward* and *Fletcher* v. *Peck* (cited in fn. 3 of this chapter). But see the surprising 4:3 decision in 1977 (*U.S. Trust Co.* v. *New Jersey*, 431 U.S. 1). Yet the Court "made up" for the latter decision in an 8:0 holding in 1984 that would have horrified Marshall: Justice O'Connor's opinion upheld a major land reform program in Hawaii that utilized the state's power of eminent domain to break up large estates and transfer land ownership to the states' tenants! (*Hawaii Housing Authority* v. *Midkiff*, 467 U.S. 229).

petititon for the redress of grievances and assembly when the right to vote is gone? Of what benefit is the right of freedom of speech and press when *prior* censorship denudes these of meaning? In short, when these most basic rights are gone, the rest become irretrievable as well. It was this reasoning that persuaded Justice Stone, with an assist from Chief Justice Hughes, to write the famous and lastingly influential Footnote Four to an otherwise unimportant 1938 case, *United States* v. *Carolene Products Co.*,[20] a footnote that must surely rank as one of the most significant in all legal history. In it he intimated with conviction that the type of judicial self-restraint that we normally have a right to expect from the judicial branch of the government would be misapplied in the civil liberties field; that in the case of the Constitution's specific prohibitions there existed more than justification, indeed an activist command, for close and even painful scrutiny. He did not believe this scrutiny to be justifiable in the economic-proprietarian field, however, where he, too, did not find the Constitution specific; that, in fine:

> ...*legislation which restricts those political processes which can ordinarily be expected to bring about repeal of undesirable legislation, is to be subjected to more exacting judicial scrutiny under the general prohibitions of the Fourteenth Amendment [as applied by the First] than are most other types of legislation.*

And he confirmed this belief in his solitary, stirring dissenting opinion in the first *Flag Salute* case [21] two years later, a dissent that became majority opinion scarcely three years thereafter:[22]

> *The very fact that we have constitutional guarantees of civil liberties and the specificity of their command when freedom of speech and of religion are concerned require some accommodation of the powers which government normally exercises, when no question of civil liberty is involved, to the constitutional demand that these liberties be protected against the action of government itself. ... The Constitution expresses more than the conviction of the people that democratic processes must be preserved at all costs. It is also an expression of faith and a command that freedom of mind and*

---

[20]304 U.S. 144 (1938). See my *Freedom and the Court*, pp. 15 ff.
[21]*Minersville School District* v. *Gobitis*, 310 U.S. 586 (1940).
[22]*West Virginia State Board of Education* v. *Barnette*, 319 U.S. 624 (1943).

spirit must be preserved, which government must obey, if it is to adhere to that justice and moderation without which no free government can exist.[23]

Third, and following logically if one accepts the first and second contentions, no other agency of our government has proved itself willing and/or capable of protecting this vital area of freedom so assertively. (Unlike Britain, for one, where the representative legislative branch continues to exert far-reaching, indeed the ultimate, power in demanding that the government preserve and defend civil liberties.) Thus it has fallen to our judiciary to afford that necessary protection—a task and a role that our traditions have always viewed as an intrinsic function of the courts staffed by jurists who are presumably eminently qualified by experience as well as instinct to play the role of guardians of our fundamental rights. It is a role procedurally enhanced by the Supreme Court's all but absolute prerogative of determining the kind of cases that will reach its docket, thus enabling it to concentrate on articulating the libertarian realm.[24]

On the other hand, the judiciary has neither the expertise nor the time, given its heavy docket, to make complex economic judgments. These would appear to belong to the legislative branch of the government, for it is there that the day-to-day process of economic planning and facilitation finds appeal and expression. As Justice Black expressed the matter once: "Whether the legislature takes for its textbook Adam Smith, Herbert Spencer, Lord Keynes or some other is of no concern of ours."[25] Probably no one ever stated the case so well as did the nonagenarian Justice Holmes, in typically colorful fashion, to his then sixty-one-year-old colleague, Justice Stone. White mustache bristling, his still-sharp, clear eyes dancing, Holmes intoned:

Young man, about 75 years ago I learned that I was not God. And so, when the people [through their elected representatives] want to do something [in that vast realm of economic and social legislation] I can't find anything in the Constitution expressly forbidding them to do, I say, whether I like it or not, "Goddamit, let 'em do it."[26]

---

[23]310 U.S. 586, *loc. cit.,* at 606–607.

[24]On that point, see Alpheus Thomas Mason, *The Supreme Court from Taft to Warren* (New York: W. W. Norton & Co., 1964), Ch. 5, "Toward Positive Responsibility."

[25]*Ferguson* v. *Skrupa,* 372 U.S. 726 (1963), at 732.

[26]As quoted by Charles P. Curtis in his *Lions Under the Throne* (Boston: Houghton Mifflin Co., 1947), p. 281.

Or, as that supreme skeptic and philosopher, while chatting about anti-trust legislation, once expressed the matter on another occasion to John W. Davis (the famed corporation and criminal lawyer and un-successful 1924 Democratic nominee for the presidency):

Of course I know, and you know, and every other sensible man knows, that the Sherman [Anti-Trust] Law is damned nonsense, but if my country wants to go to hell, I am here to help it.[27]

Yet in the area of the Bill of Rights, in general, and that of the First Amendment, in particular, Holmes firmly rejected that philosophy, for he was convinced that the Constitution neither provided nor sanctioned such an approach. In concert with many other thoughtful jurists, he simply did not regard the average American (including his legislative representatives) as being very "enlightened"—to use Justice Jackson's phrase[28]—on the subject of basic civil rights and liberties.

Fourth, it is an axiom of the American political scene that, by and large, the average economic-proprietarian or social interest or pressure group has more avenues and pathways of *access* to the legislative process, in order to obtain real or fancied redress of public policy grievances, than does the often unpopular minority in the cultural freedoms realm. After all, it is the latter that accounts for the vast bulk of civil liberties litigation, hardly the former! The difficulty is that whatever may be the views of the average American citizen toward the activities of an economic interest, he or she is more likely than not to regard those of the political minority group or individual as "troublemakers" of one sort or another. Alas, as Justice Frankfurter once observed tellingly, the average civil liberties litigants "are not very nice people."[29]

Frankfurter was referring to those accused in the criminal law realm, who have frequently been vehicles for procedural due process decisions by the Court. Increasingly, these decisions have not only proved favorable to the accused, but have become catalysts for liberal interpretations of the constitutional provisions concerned. Thus there

---

[27]As told by Francis Biddle, *Justice Holmes, Natural Law, and the Supreme Court* (New York: The Macmillan Co.,1961), p. 9.

[28]See Robert H. Jackson, *The Supreme Court in the American System of Government* (Cambridge, Mass.: Harvard University Press, 1955), p. 82.

[29]The exact quote, penned in *United States* v. *Rabinowitz*, 339 U.S. 56 (1950), was: "It is a fair summary of history to say that safeguards of liberty have been forged in controversies involving not very nice people."

was nothing particularly endearing about one Dollree Mapp, to whom we are "indebted" for the 1961 landmark decision in *Mapp* v. *Ohio*,[30] which held, in Justice Clark's words, "that the right to privacy[31] embodied in the Fourth Amendment is enforceable against the States, and that the right to be secure against rude invasions of privacy by state officers is, therefore, constitutional in origin." Neither do we admire Arthur Culombe, whose Connecticut conviction for two grisly gasoline station murders was set aside by the Supreme Court on the grounds that his confession was obtained by force and that it lacked the judicial standard of voluntariness.[32] Nor, surely, the convicted rapist and kidnapper, Ernesto Miranda, whose name has become a household word for safeguards—however contentious—in the realms of legal counsel, confession, and self-incrimination.[33] It is not easy for that type of appellant to obtain his or her day in court, let alone at the bar of legislature. One of the by-products of the rise and sustenance of civil libertarian activism as of the early 1950s, however, has been the very marked success of civil rights interest groups in having their grievances heard and litigated in increasing numbers at all levels of the governmental process—aided in considerable measure by often governmentally funded, public interest lawyers as well as civil rights and civil libertarian interest groups, such as the ACLU and the NAACP. This represents a significant change from the days of yore—indeed a revolutionary one.[34]

---

[30]367 U.S. 643. See also p. 125 of this text.

[31]For some intriguing "privacy" decisions in realms other than that of the Fourth Amendment—concentrating instead on the Ninth—see, among others: *Griswold* v. *Connecticut*, 381 U.S. 479 (1965), the "Birth Control Case"; the 1973 "Abortion Cases," *Roe* v. *Wade*, 41 U.S. 213 and *Doe* v. *Bolton*, 410 U.S. 179; *Planned Parenthood of Missouri* v. *Danforth*, 428 U.S. 52 (1976); and the three important 1983 *Abortion Cases*, affirming and extending *Roe*, 462 U.S. 416, 476, and 506, respectively. Ditto *Eisenstadt* v. *Baird*, 405 U.S. 438 (1972); *Carey* v. *Population Services International*, 431 U.S. 678 (1977); *Bellotti* v. *Baird*, 431 U.S. 678 (1979); *Caulotti* v. *Franklin*, 439 U.S. 379 (1979); and *H. L.* v. *Matheson*, 450 U.S. 398 (1981). See also the New Jersey Supreme Court's 1977 declaration of unconstitutionality of its ancient ban on fornication (*State* v. *Saunders*, 75 N.J. 200). For a general discussion of privacy, see p. 125 of this text.

[32]*Culombe* v. *Connecticut*, 367 U.S. 568 (1961).

[33]*Miranda* v. *Arizona*, 384 U.S. 436 (1966). (Miranda was killed in a barroom brawl in 1976—with the police subsequently using a "Miranda card" to read the prime suspect his rights prior to arrest.)

[34]See my *Freedom and the Court*, 4th ed., in which I argue (p. 27, fn. 89) that this fourth factor is no longer a realistic one.

This development notwithstanding, it remains true that, since the average economic-proprietarian interest group does not normally suffer from the "not-so-nice" label, and more often than not is viewed as both "respectable" *and* influential, it has little difficulty in gaining the attention of legislative representatives. There is nothing evil or wrong with this fact of public life. Yet it does point to the relative ease with which the average economic interest group can take steps to redress court-imposed grievances, should the need arise. There is a superior ability of the average economic interest to gain access to the governmental process. Of course, there is a significant, often crucial, distinction that must be made between large, powerful firms, such as du Pont de Nemours, for example, and the corner grocer. The grocer's influence is hardly on a par with du Pont's. But this does not negate the basic argument of potential access based upon notions of "respectability" and "noncriminality"—which even the lone economic individual possesses, though he or she may belong to no identifiable interest or pressure group at all.

In the 1960s, the Court modified the traditional "double standard" to give "strict judicial scrutiny" to certain types of equal protection *and* due process cases. Depending on the type of legislative statutory classification, the Court places or views the case before it in different categories or levels, which affects its treatment of the issue at hand accordingly. Thus for the economic-proprietarian cases discussed earlier in this chapter, the Court still uses the traditional "equal protection" and "due process" test of examining whether the legislature had a "reasonable" or "rational" basis for making its statutory classification.[35] Basic civil rights and liberties issues, for some time now, have led to a closer case examination by the Court—namely, if the Court is satisfied that it is dealing with a law or an executive action that affects so-called fundamental interests (e.g., voting rights,[36] the right to interstate travel[37]) or touches a "suspect" category (e.g., race,[38] national origin, or alien status[39]) it will extend particu-

---

[35]See the contentious property tax application case of *San Antonio Independent School District* v. *Ridriguez*, 411 U.S. 1 (1973).

[36]For example, *Harper* v. *Virginia Board of Elections*, 383 U.S. 663 (1966).

[37]For example, *Shapiro* v. *Thompson*, 394 U.S. 618 (1969).

[38]For example, *Loving* v. *Virginia*, 388 U.S. 1 (1967).

[39]For example, *Graham* v. *Richardson*, 403 U.S. 365 (1971); *Plyler* v. *Doe*, 457 U.S. 202 (1982); and *Bernal* v. *Fainter*, 52 LW 4669 (1984). But compare *Ambach* v. *Norwich*, 441 U.S. 68 (1979) and *Cabell* v. *Chavez-Salido*, 454 U.S. 432 (1982).

larly close and exacting judicial scrutiny to its ajudication. Although in some cases the subject matter may not be "suspect," it is still accorded especially close attention: sex discrimination, for example, is second only to race in contemporary "equal protection of the laws" litigation.[40] Once an issue has been placed on the "suspect" category level, the Court, in effect, shifts the burden of proof of its constitutionality to the government and requires that it demonstrate a *"compelling* state interest" for its legislative classification.[41] Hence, once the "fundamental interest" or *"suspect* category" classification of a case is demonstrated, the "strict judicial scrutiny" that thereby results leads to considerably greater judicial protection of these rights. In essence, then, the Court uses a complicated double standard within a double standard to accomplish this contemporary task. This has triggered widespread accusations of judicial arrogation of legislative power—quite apart from triggering constitutional confusion.[42]

See also the illegitimacy issue, as decided in *Levy* v. *Louisiana*, 391 U.S. 68 (1968); *Labine* v. *Vincent*, 401 U.S. 532 (1971); and *Weber* v. *Aetna Casualty and Insurance Company*, 406 U.S. 164 (1972). But after having enjoyed a "suspect category" standard for almost a decade, a 6:3 decision by the Court in mid-1976, ruling against a claim by illegitimate children, pronounced the subject matter no longer "suspect," and said that the sole test to be met by the legislature was the usual one of "reasonableness." (*Norton* v. *Mathews* and *Mathews* v. *Lucas*, 427 U.S. 495 (1976). Compare *Trimble* v. *Gordon*, 430 U.S. 762 (1977).

[40]For example, *Reed* v. *Reed*, 401 U.S. 71 (1971); *Frontiero* v. *Richardson*, 411 U.S. 677 (1973); *Califano* v. *Goldfarb*, 430 U.S. 199 (1977); *Califano* v. *Silbowitz*, 430 U.S. 934 (1977); *Califano* v. *Westcott*, 443 U.S. 76 (1979); *Mississippi University for Women* v. *Hogan*, 458 U.S. 718 (1982); *Arizona* v. *Norris*, 464 U.S. 808 (1983); and *Roberts* v. *U.S. Jaycees*, 465 U.S. 555 (1984). But compare *Kahn* v. *Shevin*, 416 U.S. 351 (1974); *General Electric Co.* v. *Gilbert*, 429 U.S. 125 (1976); *Personnel Administrator* v. *Feeney*, 442 U.S. 256 (1979); and *Michael M.* v. *Superior Court*, 450 U.S. 464 (1981). See also the rather strained "equal-pay-for-comparable-work" 1981 decision in *County of Washington* v. *Gunther*, 452 U.S. 161 and that same year's dramatic armed forces registration case of *Rostker* v. *Goldberg*, 453 U.S. 57. Compare *McCarty* v. *McCarty*, 453 U.S. 210 (1981) and *Hishon* v. *King and Spaulding*, 467 U.S. 69 (1984).

[41]As it did successfully in the highly controversial *Korematsu* v. *United States*, 323 U.S. 214 (1944), the famed "Japanese Exclusion-from-the-West-Coast" World War II case.

[42]For two excellent treatments of this vexatious and complicated issue, see Gerald Gunther, "The Supreme Court: 1971 Term: In Search of Evolving Doctrine on a Changing Court: A Model for a Newer Equal Protection," 86 *Harvard Law Review* 1 (1972); and J. Harvie Wilkinson, III, "The Supreme Court, the Equal Protection Clause, and the Three Faces of Constitutional Equality," 61 *Virginia Law*

Taken together, as well as separately, the four reasons outlined above represent the case for a justification of a double standard (or standards). The latter may not be entirely convincing either morally or logically. It raises very serious, indeed fundamental, questions about the nature of judicial power and judicial process under our system. Yet it is a practical recognition of one of the latter's crucial and realistic facets of government and politics. Within often ill-defined limits, the case of the special judicial protection of civil liberties is strong. But there is an additional consideration related to the concept of a double standard: the vexatious and contentious matter of the "incorporation," "nationalization," or "absorption" of the provisions of the federal Bill of Rights to the several states via the first section of the Fourteenth Amendment, in general, and the due process of law clause, in particular. The due process clause of the Fourteenth Amendment reads as follows:

No State shall make or enforce any law which shall abridge the privileges or immunities of citizens of the United States; nor shall any state deprive any person of life, liberty, or property, without due process of law; nor deny to any person within its jurisdiction the equal protection of the laws.

"Incorporation," Due Process of Law, Privacy, and Criminal Justice

TWO TYPES OF DUE PROCESS OF LAW

There are two types of due process of law: *substantive* and *procedural*. They are not as clearly separable as we might wish, or as some members of the legal profession at times pretend, but it is both possible and vital to understand the basic distinction. Simply, *substantive due process* refers to the contents or subject matter of legislation or an executive ordinance; *procedural due process* refers to the manner in which the fruits of the legislative and/or administrative process are carried out by public officials, be they executives, policy-making or subordinate civil servants, or members of the judicial branch. In both

---

Review 945 (1975). See also Chapter II, "The Double Standard," of my *Freedom and the Court,* and Richard Funston's *A Vital National Seminar: The Supreme Court in American Political Life* (Palo Alto, Calif.: Mayfield Publishing Co., 1978).

substantive and procedural concepts, the test of constitutionality or legality applied by the judiciary under the due process clauses answers the question of whether or not an action by a member of the government, in content or in procedure, has been "capricious," "invidious," "irrational," "irrelevant," "arbitrary," or "unreasonable,"[43] as applied to the constitutional powers and guarantees. If the judicial response to this question is affirmative, the law or order presumably falls on either substantive grounds or procedural grounds; sometimes both violations are present. (It ought to be noted here that until the latter part of the nineteenth century the concept of due process of law was viewed as a wholly procedural one. But as a result of the now famous (or infamous) New York state court decision in *Wynehamer* v. *People*,[44] courts began to examine the substance of legislation as well.) Substantive versus procedural due process has proved to be one of the most controversial aspects of the judicial role because it involves the ever present basic question as to the extent, if any, the judicial branch may, in effect, authoritatively "legislate" as well as "judge."[45]

Substantive Due Process. A fairly recent and admittedly extreme illustration of violation of substantive due process was a Jacksonville, Florida, ordinance that inherited some of its language from the "poor laws" of Elizabethan England. This ordinance outlawed as vagrants and "rogues and vagabonds" persons who, among other things, "use juggling or unlawful games," are "common nightwalkers" or "habitual loafers," and who are "able to work but habitually live upon the earnings of their wives or minor children." Plaintiff Papachristou had been convicted under the quaint statute for "prowling by auto." In an opinion for the unanimous Supreme Court, Justice Douglas declared the law unconstitutionally vague, because it did not tell citizens what conduct was forbidden and encouraged arbitrary and erratic arrests and convictions.[46]

---

[43]Mr. Justice Black's enumeration in his dissenting opinion in *Harper* v. *Virginia Board of Education*, 383 U.S. 663 (1966), at 677–79.

[44]13 N.Y. 358 (1856), declaring a law banning the sale of liquor unconstitutional.

[45]Justice Frankfurter, a strong opponent of judicial examination of substantive, as contrasted with procedural, due process, had the satisfaction of seeing his conviction enshrined—on his direct advice—in the Indian Constitution of 1950 (Art. 21), to wit: "No person shall be deprived of his life or liberty *except according to procedure established by law*" (italics added). "The due process clause ought to go," he wrote in *The New Republic* on October 1, 1924.

[46]*Papachristou* v. *City of Jacksonville*, 405 U.S. 156 (1972).

Another example from three decades earlier is *Skinner* v. *Oklahoma*,[47] which challenged the Oklahoma Habitual Criminal Sterilization Act of 1935. Oklahoma's legislature had passed the statute in a burst of moralistic enthusiasm, confident of both its wisdom and constitutionality. It provided that thrice-convicted criminal offenders, whose crimes amounted to felonies involving "moral turpitude," could be legally compelled to undergo sterilization.

Arthur Skinner "qualified" under the statute and was advised that his time as a procreator had run its course. He appealed the order and ultimately attained a hearing in the United States Supreme Court. In one of Douglas's earliest opinions, the highest tribunal unanimously declared the law unconstitutional on the grounds that the classification of "criminal" was "too loose for so serious a business," especially since it included larceny by fraud (Skinner had stolen three chickens, which "counted" as one of the three offenses to be punished by sterilization), but it *excluded* embezzlement. The Court thus refused to be persuaded that "a man in Skinner's category was more likely to transmit biologically inheritable traits than one who had embezzled." Although the basic issue in this case, as presented by Skinner's attorneys, was an alleged violation of the "equal protection of the laws" clause of Amendment Fourteen rather than its "due process" clause, the law in fact fell as a violation of substantive due process because of its arbitrary nature.

On the other hand, a Virginia sterilization law enacted in 1924 had already been upheld against substantive challenges. It provided that inmates of state-supported institutions who had been found to be afflicted with "an *hereditary* form of insanity, idiocy, imbecility, feeble-mindedness, or epilepsy" might be sterilized by state action. Carrie Buck was a seventeen-year-old feeble-minded inmate of a state institution; her feeble-minded mother, Emma, was also confined there. Carrie had given birth out of wedlock to an allegedly mentally deficient baby just prior to her admission to the institution. Over Carrie's lawyer's argument that the Virginia statute should fall, among other reasons because it applied only to the mentally deficient persons confined to state institutions and not "to the multitude outside," the Supreme Court upheld it on appeal by an 8:1 vote. Speaking through the eighty-six-year-old Justice Holmes—a Malthusian since his boyhood—the Court ruled that the "principle that sustains compulsory vaccination is broad enough to cover cutting the Fallopian

---

[47]316 U.S. 535 (1942).

tubes [under the given circumstances] . . . three generations of imbeciles are enough."[48] And Carrie was duly sterilized—one of 8,300 to be thus victimized in the next fifty years, until such sterilizations were discontinued in 1972.[49]

Procedural Due Process. Procedural violations are naturally much more common. The concept requires a general standard of fair procedure. In other words, the procedural due process guarantee denies to agents of government what has been called "the power to filch away private rights by hole-and-corner methods."[50] Obvious examples are coerced confessions, denial of counsel, "stacked juries," and *unreasonable* searches and seizures. A specific illustration of a clear-cut violation of procedural due process is the famous case of *Rochin* v. *California.*[51] Here, Antonio Richard Rochin was surprised in his bedroom by three Los Angeles County deputy sheriffs, who had some information that he was selling narcotics. Without arrest or search warrant, they broke into the two-story house where Rochin lived with his mother, common-law wife, brother, and sisters. Two morphine capsules that he had allegedly obtained illegally (which happened to be true) lay on the night table by the bed. When the agents spied them and asked, "Whose stuff is this?" Rochin won the ensuing race for the capsules and stuffed them into his mouth. The agents of the law pummeled and kicked him in the unsuccessful hope that he would relinquish the evidence; to the contrary, he swallowed it. They then inflicted on him a rather thorough beating, hoping, again unsuccessfully, that he might vomit the capsules. Ultimately, they tied, gagged, and transported him to a hospital, where they ordered a resident physician to give the immobilized and irate Rochin an emetic through a stomach tube. This inevitably successful procedure resulted in the vomiting of the two capsules, which the heroic police then presented as evidence at his subsequent trial.

Rochin was convicted on the strength of that evidence against his hardly unreasonable contention that he had been deprived of procedural due process. Yet when he appealed, the entire appellate structure of the California judicial hierarchy rejected his contentions on

---

[48]*Buck* v. *Bell*, 247 U.S. 200 (1927).

[49]The law continues on the statute books; but the 1981 session of the Virginia legislature eliminated those provisions that permitted involuntary sterilization of minors "for the good of society."

[50]Corry and Abraham, *Elements of Democratic Government*, p. 267.

[51]342 U.S. 165 (1952).

the ground that although the evidence was the fruit of what would have clearly been an unconstitutional search and seizure on the *federal* level of government, California did not [then] bar the admission at the trial stage of such evidence. This despite the ready acknowledgment by the District Court of Appeal (the state's intermediate appellate tribunal) that Rochin had been treated outrageously and brutally! When the case ultimately reached the United States Supreme Court on certiorari, that body unanimously reversed Rochin's conviction on grounds of rank violation of *procedural* due process of law guaranteed by the Fourteenth Amendment. Speaking through Justice Frankfurter, the Court held that the proceedings constituted "conduct that shocks the conscience"; that this "course of proceedings by agents of government to obtain evidence is bound to offend even hardened sensibilities. . . . States in their prosecutions [must] respect certain decencies of civilized conduct." And, concluded Frankfurter in words symptomatic of his judicial posture on the entire problem of "incorporation":

> *Due process of law, as a historic and generative principle, precludes defining, and thereby confining, these standards of conduct more precisely than to say that convictions cannot be brought about by methods that offend "a sense of justice."*[52]

Yet in the firmly held view of Justices Black and Douglas, expressed in separate *concurring* opinions, the case was rightly decided, but for the wrong reasons. These concurring opinions preview the basic clash over the applicability of the Bill of Rights via the Fourteenth Amendment that existed, and still exists, between what we might loosely call the Frankfurter and Black "camps." In Black's and Douglas's opinion, the constitutional issue was not the Frankfurter-expressed matter of violation of procedural due process of law under Amendment Fourteen. The vagueness of Felix Frankfurter's notion of "a sense of justice" was not for them! Rather, these two staunch champions of basic freedoms held that California's agents had in fact clearly violated individual liberties expressed by, and safeguarded under, *specific* provisions of the Bill of Rights, such as the self-incrimination provisions of the Fifth Amendment.[53] In their repeated-

---

[52]Ibid., at 173. (Italics added.)

[53]Twelve years later their viewpoint regarding that particular provision triumphed, when in 1964 the Court held 5:4 that "the Fourteenth Amendment secures against invasion by states the same privilege that the Fifth Amendment guarantees against Federal infringement" (*Malloy* v. *Hogan*, 378 U.S. 1).

ly expressed judgment, these rights are ipso facto applicable to the several states as well as to the federal government. Here, of course, is the basic dilemma with which we are now concerned.

SOME HISTORICAL CONSIDERATIONS

In the search for a solution of the incorporation problem, we turn to the past. There is multiple and conclusive historical evidence that the framers of the Bill of Rights intended it to be a barrier against the *federal* government *only*. Indeed, it was the then existing states, under the leadership of James Madison, that had insisted that a Bill of Rights, applicable to the national government, be added to the Constitution. The states had their own bills of rights; they saw to it that the First Congress proposed the series of ten amendments we now know as the Bill of Rights, and they ratified them in December 1791.[54] Certainly there can be no doubt about the initial reach of the First Amendment, for example, for its specific language begins with the words, "Congress shall make no law. . . ." The other amendments are couched in more general language, however, and despite the aforementioned incontrovertible evidence, some observers held that they ought to be construed so as to apply to the states as well as to the federal government. The matter came to a head and was settled (until the passage of the Fourteenth Amendment thirty-five years later) in the famous case of *Barron* v. *Baltimore*,[55] Chief Justice Marshall's last constitutional law decision, one that has never been overruled per se.

Barron v. *Baltimore.*   The case arose as a result of plaintiff Barron's claim that the City of Baltimore had deprived him of his property without due process of law. That property, he protested, was protected by the spirit and the letter of that portion of the Fifth Amendment that forbids the taking of private property for public use without just compensation—also known as the right of "eminent domain." Barron had owned a fine wharf, but the city's street-paving and stream-diverting operations caused deposits of sand and gravel to form near it, shallowed the water, and thus prevented the approach of vessels. *Today,* Mr. Barron would seek redress under the *Fourteenth* Amendment, but his only recourse *then* was the *Fifth.* Mar-

---

[54]In a speech on the floor of the House of Representatives on June 8, 1789, Madison proposed that the putative Bill of Rights restrict the states as well as the federal government, but the First Congress firmly refused.

[55]7 Peters 243 (1833).

shall made short shrift of Barron's argument: Speaking for his unanimous Court, the chief held that the tribunal had "no jurisdiction of the case; and it is dismissed." His opinion stressed the view that "the question...presented is...of great importance, but not of much difficulty." Thus he ruled that the Bill of Rights, generally, and here the Fifth Amendment, particularly, was "intended solely as a limitation on the exercise of power by the government of the United States, and is not applicable to the legislatures of the States.... This court cannot so apply them."[56] He saw no "repugnancy between the several acts of the general assembly of Maryland...and the Constitution of the United States." Mr. Barron had no further legal recourse.[57]

The Slaughterhouse Cases. No other litigation of significance arose on the point at issue until after the ratification of the Fourteenth Amendment in 1868. In 1873, however, the Court reconfirmed the *Barron* doctrine by widening the gulf between the Constitution's applicability to the two levels of government in the very first cases involving the new Amendment. It did this by holding that its "privileges or immunities" clause did not, and was not intended to, protect the rights of *state* citizenship, but solely those of *federal* citizenship; that, in the words of Justice Samuel F. Miller's majority opinion for the closely divided (5:4) Court:

> *It is quite clear, then, that there is a citizenship of the United States, and a citizenship of a state, which are distinct from each other, and which depend upon different characteristics or circumstances in the individual.*[58]

Having made that distinction, Miller was able to draw a sharp line between those "privileges or immunities" that accrued to an individual by virtue of his or her *state* citizenship, and those which accrued by virtue of his or her citizenship in the *national* government. Only the latter, then, fell under the protective umbrella of the Fourteenth Amendment.

---

[56]*Loc. cit.*, pp. 250–251.

[57]Actually, Barron had won his argument at the level of the trial court, which awarded him $4500 in damages, but when the City of Baltimore appealed that decision to the Maryland State Court of Appeals, it won a reversal.

[58]*The Slaughterhouse Cases (The Butchers' Benevolent Association of New Orleans v. Crescent City Live Stock Landing and Slaughterhouse Co.,),* 16 Wallace 36 (1873), at 74.

This was bad news for the plaintiffs in the case, the Butchers' Benevolent Association of New Orleans, who had contended that the Louisiana "Carpetbag" legislature, unquestionably under corrupt influence, had in 1867 conferred upon one firm what was virtually a monopoly of the slaughterhouse business in New Orleans. It was a monopoly forbidden under Amendment Fourteen, they insisted, and one that now prevented over 1,000 firms and individuals from continuing in the slaughterhouse business. It was also bad news for the many supporters of the language of the Fourteenth Amendment, especially its first section.[59] These supporters had been confident that its adoption would provide certain minimum federal standards below which a state would not be permitted to fall. It was equally bad news to those who held the position, later expressed by the magisterial John W. Burgess, that "if history has taught us anything in political science, it is that liberty is *national* in its origin, content and sanction."[60] Yet, had the *Slaughterhouse Cases* been decided twenty-five years later, under the substantive due process-oriented Fuller Court, or even thirteen years later under Chief Justice Morrison R. Waite, the grievance by the New Orleans butchers would almost certainly have been adjudged a violation of the (substantive) "due process of law" clause of the Fourteenth Amendment. It was in 1886 that Waite ruled for a unanimous Court—casually, and without hearing argument —that *corporations* were henceforth to be regarded as "persons" under the Fourteenth Amendment, and were thus protected by the Constitution against invalid state infringement.[61] This decision gladdened the judicial and philosophical heart of Justice Stephen J. Field, who had written the leading dissenting opinion in the *Slaughterhouse Cases:* to him an absolute right to engage in the trade of butchering was *the* privilege or immunity in need of protection there.[62]

The Fourteenth Amendment Controversy. We now turn to a far less clear or certain historical question, one still unresolved, and

[59]". . . No State shall make or enforce any law which shall abridge the privileges or immunities of citizens of the United States; nor shall any State deprive any person of life, liberty, or property, without due process of law; nor deny to any person within its jurisdiction the equal protection of the laws."

[60]*Political Science and Comparative Constitutional Law* (Boston: Ginn and Co., 1890), I, p. 2250.

[61]*Santa Clara County* v. *Southern Pacific Railroad Co.*, 118 U.S. 394 (1886).

[62]16 Wallace 36 (1873).

one that has presented us through the years with one of the bitterest of constitutional arguments: When its framers in the Thirty-Ninth Congress worded Section I of the Fourteenth Amendment, did they or did they not intend to have it "incorporate" or "nationalize" or "absorb" the provisions of the federal Bill of Rights, and thus make it applicable *in toto* to the several states? Or, put somewhat differently, how far, if at all, does the language of the first section of that most litigious amendment of all apply to the states the twenty-five or so specific rights listed in the 462-word Bill of Rights as a prohibition upon state action?

This grave and perplexing question has not been settled. But since 1925 it has been resolved on a piecemeal, gradualist, pragmatic basis in favor of the contention that many, if not all, of the enumerated rights must be applied to the states, although that enumeration remains incomplete and contentious. Those who would prefer an historical justification, however, have never really been satisfied, despite a torrent of research and comment alleged to provide *the* answer. The question may well be beyond authentic response, for historical evidence is not conclusive. It may well be that the affirmative respondents have a slight edge, based on the duly recorded assertions by the two floor managers of the amendment, Republican Representative James A. Bingham of Ohio and Republican Senator Jacob Howard of Michigan.[63]

But it is simply a matter of fact that it is entirely possible to come up with opposite conclusions based on almost identical primary data—to wit, the records of the congressional debates on the subject. Thus, Justice Black, in what is one of the longest extant and most elaborately researched dissenting opinions (in *Adamson* v. *California*[64]) insisted that one of the chief objectives of the provisions of the Fourteenth Amendment's first section, "separately and as a whole," was to make the *entire* Bill of Rights applicable to the states. He never wavered from this interpretation and advocacy, one supported *ante* by Professor Horace Flack's 1908 book.[65] Yet, answering Justice Black and basing his response on substantially similar data, Professor

---

[63]For a lengthy discussion and analysis, see my *Freedom and the Court*, pp. 30 ff.

[64]332 U.S. 46 (1947). The specific *holding* in the case was overruled eighteen years later in *Griffin* v. *California*, 380 U.S. 609 (1965). In 1981 the Court required 8:1 that, on a defendant's demand, the presiding judge must advise the jury *not* to regard silence as implied guilt (*Carter* v. *Kentucky*, 450 U.S. 288).

[65]*The Adoption of the Fourteenth Amendment* (Baltimore: The Johns Hopkins Press, 1908).

Charles Fairman, a well-known expert on constitutional law and history, came to a precisely opposite conclusion and, in the process, accused Black of deliberate distortion in order to prove his point.[66] Another expert in the area, Professor Stanley Morrison of Stanford University, inclined toward the Fairman interpretation, but believed that the latter's categorical negative went a bit too far.[67] Almost three decades later, the Fairman-Morrison position received highly vocal support with the publication of Professor Raoul Berger's fascinating and controversial *Government by Judiciary: The Transformation of the Fourteenth Amendment*.[68] A sixth protagonist, Professor J. B. James, who like Flack wrote an entire book[69] on the subject, attacked the sweeping Black interpretation of the congressional debates as erroneous but, with some reservations, shared Black's conclusion that the framers of the Fourteenth Amendment did indeed intend to have the Bill of Rights incorporated.

These six positions indicate only too well how difficult it is to prove speculative history—and how little authenticity can result from the popular game of psychoanalyzing history! The famed German historian Ranke's outburst that it is essential to determine "*wie es eigentlich gewesen*,"[70] is understandable, but its application is at times rather futile, as in this instance. "This [the incorporation issue] is an argument no one can win," understandably concluded John Hart Ely in his recent examination of the issue.[71] Not futile, however, and indeed crucial to an understanding of the problem, are a discussion and an analysis of the various positions that have been taken by members of the Supreme Court.

TO INCORPORATE OR NOT, AND IF SO, HOW?

Pre-Gitlow Developments. This century's preoccupation with the question and problem dates from Justice Edward T. Sanford's

---

[66]"Critique of the Black Dissent in *Adamson* v. *California*," 2 *Stanford Law Review* 5 (December 1949).

[67]"Does the Fourteenth Amendment Incorporate the Bill of Rights—The Judicial Interpretation," 2 *Stanford Law Review* 140 (December 1949).

[68](Cambridge: Harvard University Press, 1977), Ch. 8, "Incorporation of the Bill of Rights in the Fourteenth Amendment," pp. 134–156.

[69]*The Framing of the Fourteenth Amendment* (Urbana: University of Illinois Press, 1956).

[70]"How it actually was."

[71]*Democracy and Distrust: A Theory of Judicial Review* (Cambridge, Mass.: Harvard University Press, 1980), p. 25.

historic "assumption" in the 1925 landmark case of *Gitlow* v. *New York*.[72] There, although the appellant lost his free speech and press claims against New York's Criminal Anarchy Act of 1902—the Court dividing 7:2 with Justices Holmes and Brandeis in outraged dissent—Sanford accepted Gitlow's plea for incorporation of First Amendment freedoms by stating that

> *for present purposes we may and do assume that freedom of speech and of the press—which are protected by the First Amendment from abridgement by Congress—are among the fundamental personal rights and "liberties" protected by the due process clause of the Fourteenth Amendment from impairment by the states.*[73]

This did not help Gitlow, who went to jail (although he was later pardoned and commenced a lucrative career as a paid informer for the federal government in internal security cases in the 1940s and 1950s), yet it proved of momentous significance within little more than a decade.

But *Gitlow* was not, of course, the first case to raise—or raise again, given the decision in the *Slaughterhouse Cases*[74]—the basic problem; it was certainly not unknown to the judicial profession. Notably, the first Justice John Marshall Harlan had, time and again in dissent, proved receptive to petitioners' claims in behalf of the incorporation theory. Thus his lonely dissenting opinions in *Hurtado* v. *California* (1884),[75] *Maxwell* v. *Dow* (1900),[76] and *Twining* v. *New Jersey* (1908)[77] demonstrated his unshakable conviction that the Fourteenth Amendment was intended to incorporate the *entire* Bill of Rights, for he regarded *every* right in the Bill as a "fundamental" one. The first of these cases involved a claim under the grand jury indictment privilege of the Fifth Amendment; the second involved the same provision of the Fifth *and* trial by a petit jury under the Sixth Amendment; and the last, the privilege against self-incrimination under the Fifth. Yet in each of the cases, Harlan lost to a solid eight-man majority (although the Court had unanimously applied the Fifth Amendment's eminent domain concept to the states, via the "due pro-

---

[72]268 U.S. 652.
[73]Ibid., at 666.
[74]16 Wallace 36 (1873).
[75]110 U.S. 516.
[76]176 U.S. 581.
[77]211 U.S. 78.

cess of law" component of Amendment Fourteen, in an 1897 opinion by Harlan[78]). That majority not only rejected his view of the incorporation theory, but also denied that petitioners Hurtado, Maxwell, and Twining had been deprived by California, Utah, or New Jersey of *any* Fourteenth Amendment "privileges or immunities" or "liberty and/or property" rights. Yet seventeen years after the *Twining* decision, *Gitlow* appeared on the horizon, destined to provide us with the doorway to the crucial and exciting constitutional developments to which we now briefly turn.

Enter the "Honor Roll" Approach: Palko v. Connecticut.[79] Within a few years after the 1925 decision in *Gitlow*, the Supreme Court confirmed the freedom of speech aspect of the Sanford "assumption" in a Kansas case,[80] and that of freedom of the press in two important cases decided after Justice Sanford's death in 1930.[81] But the Court was to expand the doctrine: First, in the celebrated *Scottsboro Case*[82]—replete with evidence of the shocking miscarriage of justice in Alabama courts—the Court broke new ground by incorporating the concept of benefit of counsel in *capital* criminal cases. Second, it extended the First Amendment coverage to free exercise of religion in a California case involving Albert Hamilton, a University of California student, who objected to participation in military drill (although the Court held that his religious liberty had not been abridged by compelling him to participate in the exercises as a condition of attending the state institution of higher learning).[83] And third, it included two of the still "left out" guarantees of the First Amendment by incorporating the freedoms of assembly and petition in *De Jonge* v. *Oregon*[84] in 1937, just a few months prior to *Palko* v. *Connecticut.*[85]

In the latter case Frank Palko had been indicted by Connecticut for *first degree* murder; a jury found him guilty of *second degree* mur-

---

[78]*Chicago, Burlington & Quincy R.R.* v. *Chicago,* 166 U.S. 226. Here Harlan spoke for a unanimous—and property-conscious—Court.

[79]302 U.S. 319 (1937).

[80]*Fiske* v. *Kansas,* 274 U.S. 380 (1927).

[81]*Near* v. *Minnesota,* 283 U.S. 697 (1931) and *Grosjean* v. *American Press Co.,* 297 U.S. 233 (1936).

[82]*Powell* v. *Alabama,* 287 U.S. 45 (1932).

[83]*Hamilton* v. *Regents of the U. of California,* 293 U.S. 245 (1934).

[84]299 U.S. 253.

[85]*Palko* v. *Connecticut,* 302 U.S. 319 (1937).

der, and he was given a life sentence with a recommendation that he never be paroled. Pursuant to a statute of 1886, the state, with the permission of the presiding judge of the trial court, appealed the conviction on the lesser count by charging legal error. The Connecticut Supreme Court held that there had indeed been "error of law to the prejudice of the state," so that court reversed the judgment below and ordered a new trial. Over Palko's objections that the second trial would place him twice in jeopardy for the same offense, forbidden by terms of the Fifth Amendment and, according to his contention, consequently also by those of the "due process of law" clause of the Fourteenth, he was retried. This time the jury returned a *first degree* murder verdict and the trial court imposed the death sentence. Palko appealed to the United States Supreme Court, contending that whatever is forbidden by the language of the Fifth is also forbidden by that of the Fourteenth Amendment. For the important reasons given below, the Court ruled 8:1 against Palko, Justice Butler dissenting without opinion—and the appellant was subsequently executed. A cynic might say that in view of the importance of the Supreme Court's pronouncements in the case, Palko did not die in vain.

Justice Cardozo's eloquently written opinion for the eight-man majority is probably the best known of the decisions he penned during his all-too-brief term of six years on the Court. It is a judicial landmark for many reasons, but for present purposes two closely related aspects should be cited: First, it recognized justification for the claim that, under certain conditions and in certain areas, the several states *are* bound by the verbiage of the Bill of Rights via that of the Fourteenth Amendment. Second, it provided a formula by which a modicum of certainty could govern the judicial process in this sphere. In essence, the Cardozo opinion firmly denied the existence of a "general rule" of "incorporation" or "carrying over" via Amendment Fourteen, *but* stated that there are *some* rights in the Bill of Rights that are and must be so "absorbed" because they are "fundamental."

How and where did Cardozo draw the line? How did he establish this "honor roll" of rights to which Justice Frankfurter, Cardozo's successor and lifelong admirer, irreverently referred as "the slot machine theory...some are in and some are out"? Refusing to regard the "due process of law" clause of the Fourteenth Amendment as "shorthand" for the Bill of Rights, Cardozo nonetheless established a dichotomy of those fundamental rights that are "of the very essence of a scheme of ordered liberty" and those without which "justice would not perish" because, unlike the former group, he did not regard them as "implicit in the concept of ordered liberty." To expand somewhat on his justification for the "fundamental" group, he wrote movingly of "those fundamental principles of liberty and justice which lie at the base of all our civil and political institutions," and of a "principle of justice so rooted in the traditions and conscience of our people as to be ranked as fundamental." (Note the recurrent theme of the concept *fundamental* versus what might be called the merely *formal*.) Recognizing the difficulty inherent in this dichotomy, and correctly anticipating some of the problems as well as the criticism that would follow, Justice Cardozo resorted to the "freedom of thought and speech" as his chief illustration, writing: "Of that freedom one may say that it is the matrix, the indispensable condition, of nearly every other form of freedom." And so it is.

As for the "formal" rights, he contended, speaking of the privilege against self-incrimination, that "[J]ustice would not perish if the accused were subject to a duty to respond to orderly inquiry." He insisted that in the realm of these chiefly procedural rights, in general, and the double jeopardy safeguards of the Fifth Amendment, in particular—since it was at issue in *Palko*—the question to be posed by the Court is whether the state action complained of represents "a hardship so acute and shocking that our polity will not endure it? Does it violate those fundamental principles of liberty and justice which lie at the base of our civil and political institutions?... The answer surely must be 'no.' " In Cardozo's view, Connecticut had sought no more than parity with the defendant in the right to continue a case "until there shall be a trial free from the corrosion of substantial legal error." A defendant was given the right to appeal errors adverse to him. "A reciprocal privilege... has now been granted to the state...." And he concluded: "The edifice of justice stands, its symmetry, to many, greater than before."[86]

Despite the *Palko* double standard between those rights that are and those that are not "implicit in the concept of ordered liberty," Cardozo made it clear that the states would still be subject to the judicial test of whether a properly contested action by a state involved a violation of the "due process of law" clause of the Fourteenth Amendment per se. In other words, the fact that only some of the rights of the federal Bill of Rights are ipso facto applicable to the states via the Fourteenth Amendment does not mean that the states are free to violate the constitutional concept of "due process of law" to which all persons in their jurisdictions are entitled. The judicial test here be-

[86]Ibid., at 328.

comes that contentious one, so ardently and consistently embraced by Justice Frankfurter and his adherents, of whether or not the state conduct complained of "shocks the conscience"—or, in the less delicate language of Justice Holmes, "Does it make you puke?" Or, to put the matter somewhat differently, the judicial test represents a case-by-case approach to each litigation, always turning on the question of whether the action by a state official has transgressed the bounds of constitutionality inherent in the "due process of law clause" of the Fourteenth Amendment, as tested by the judges. The case of *Rochin* v. *California*,[87] discussed above, illustrates this judicial test, with Justice Frankfurter holding for the Court that the conduct of the Los Angeles sheriff's deputies "shocked the conscience," and hence violated due process of law. The concurring opinions of Justices Black and Douglas, although naturally agreeing with the reversal of Rochin's conviction, stressed their judgment that the reversal should have been based upon a violation of the Fifth Amendment's provision against self-incrimination, which they would have incorporated verbatim then and there, along with *all* the provisions of the Bill of Rights.

This basic disagreement, between what will henceforth be referred to as the "Frankfurter" and "Black" dichotomy, was sharpened in a later state case involving self-incrimination and unreasonable search and seizure.

Breithaupt v. *Abram*.[88]   This case well illustrates the basic problem raised in *Rochin* and our discussion of the entire incorporation matter. While driving a pickup truck on a New Mexico highway, Paul H. Breithaupt was involved in a collision with a passenger car. The three occupants of the car were killed and Breithaupt was seriously injured. An almost empty pint bottle of whiskey was found in the glove compartment of Breithaupt's truck. He was taken to a hospital, and while he was lying unconscious in the emergency room, attendants detected a strong odor of liquor on his breath. Upon the request of a state patrolman, an attending physician withdrew 22 cc. of blood from the unconscious man. The sample contained .17 percent of alcohol, and Breithaupt, who recovered, was ultimately charged with involuntary manslaughter, with the blood test submitted as important and damaging evidence. Largely following the Court's reasoning in

[87]342 U.S. 165 (1952).
[88]352 U.S. 432 (1957).

Rochin, Breithaupt charged violation of "due process of law" of the Fourteenth Amendment. Speaking for a six-member majority of the Court, Justice Clark, however, pointed out that "the blood test procedure has become routine in our day," and, responding to the petitioner's charge that the procedure involved constituted "conduct that shocks the conscience" (the *Rochin* test), ruled that "a blood test taken by a skilled technician is not such conduct that shocks the conscience," and does not offend a sense of justice.[89] But there were dissenting opinions by Chief Justice Warren and Justice Douglas, both joined by Justice Black. The three jurists contended with feeling that there was no basic distinction between the two cases, since both involved involuntary incrimination; they rejected any "analysis that would make physical resistance by a prisoner a prerequisite to the existence of his constitutional rights"; and held that, in any case, the Fourth and Fifth Amendments of the Bill of Rights, barring unreasonable searches and seizures and self-incrimination, should be made applicable to the states via the Fourteenth. Again, the basic clash is evident.

On the other hand, almost three decades later the Court ruled 9:0 that the Constitution bars the forced removal of a bullet from the chest of an armed robbery suspect. Justice Brennan, speaking for the unanimous Court, held that under the circumstances the operation would violate the suspect's Fourth Amendment

> *right to be secure in his person. . . . A compelled surgical intrusion into an individual's body for evidence implicates expectations of privacy and security of such magnitude that the intrusion may be "unreasonable" even if likely to produce evidence of a crime.*[90]

Yet there are still other positions on "incorporation" worthy of mention, to which we shall turn after an analysis of the division determined by Justice Cardozo in *Palko* and subsequent developments.

The Two Sides of the Palko Line, et seq. Few determinations are as clearly outlined in a case at law as is Justice Cardozo's "honor

---

[89]The *Breithaupt* decision was confirmed 5:4 in *Schmerber* v. *California*, 384 U.S. 757 (1966), Justice Brennan writing the opinion, with the three *Breithaupt* dissenters joined by Justice Fortas in the minority. See also the related supportive opinion, written in 1983 by Justice O'Connor for a 7:2 Court in *South Dakota* v. *Neville*, 459 U.S. 553.

[90]*Winston* v. *Lee*, 105 S. Ct. 1611 (1985).

roll" in *Palko* v. *Connecticut*,[91] and it is quite easy to build a table or draw a chart based upon it. Those rights viewed by the terms of Cardozo's 1937 opinion as being "of the very essence of a scheme of ordered liberty," and thus incorporated via Amendment Fourteen, were as follows:

Amendment I:	Speech
	Press
	Free Exercise of Religion
	Peaceable Assembly (and Petition)
Amendment V:	Eminent Domain
Amendment VI:	Counsel in Capital Criminal Cases

And, he added, there may be other similar situations, including the right to a "fair trial" generally.

But Cardozo *expressly exempted* from his incorporation classification certain rights in Articles IV–VIII of the Bill of Rights that he did not deem to be "of the very essence of a scheme of ordered liberty." His specific 1937 roster of *non*incorporation:

Amendment IV:	Evidence Admitted as a Result of an Unreasonable Search and Seizure
Amendment V:	Double Jeopardy
	Grand Jury Indictment or Presentment
	Self-Incrimination
Amendment VI:	Jury Trial in Criminal Cases
Amendment VII:	Jury Trial in Civil Cases

Cardozo thus did not specifically treat *every* area of the Bill of Rights—he did not address Amendments II, III, and VIII at all—but he made quite clear that in his judgment the federal principle demanded that the states be permitted to follow their own discretion in much of the area of procedural due process of law, *so long as due process of law was indeed provided in every instance.*

The Cardozo "honor roll" stood for almost a quarter of a century—save that, in an opinion by Justice Black, the First Amendment's separation of state and church clause was specifically incorporated and thus made applicable to the states via Amendment Fourteen in the 1947 *New Jersey Bus Case*,[92] and that the concept of a *public* trial

---

[91]302 U.S. 319 (1937).

[92]*Everson* v. *Board of Education of Ewing Township*, 330 U.S. 1.

was carried over in 1948.[93] Despite repeated calls by Justices Stone, Black, Douglas, Murphy, and Rutledge for further, if not total, incorporation, it was not until 1961 that an additional one was effected. It came as a result of the 6:3 opinion in *Mapp* v. *Ohio*,[94] written by Justice Clark, which overruled long-standing precedents[95] to hold that "all evidence obtained by searches and seizures, in violation of the Constitution is, by that same authority, inadmissible in a state court. . . ." and:

> *Since the Fourth Amendment's right of privacy has been declared enforceable against the States through the Due Process Clause of the Fourteenth, it is enforceable against them by the same sanction of exclusion as it used against the Federal Government.*[96]

Privacy.   The Fourth Amendment's implications of and for privacy point to what is arguably the newest and still broadly undefined realm of constitutional law, that of *privacy.* Any satisfactory elucida-

---

[93]*In re Oliver*, 333 U.S. 257 (the Michigan "one-man grand jury" case). But note the 5:4 limitation of the "public" concept in 1979 in *Gannett* v. *DePasquale*, 443 U.S. 368, which was more or less removed in 1980 in *Richmond Newspapers* v. *Virginia*, 448 U.S. 555; in *Globe Newspapers Co.* v. *Superior Court*, 457 U.S. 596 (1982); and in *Waller* v. *Georgia*, 467 U.S. 39 (1984), in which the Court ruled unanimously that pre-trial procedures in criminal cases should not generally be closed to the public when the defendant wants them open. On the other hand, the Court, on the same day and in a first-of-its-kind decision, held equally unanimously that a judge in Washington state had acted properly when he ordered newspapers *not* to publish material they had obtained during pre-trial "discovery" proceedings in a libel suit against them. (*Seattle Times Co.* v. *Rinehart*, 467 U.S. 20). See also the "television-presence" approval by the Court in *Chandler* v. *Florida*, 449 U.S. 560 (1981).

[94]367 U.S. 643.

[95]See especially the famous case of *Wolf* v. *Colorado*, 338 U.S. 25 (1949). In *Wolf*, Justice Frankfurter had held for the Court that the safeguards of the Fourth Amendment are "implicit in the concept of ordered liberty," and enforceable against the states via Amendment Fourteen—*but* that it does *not* forbid the admission of illegally obtained evidence in a *state* court! For in the latter, the common-law doctrine then still governed (as it does to this day in British courts and most of the other countries of the world), namely: that if the evidence is trustworthy, it is admissible regardless of how it was obtained.

[96]*Mapp* v. *Ohio, loc. cit.*, at 654–55. More than two decades later the Court's 5:4 decision rendered the "exclusionary rule" retroactive in *United States* v. *Johnson*, 457 U.S. 537. For some later key Fourth Amendment cases, compare *Katz* v. *United States*, 389 U.S. 347 (1967); *United States* v. *Chadwick*, 433 U.S. 1 (1977); *United States* v. *Mendenhall*, 446 U.S. 554 (1980); *Reid* v. *Georgia*, 448 U.S. 438 (1980); *Florida* v. *Royer*, 460 U.S. 419 (1983); and *Zurcher* v. *Stanford Daily*, 436

tion of the concept is rendered extremely difficult because, as the aforegone and subsequent discussions of fundamental rights manifest, not only is privacy a vexatious universe, there are at least three different notions of "privacy"—all of which the Court has recognized at one time or another, and these recognitions promise to escalate in the years ahead.

One claim *cum* right or privacy is, in the classification by two leading students of the issue,[97] the "place-oriented conception of privacy" or "privacy that inheres in the place or property." Mrs. Dollree Mapp's claim, elucidated above, falls squarely into that category. So did those of the wiretapped Messrs. Olmstead and Katz.[98] So did that of "T.L.O.," a fourteen-year old New Jersey high school freshman,

---

U.S. 547 (1978). See also the historic wiretapping decision, overruled by *Katz*, of *Olmstead* v. *United States*, 277 U.S. 438 (1928). But compare *United States* v. *Watson*, 423 U.S. 411 (1976); *Payton* v. *New York*, 445 U.S. 573 (1980); and *Welsh* v. *Wisconsin*, 466 U.S. 740 (1984). See also the two opposite-in-effect automobile search-and-seizure decisions in *New York* v. *Belton*, 453 U.S. 454 and *Robbins* v. *California*, 453 U.S. 320 (both 1981), perhaps at last clarified by the Court's significant 6:3 broadening of police powers in such cases in 1982 (*United States* v. *Ross*, 456 U.S. 798) and in the 1986 decision in *Lowe* v. *Virginia*, 54 LW 3630. Given probable cause-belief of the presence of contraband in a police-stopped automobile, a probing search of compartments and containers not "in plain view" may thus henceforth be undertaken. Also note the 1981 approval of "temporary detention" during a contraband search in *Michigan* v. *Summers*, 452 U.S. 692. *Watson* and *Payton*, loc. cit., should be compared and contrasted with the Court's 1981 holding in *Donovan* v. *Dewey* mine inspection case, 452 U.S. 594. See also the Court's public apology ("we apologize to all") in its abortive attempt to redefine the exclusionary rule in 1983. (*Illinois* v. *Gates*, 462 U.S. 213.) The heated and continuing controversy over the exclusionary rule came to a head seventy years after its birth in *Weeks* v. *United States*, 232 U.S. 283 (1914), and thirty-five years after *Wolf*, *loc. cit.*: In two long-awaited dramatic decisions, the Court held 6:3 and 7:2 that probative, relevant, material evidence, seized *with* a search warrant that later proved to be technically defective, would be entitled to a narrow exception, and thus admissible when the police act "in objectively reasonable reliance" on the warrant—in other words, when the officers acted in "good faith." (*United States* v. *Leon* and *Massachusetts* v. *Sheppard*, 468 U.S. 897 and 52 LW 5177 (1984), respectively.) The Court has refused to apply the Fourth Amendment's basic protection to prisoners in their cells (*Hudson* v. *Palmer*, 468 U.S. 517 [1984]) nor to civil deportation hearings (*I.N.S.* v. *Lopez-Mendoza*, 468 U.S. 1032 [1984]). Note also the "reasonable grounds"-based 1985 approval of searches of school pupils on the school premises. (*New Jersey* v. *T.L.O.*, 53 LW 4083.)

[97]P. Allan Dionisopoulos and Craig Ducat, *The Right to Privacy: Essays and Cases* (St. Paul, Minn.: West Publishing Co., 1976).

[98]*Olmstead* v. *United States*, 277 U.S. 438 (1928) and *Katz* v. *United States*, 389 U.S. 347 (1967), respectively. Olmstead lost 5:4; Katz won 8:1, his victory overturning *Olmstead*.

whose private property was searched after an administrator had been repeatedly alerted to smoking violations by the young woman, as well as suspicions of selling and using marijuana. With her consent, the school official thus searched her purse where he found a pack of cigarettes, a packet of rolling papers, a pipe, a small amount of marijuana, some empty plastic bags, $40 in cash, a card that appeared to be a list of students who owed the girl money, and two letters indicating clearly that she dealt in "pot." She was tried as a juvenile, found delinquent, and sentenced to one year on probation. On appeal, the New Jersey Supreme Court overturned "T.L.O.'s" conviction on Fourth Amendment unreasonable search and seizure grounds. But the U.S. Supreme Court reversed 6:3, ruling that while the Amendment indubitably applied to students as well as others, drug use and violence in public schools are "major social problems" that give school officials broad power to search students suspected of carrying weapons, dealing drugs, or even violating school rules.[99] A host of similar, and indeed different, "place or property oriented" illustrations of privacy claims are apposite here, many of them listed in footnote 96. Among the "different" examples would be the right of one Stanley, sitting in the assumed privacy of his own home, amusing himself with reels of film that depicted "successive orgies of seduction, sodomy, and sexual intercourse," who found himself arrested and convicted for violating Georgia's law forbidding possession of obscene matter. Speaking for a 9:0 Court, Justice Marshall held that "a State has no business telling a man, sitting alone in his own house, what books he may read or what films he may watch...."[100]

A second category or concept of claims to privacy is person-oriented rather than place-oriented—although the two are naturally related and may overlap. It is possible, however, to distinguish them. An illustration of a demonstrably "person-oriented" privacy might be the successfully propounded right of the comatose Karen Ann Quinlan, collateral with that of her parents, to have life-sustaining apparatus disconnected. The New Jersey Supreme Court was unanimous in upholding the aggrieved family's Ninth and Fourteenth Amendment-based privacy claims, with the U.S. Supreme Court denying certiorari.[101] Other illustrations are the aforementioned *Rochin, Breithaupt,* and *Schmerber* cases, that reached the Court on

---

[99]*New Jersey* v. *T.L.O.*, 53 LW 4083 (1985).

[100]*Stanley* v. *Georgia*, 394 U.S. 557, at 565.

[101]*Garger* v. *New Jersey*, 429 U.S. 922 (1976).

Fourth, Fifth, and Fourteenth Amendment grounds—Rochin winning, Breithaupt and Schmerber losing.[102] A different "person-oriented" privacy claim, which ultimately failed at the bar of the Supreme Court 5:4, was that of the Hill family of Connecticut, who sued Time, Inc. for breach of privacy. *Life* magazine, a Time subsidiary, over the family's objections and in the face of a New York statute that appeared to proscribe *Life's* particular photographic and textual invasion of privacy, had reviewed the play "The Desperate Hours," which was based on the Hill's horrifying struggle with an intruder.[103] Their privacy claims lost, albeit narrowly, at the bar of the stronger First Amendment constitutional contentions by Time, Inc. So did, on similar grounds, the agonized, tragic plea by a Florida father, whose daughter had been brutally raped and murdered, and who desperately attempted to keep the Cox Broadcasting Corporation from publishing her name.[104] Not only did the parents' privacy claim—which was buttressed by a Florida statute—lose to counter claims on First and Fourteenth Amendment grounds, it lost 9:0 (although it had triumphed in the courts below). Press freedom, of which much more will be discussed in the following chapter, is usually a good bet to win over competing constitutional claims.

The third classification or category of privacy, so ably conceptualized by Professors Dionisopoulos and Ducat, pertains to those claims that inhere in what, for want of a better term, may be called "certain personal relationships." The latter are particularly prevalent in the sexual realm. Thus what is indubitably the constitutional father and mother of the privacy child, *Griswold* v. *Connecticut*, found a basic right of privacy to inhere in a host of "radiations," "emanations," and "penumbras" implicit in five provisions of the Bill of Rights and two constitutional amendments, here to strike down Connecticut's silly old birth control statute that prohibited not only the sale of contraceptives and the tendering of advice but also the *use* of such implements—making no distinction between married or unmarried utilizers![105] The capstone of the 7:2 opinion, penned with glee by Justice Douglas, was his contention that the Ninth Amendment is a veritable beacon that illuminates "the zone of privacy created by [the] several

---

[102]See text, pp. 122ff and fns. 88–90 of this text.
[103]*Time, Inc.* v. *Hill*, 385 U.S. 374 (1967).
[104]*Cox Broadcasting Corp.* v. *Cohn*, 420 U.S. 469 (1975).
[105]*Griswold* v. *Connecticut*, 381 U.S. 479 (1965).

fundamental constitutional guarantees" outlined above.[106] Utilizing *Griswold* with alacrity, subsequent privacy claims on the contraception front won easily: e.g., down went New York's ban on the sale of contraceptives to minors in 1972 and, five years later, that state's proscription of their advertisement.[107] Most famous—or most notorious, depending upon one's *Weltanschauung*—among privacy claims in this third category is the Supreme Court's momentous series of decisions, spearheaded by its 1973 holding in *Roe* v. *Wade*,[108] that have served to create a woman's fundamental constitutional right, within certain calendar restrictions, to obtain an abortion as a matter of "free choice." The Court's 7:2 ruling was based upon claims of privacy now rooted in the Ninth and Fourteenth Amendments, the privacy of a woman's body (a concept that might also fit into the second category of privacy claims).

Whereas privacy claims triumphed in each of the several illustrations presented so far in this third category of "personal relationships," those who have attempted to profess the existence of a constitutional privacy right to "sexual preference", i.e., to the practice or condition of homosexuality, have not fared well at the hand of the courts to date. While there have been repeated indications of the Supreme Court's interest in ultimately coming to constitutional (or at least statutory) grips with that delicate and emotion-charged issue —rendered even more so by the AIDS outbreak—it has not squarely faced the issue (although cases were on its 1986 docket as these lines are written). When it has handed down rulings, they have customarily been prone to affirm decisions below, as was the case with its upholding, without formal opinion, of a lower tribunal's sanctioning of the constitutionality of Virginia's anti-sodomy statute in 1976, a decision it reconfirmed similarly in 1978.[109] Whether time will effect a change remains to be seen.

Returning to the "incorporation" discussion, barely a year had passed before another formerly "nonincorporated" segment of the Bill of Rights was carried over: the Eighth Amendment's injunction against "cruel and unusual punishment." Cardozo's opinion in *Palko* had not specifically dealt with that clause, and doubt existed as to the

---

[106]Ibid., at 485.

[107]*Eisenstadt* v. *Baird*, 405 U.S. 438 and *Carey* v. *Population Services International*, 431 U.S. 678, respectively.

[108]410 U.S. 113.

[109]*Doe* v. *Commonwealth Attorney*, 425 U.S. 901 and *Enslin* v. *Bean*, 436 U.S. 912, respectively.

limits a state—or the national government, for that matter—could go before its actions in this sphere would constitute a constitutional violation. But as a result of Justice Stewart's opinion in a decision in 1962, involving the validity of a sweeping California criminal statute against narcotics addiction,[110] the prohibition against cruel and unusual punishment is now one of the "nationalized" safeguards. It became the constitutional hook on which the Court, in a welter of nine opinions running to 243 pages, hung its historic 5:4 decision in 1972 that outlawed capital punishment "as it was then imposed under statutes."[111] But in July 1976, in a series of cases reaching it from five states that had carefully redrawn their laws to meet the objections of the 1972 decision, the Court, by a decisive margin of 7:2, upheld the constitutionality of capital punishment, given the presence of precise statutory safeguards and the absence of either impermissible discretionary imposition or a mandatory death sentence.[112]

Of undoubtedly seminal importance is the celebrated 1963 decision in *Gideon* v. *Wainwright*,[113] which incorporated the right to counsel in *all* criminal cases, be they capital or noncapital. Some observers had assumed that Justice George Sutherland's opinion in the

---

[110]*Robinson* v. *California*, 370 U.S. 660, at 666–667. The Court began to wrestle with the related issue of chronic alcoholics in the 1968 case of *Powell* v. *Texas*, 392 U.S. 514, but for the present refused 5:4 to apply the *Robinson* rationale since, as Justice Thurgood Marshall wrote in the majority opinion, Powell was not "convicted for being a chronic alcoholic, but for being in public while drunk on a particular occasion" (at 532). See also the Court's 1982 *per curiam* 6:3 upholding of a 40-year sentence for trafficking in marijuana. (*Hutto* v. *Davis*, 454 U.S. 370.)

[111]*Furman* v. *Georgia*, 408 U.S. 238.

[112]*Gregg* v. *Georgia* and *Roberts* v. *Louisiana*, 428 U.S. 153, 325 (1976). See the latter's reconfirmation in 1977 in a different context (431 U.S. 633). See also the Court's "no" on capital punishment for rape in a 7:2 opinion that adjudged the ultimate penalty therefore to be "grossly disproportionate and excessive" (*Coker* v. *Georgia*, 433 U.S. 584, 1977, and in the particularly brutal murder of a policeman by a sixteen-year old, *Eddings* v. *Oklahoma*, 455 U.S. 104 [1982]).

[113]372 U.S. 335. Chief Justice Warren placed the *Gideon* case third in importance in the cases decided during his sixteen-year career on the bench. Its liberal extensions in such famed and controversial decisions as *Escobedo* v. *Illinois*, 378 U.S. 478 (1964), *Miranda* v. *Arizona*, 384 U.S. 436 (1966), and *Orozco* v. *Texas*, 394 U.S. 324 (1969) underscore *Gideon's* significance. A contraction of *Miranda* came in *Harris* v. *New York*, 401 U.S. 222 (1971); others in *Oregon* v. *Haas*, 420 U.S. 714 (1975); *Michigan* v. *Mosley*, 423 U.S. 96 (1975); *United States* v. *Mandujano*, 425 U.S. 564 (1976); and *United States* v. *Havens*, 446 U.S. 620 (1980). But 1976 and 1984 also saw a significant expansion of the embattled *Miranda* decision (*Doyle* v. *Ohio* and *Wood* v. *Ohio*, 426 U.S. 610 and *Berkemer* v. *McCarty*, 468 U.S. 420, respectively). In 1977 there was both a narrowing in *Oregon* v.

Scottsboro Case[114] had made that aspect of the Sixth Amendment applicable to the states in all criminal cases. But the Court subsequently ruled otherwise in a highly contentious case in 1942: Justice Roberts's opinion held 6:3 that the Fourteenth Amendment did *not* require that counsel be furnished to an indigent by a state (here Maryland) in *noncapital* crimes,[115] unless "special or exceptional circumstances" existed—such as "youth," "lack of education," or "mental illness." It was this holding that was specifically overruled in *Gideon*, a case that came to the Supreme Court through Clarence Earl Gideon's pencilled *in forma pauperis* petition to it. Lawyerless and penniless, Gideon had been committed to a Florida jail as a result of the conviction of a crime (which, with the aid of a court-appointed lawyer following the mandate of *Gideon*, he was later easily able to prove a frame-up). Speaking with evident satisfaction for a unanimous Court, Justice Black wrote in *Gideon* that it was an "obvious truth" that "in our adversary system of criminal justice any person hauled into court who is too poor to hire a lawyer cannot be assured a fair trial unless counsel is provided for him."[116] Since 1972 the *Gideon* holding extends to *all*

Mathiason, 429 U.S. 492 *and* a patent refusal to overrule *Miranda* in an emotion-charged 5:4 decision in a grisly Iowa child-murder case, *Brewer* v. *Williams* (430 U.S. 387) that became known as the "Christian Burial Speech Case." See also the 1979 holding in *North Carlina* v. *Butler*, 441 U.S. 369. Ditto the 1980 decision in *Rhode Island* v. *Innis*, 446 U.S. 291 that attempted to distinguish the *Brewer* decision and to define "interrogation" in light of those two intriguing cases. The same year witnessed an 8:1 underscoring of the requirement of a genuinely *voluntary* waiver of *Miranda* rights in *Tague* v. *Louisiana*, 444 U.S. 469. Nor, as the Court ruled 6:3 in 1981, does a reading of the *Miranda* rules require a "talismanic incantation" of warnings (*California* v. *Prysock*, 453 U.S. 355). And in 1984, in a reprise of the *Williams* case, *loc. cit.*, the Court ruled 7:2 that illegally obtained evidence *may* be admitted at trial if the prosecutor can prove—as he did here—that the evidence would "inevitably" have been discovered by lawful means. Moreover, "overriding considerations of public policy" may justify immediate questioning without giving a suspect the *Miranda* warnings *first*. (*New York* v. *Quarles*, 467 U.S. 649.)

[114]*Powell* v. *Alabama*, 289 U.S. 45 (1932).

[115]*Betts* v. *Brady*, 316 U.S. 455 (1932).

[116]*Gideon* v. *Wainwright*, 372 U.S. 355. See Anthony Lewis's excellent account of Gideon's trials and tribulations in *Gideon's Trumpet* (New York: Random House, 1964).

[117]*Argersinger* v. *Hamlin*, 407 U.S. 25, which was made retroactive in 1973 (*Berry* v. *Cincinnati*, 414 U.S. 29). *Argersinger* was interpreted in 1979 as reaching only those instances in which there was at least a *likelihood* of actual imprisonment rather than a mere possibility (*Scott* v. *Illinois*, 440 U.S. 367.) Thus a mere fine in a petty case would not provide the right to be assigned counsel.

imprisonable crimes, even misdemeanors,[117] but not to prison inmates held in a special detention unit while under investigation for a crime committed in prison;[118] since 1981 to post-arrest questioning by psychiatrists in capital punishment cases;[119] and, as of 1985, to free psychiatric assistance to indigent criminal case defendants in preparing an insanity defense, *if* the defendant's sanity at the time of the crime was seriously in question.[120]

In order to limit cascading claims of "poor representation," the Court, in an interesting and important 8:1 decision in 1984, ruled that, to prevail, a defendant must demonstrate that the lawyer's work fell below "prevailing professional norms" and that, except for counsel's professional errors, the outcome would have been different.[121] Perhaps believing that amplification of that holding was desirable, the Court ruled 7:2 in 1985—and clearly for the first time—that a criminal defendant has a constitutional right to "effective assistance of counsel on appeal."[122] However, future ligitation on the meaning of the adjective "effective" is all but certain.

The highly significant self-incrimination safeguards of the Fifth Amendment were incorporated in 1964. In a dramatic overruling of its 1908 precedent of *Twining* v. *New Jersey*,[123] the Court broadened the scope of the Constitution's protection for individuals who refuse to testify against themselves in criminal cases. It did this in two rulings of major importance to jurisprudence: first, by holding 5:4 that the Fourteenth Amendment, which assures all citizens due process of law, "secures against states' invasion the same privilege that the Fifth Amendment guarantees against Federal infringement";[124] and second, by rejecting unanimously "the rule that one jurisdiction within our federal structure may compel a witness to give testimony which could be used to convict him of a crime in another."[125] To emphasize the Court's full intent of its judgment, Justice Goldberg, speaking for

---

[118]*United States* v. *Gonveia*, 467 U.S. 180 (1984).

[119]*Estelle* v. *Smith*, 49 LW 4490. But *not*, ruled the Court 5:4 in the same term, to free legal assistance to indigent parents in civil proceedings on the issue of terminating their legal relationship with their children (*Lassiter* v. *Department of Social Services*, 49 LW 4586).

[120]*Ake* v. *Oklahoma*, 53 LW 4179.

[121]*Strickland* v. *Washington*, 467 U.S. 1267.

[122]*Evitts* v. *Lucy*, 53 LW 4101.

[123]211 U.S. 78.

[124]*Malloy* v. *Hogan*, 378 U.S. 1.

[125]*Murphy* v. *Waterfront Commission*, 378 U.S. 52.

the unanimous bench in the second case, made matters crystal clear: "We hold that the Constitutional privilege against self-incrimination protects a state witness against incrimination under Federal as well as state law and a Federal witness against incrimination under state as well as Federal law." Another corner along the road of incorporation had thus been reached and turned.[126]

Still more were to come. In 1965, in a Black opinion, the Court incorporated, 7:2, the Sixth Amendment's right of an accused in a criminal case to confront *adverse* witnesses[127]—a right expanded two years later in a dissent-free opinion by Chief Justice Warren to the privilege of having compulsory process also for obtaining and confronting *favorable* witnesses.[128] A short while earlier, the Court, in yet another Warren opinion, had unanimously incorporated that same Amendment's provision to the right of a *speedy* trial.[129] In 1968 it then voted 7:2 to incorporate the right to a trial by jury in all non-petty *criminal* cases.[130] It had already so held 8:1 as to the basic right to a trial by an "impartial" jury one year earlier.[131]

---

[126]On the merits of the self-incrimination issue itself, on the other hand, see the narrowing of the immunity concept by the Burger Court in two 1975 (5:2) opinions, written by Justice Powell. In them the Court upheld the use of a new type of immunity of witnesses, the 1970 legislatively sanctioned "use" immunity (*Kastigar* v. *United States*, 406 U.S. 441 and *Zicarelli* v. *New Jersey*, 406 U.S. 472). The complete immunity from prosecution ("transactional") is thus evidently now replaceable with the more limited type ("use"); the latter allows the prosecution to use evidence in a case about which the witness was compelled to testify under an immunity grant, *provided* it is able to prove that it derived that evidence "wholly independent" of his or her testimony and that it did so "wholly legitimately."

[127]*Pointer* v. *Texas*, 380 U.S. 400.

[128]*Washington* v. *Texas*, 388 U.S. 14 (1967).

[129]*Klopfer* v. *North Carolina*, 386 U.S. 213 (1967). In 1974 Congress, led by the retiring Senator Sam J. Ervin, Jr. (D.-N.C.), passed the Federal Speedy Trial Act. This provided for setting up a schedule to be implemented over a five-year period of time limits, ultimately reaching a low of 100 days, during which criminal charges must either be brought to trial or dropped. (A number of states have adopted similar laws.) But the Act was declared unconstitutional by a federal district court in November 1977, the government filing an immediate appeal (*United States* v. *Howard*, 440, F. Supp. 1106). The Court of Appeals affirmed, but on other-than-constitutional grounds (590 F.2d 564) and the Supreme Court denied *certiorari* later in 1979 (440 U.S. 976). In 1979, Congress postponed the Act's implementation until mid-1980, but amended and strengthened it

[130]*Duncan* v. *Louisiana*, 391 U.S. 145. But earlier in 1968 it had declined to review the same issue for *civil* cases. (*McBeth* v. *Texas & Pacific Railway Co.*, 390 U.S. 987.) A "petty" case was held (7:1) in 1970 to be one for which incarcerability could not exceed six months. (*Baldwin* v. *New York*, 399 U.S. 66.) In a 5:4 ruling in

But the Court ruled by a narrow margin in 1972 that the right to a trial by an impartial jury neither encompasses a constitutional requirement for states to provide a twelve-member jury[132] (although one of less than six, i.e., five, was declared unconstitutional, as was a six-member one that split 5:1[133] nor a unanimous jury[134]). Nor does the Seventh Amendment's guarantee of a right to a trial by jury in *civil* cases in suits valued above $20 mandate a twelve-member jury even at the *federal* level (let alone at that of the states).[135] And in 1969, on the last day of Chief Justice Warren's tenure on the highest bench, the Court, in a 6:2 opinion written by Justice Marshall, at last held the double jeopardy safeguards of the Fifth Amendment to be "a fundamental ideal in our constitutional heritage . . . that . . . should apply to the States through the Fourteenth Amendment."[136] He added that insofar as this new holding was inconsistent with *Palko* v. *Connecticut*,[137] the latter stood overruled.[138]

By early 1986 no other provisions of the Bill of Rights had been incorporated (the concepts of a fair trial and eminent domain safeguards are regarded as having been absorbed long ago). Whether the Bill of Rights will ever be incorporated *in toto* is highly problematical because of the strong implications of federalism in, and the relatively lesser significance to basic human rights of those very few enumerated rights still remaining "out"—namely, those dealing with grand jury

---

1976, however, the Court seemed to narrow *Duncan* by holding that a state may deny a defendant a jury in his initial trial on a criminal charge *if* it allows that defendant, through an appeal, to get a second trial in which there is a jury, *Ludwig* v. *Massachusetts*, 427 U.S. 618 (1976).

[131]*Parker* v. *Gladden*, 385 U.S. 363 (1967), decided *per curiam*, Harlan dissenting.

[132]*Williams* v. *Florida*, 399 U.S. 78 (1970).

[133]*Ballew* v. *Georgia*, 435 U.S. 223 (1978) and *Burch* v. *Louisiana*, 441 U.S. 130 (1979), respectively.

[134]*Johnson* v. *Louisiana*, 406 U.S. 356 and *Apodaca* v. *Oregon*, 406 U.S. 404.

[135]*Colgrove* v. *Battin*, 413 U.S. 149 (1973).

[136]*Benton* v. *Maryland*, 395 U.S. 784, at 795–796. For two 1981 double-jeopardy decisions elaborating on this, see *Albernaz.* v. *United States*, 455 U.S. 333 and *Bullington* v. *Missouri*, 451 U.S. 430, respectively.

[137]302 U.S. 319 (1937).

[138]*Benton* v. *Maryland*, loc. cit. What was thus overruled was the erstwhile nonapplicability of the double-jeopardy provision of the Fifth Amendment to the states, *not*, of course, the Cardozo-authored philosophy of "selective" incorporation as such. The latter remains the law of the land as pronounced by its highest tribunal.

indictment,[139] trial by jury in civil cases, excessive fines and bail (the question of whether the Constitution provides for a *guarantee* of bail per se was before the Court in 1983[140]) the right to bear arms,[141] and the Article III safeguards against voluntary quartering of troops in private homes. But given the now well-established belief that if there is anything at all "national" in scope and application under the Constitution of the United States of America, it is the matter of civil rights and liberties—total incorporation is no longer of primary importance save as a matter of constitutional theory. With the incorporation of double jeopardy, the last crucial fundamental right then still "out" was nationalized.

Major "Positions" on Incorporation. In summary—and at the risk of oversimplification—there are essentially four major positions held by prominent past and present members of the Supreme Court on the key questions of incorporation. The *first* position is probably still current Court doctrine, growing out of the Cardozo opinion in *Palko* v. *Connecticut:* the concept of the "honor roll" or "selective incorporation."[142] Consistently rejected by such champions of judicial self-restraint as Justices Frankfurter and the second Harlan, it has commanded a majority approval of the Court since its pronouncement in 1937. It has the virtues of emphasizing generally agreed-upon essentials while retaining some flexibility and it has the vices of weighted selectivity and uncertainty.

---

[139]The Supreme Court again denied *certiorari* on that issue late in 1968 (*Gyuro* v. *Connecticut*, 393 U.S. 937).

[140]The Court "ducked" the issue by mooting it: *Murphy* v. *Hunt*, 455 U.S. 478.

[141]If any provision seems to need no judicial protection, this Amendment Two safeguard would seem to be it—so influential have been the anti-gun control forces. In the first major case on record that did reach the Supreme Court, the high tribunal (in 1969) denied review for want of a substantial federal question, the tribunal below having held categorically that Amendment Two does not apply to the states—that, indeed, "as the language of the Amendment indicates, it was not framed with individual rights in mind. . . ." (*Burton* v. *Sills*, 394 U.S. 812, appeal dismissed). See also *Quilici* v. *Village of Morton Grove*, 532 F. Supp. 1169 (D. Ill.) (1981), in which a ban upon the sale and possession of hand guns was upheld, a decision that was reconfirmed by the Court in 1983 by letting the lower court's decision upholding the ban stand. (Ibid. 464 U.S. 863.)

[142]For a view that "selective incorporation is a misnomer, see Jacob W. Landynski, "Due Process and the Concept of Ordered Liberty: 'A Screen of Words Expressing Will in the Service of Desire,' " 2 *Hofstra University Law Review* 1 (Winter 1974).

The *second* major doctrine is that initially advocated by the first Justice Harlan at the turn of the century: *simply to incorporate the Bill of Rights lock, stock, and barrel.*[143] This doctrine has been consistently espoused through the years by Justice Black and, with reservations (see below), by such Justices as Douglas, Murphy, Rutledge, Goldberg, and probably Chief Justices Stone and Warren and Justices Brennan and the second Marshall. It has been the confirmed and warmly embraced conviction of most of these justices that not only does the Fourteenth Amendment mandate the Bill of Rights' incorporation, but that even if history does not provide an entirely adequate guide on this point, both the logic and necessity of democratic society in the last quarter of the twentieth century requires such a position. It possesses the virtues of certainty and simplicity and the vices of dogmatism and questionable interpretation of the basic document.

The *third* position is really an extension of the second: namely, that the Bill of Rights in all its majestic guarantees may not suffice to ascertain full "due process of law" and that therefore it may be necessary to embrace a "total incorporation *plus*" approach in order to achieve full justice for the allegedly aggrieved involved. This posture was most prominently expounded by Justices Murphy and Rutledge in their dissenting opinion in the *Adamson* case. In Justice Murphy's words, they agreed that the specific guarantees of the Bill of Rights should be "carried over intact" into the first section of the Fourteenth Amendment, but that "occasions may arise where a proceeding falls so short of conforming to fundamental standards of procedure *as to warrant constitutional condemnation in terms of a lack of due process despite the absence of a specific provision in the Bill of Rights.*[144] Justices Douglas and Goldberg emphatically voiced their adherence to the "incorporation *plus*" doctrine in the *Connecticut Birth Control Case* in 1965,[145] with Douglas remaining its most forceful advocate until ill health dictated his retirement in 1975 (after more than thirty-six years of service on the Court).

---

[143]Harlan did not use those words: His emphasis fell on the universally *fundamental* nature of *all* the provisions of the Bill of Rights, thus calling for their absorption via the Fourteenth Amendment.

[144]*Adamson* v. *California*, 332 U.S. 46 (1947), at 124. (Italics added.)

[145]*Griswold* v. *Connecticut*, 381 U.S. 479. In that case Chief Justice Warren and Justice Brennan seemed to embrace that doctrine as well. After Justice Douglas's departure from the Court in 1974, Justice Brennan and Marshall moved demonstrably close to his "incorporation plus" posture.

The *fourth* position is that so prominently associated with the name of Justice Frankfurter, for nearly a quarter of a century the occupant of the Holmes-Cardozo "chair" on the Court. He and his supporters—notable among them the first Justice John Marshall Harlan's grandson by the same name and Justice Lewis F. Powell, Jr.—reject total incorporation as not only foolhardy and contrary to the commands of the Constitution, but as clearly violative of the structure and principles of federalism, and, moreover, as a rank example of "judicial legislating." They reject the *Palko* rule of selective incorporation as "natural law," as creating unwarranted, artificial distinctions among basic rights. Instead, the Frankfurter position advocates the so-called "fair trial" or "case-by-case" approach described earlier, under which the Court would examine each case on its own merits, testing it against the requirements of "due process of law." This position, which has generally appealed to the four Nixon appointees to the Burger Court,[146] as well as to Mr. Ford's appointee[147] (it is too early to characterize the posture on the matter by the first woman justice[148] to sit on the Court) has the virtues of considerable judicial latitude and close examination of individual cases and the vices of unpredictability and subjectivity.

These are some of the significant considerations that attend the overriding problem of the application to our governmental institutions of both the substantive and procedural rights that constitute the lifeblood of our constitutional system.

---

[146]Chief Justice Warren E. Burger (1969); Justice Harry A. Blackmun (1970); Justice Lewis F. Powell, Jr. (1972); and Justice William H. Rehnquist (1972).

[147]Justice John Paul Stevens (1975), who succeeded Douglas.

[148]Justice Sandra Day O'Connor, appointed by President Reagan in September 1981 to succeed the retired Justice Stewart.

4

Fundamental Freedoms:

Religion, Expression, and Racial, Sexual, and Political Equality

It is axiomatic that the Supreme Court's role in each of these five fundamental freedoms and attendant collateral constitutional rights is enormously significant. The Court has been called upon to adjudicate cases arising under them since the end of World War I, and with increasing frequency. Although it has strived to establish ascertainable lines, some of these remain almost necessarily serpentine. No value judgment should be imputed to the order in which the freedoms are discussed here. They are presented as they appear in the Bill of Rights and subsequent amendments: the First Amendment, the Civil War amendments (Thirteenth, Fourteenth, and Fifteenth amendments), and the Nineteenth Amendment. We thus begin with the subject matter of the very first sentence of the first article in the Bill of Rights, Amendment One.

Religion

The First Amendment of the Bill of Rights—which, as we have seen, is now fully applicable to the states via the Fourteenth—declares that "Congress shall make no law respecting an establishment of religion, or prohibiting the free exercise thereof. . . ." To state the guarantees is

to state the problem—obviously one of the most complex constitutional ones. The amendment's implied injunction to render unto Caesar
what belongs to Caesar recognizes the difficulty, but hardly solves it.
Basically, two major concepts are involved in the field of religion as
viewed under the terminology of the First Amendment: (1) *free exercise of religion* (to what extent does this clause require deference to
action?) and (2) *separation of church and state* (does this vexatious
concept prohibit *any* aid to all religion, only *some* aid, or only discriminatory treatment?).

There is probably no other area in the realm of cultural freedom
that is so prone to emotionalism and considerations of privacy for, as
Professor Allport so well put it, religion encompasses a value that
every democrat "must hold: the right of each individual to work out
his own philosophy of life, to find his personal niche in creation, as
best he can."[1] Happily, America's general record in the religious toler-
ance realm has been a good, even excellent, one since post-Civil War
days, especially in that of the free exercise of religion, which the Court
seems consistently to have viewed as a "preferred freedom area." It is
widely accepted that, as a minimum, the free exercise clause was
clearly intended to protect a wide range of religious observances from
government activity, and the establishment clause both prohibited
the national government from founding or perpetuating a state religion and prevented it from favoring any one religion or religious sect.

FREE EXERCISE OF RELIGION

Although it is difficult to separate clearly the two aspects of the religion clause, the Court has been moved to try to distinguish between
"prohibiting the free exercise thereof" and the preceding mandate
that "Congress shall make no law respecting an establishment of religion." Turning to the former first, we are at once confronted with a
basic dilemma, for the phrase embraces two concepts: freedom to believe and freedom to act. As Justice Roberts stated it so succinctly for
the Court some four decades ago in the leading case of *Cantwell* v.
Connecticut,[2] "[T]he first is absolute but in the nature of things, the
second cannot be. Conduct remains subject to regulation for the protection of society." Hence, acting upon that philosophy, both the legislative and judicial branches have from time to time deemed it neces-

---

[1]Gordon W. Allport, *The Individual and His Religion* (New York: The Macmillan
Co., 1963), p. vii.
[2]310 U.S. 296 (1940).

sary and appropriate to curb the "action" realm of the free exercise of religion.

Thus the Supreme Court upheld federal laws forbidding the practice or advocacy of polygamy in the face of the constitutional challenge by Mormons that it violated their freedom of religion, and those regulating the use of marijuana and LSD against similar claims by the "Neo-American Church";[3] rejected sundry attacks upon so-called state blue laws, based on the same constitutional objectives;[4] denied the claim that freedom of religion includes the right to exhibit poisonous snakes in a church;[5] and, while the Supreme Court had not rendered a formal opinion on the issue as of early 1983, most lower courts have rejected the free-exercise-of-religion claim of a *constitutional* "right to die" by disconnecting life-prolonging mechanical respirators (the *Karen Ann Quinlan Case*[6] being a notable exception, and possibly a harbinger of change). On the other hand, a state may neither legally require a declaration of belief in God as a qualification for public office,[7] nor ban clergy from running for public office;[8] parents

---

[3]*Reynolds* v. *United States*, 98 U.S. 145 (1878) and *United States* v. *Kuch*, 288 F. Supp. 439 (1968), respectively.

[4]*McGowan* v. *Maryland*, 366 U.S. 420 (1961) and three other cases in the same volume. But *cf.* the related decisions in *Sherbert* v. *Verner*, 374 U.S. 398 (1966); *Parker Seal Co.* v. *Cummins*, 429 U.S. 65 (1976); *T.W.A.* v. *Hardesty*, 432 U.S. 93 (1977); *Thomas* v. *Review Board of the Indiana Empl. Sec'y. System*, 450 U.S. 707 (1981); and *Thornton* v. *Caldor*, 53 LW 4853 (1985), which provided diverse results.

[5]*Thompson* v. *Lawson*, 319 U.S. 759 (1943). Reconfirmed in *Pack* v. *Tennessee* ex rel *Swann*, 424 U.S. 954 (1976).

[6]In the *Quinlan Respirator Case*, Judge Robert Muir, Jr., of the New Jersey Superior Court, had initially ruled against the Quinlan family's pleas for a court-sanctioned medical termination of the year-long, utterly hopeless, vegetable-life, machine-supported existence of Karen Ann Quinlan (decision of November 10, 1975). But, on appeal, the New Jersey Supreme Court unanimously *reversed* Judge Muir 7:0 (March 31, 1976), structuring its holding largely on a "right to privacy," based on "religious beliefs" on the part of Karen's father to act in his daughter's best interest. The State of New Jersey declined to appeal the decision, and the United States Supreme Court denied *certiorari* that November, thus affirming *sub silentio* the decision of its New Jersey counterpart (429 U.S. 922). The respirators were disconnected, but Miss Quinlan lived until June 1985 (almost a decade after the initial disconnecting). A similar case, that of Mrs. Celia Cain, resulted in instantaneous death, however. (Duval County, Florida, December 4, 1976.) Ditto that of Rodney Pointdexter (Los Angeles, California, October 8, 1980). See the discussion of privacy in the preceding chapter, pp. 125ff.

[7]*Torcaso* v. *Watkins*, 367 U.S. 488 (1961).

[8]*McDaniel* v. *Paty*, 435 U.S. 618 (1978).

may not be compelled to send their children to a public school[9] (although they must send them to a properly accredited school[10]), nor may children be forced to go beyond the eighth grade if such compulsory attendance violates established religious beliefs (i.e., those of the Amish[11]); and—since an overruling of a series of precedents in 1946—citizenship may not be denied to otherwise qualified applicants if their religious creed prevents them from bearing arms (so long as they declare a willingness to perform some other type of service).[12] On the other hand, whereas conscientious objection to military service is entitled to every benefit of doubt under the law and the First Amendment,[13] there are limits: for example, claims to "selective" conscientious objection, which would see the claimant serve in "justifiable" but not "unjustifiable" wars.[14]

The saga of the Jehovah's Witnesses—a militantly evangelicalistic, fundamentalist, minority Protestant religion—perhaps best illustrates the Court's readiness to bend over backwards in behalf of freedom of religion even for those beliefs that may well be obnoxious to the vast majority of the body politic. In the four decades following 1937, the Witnesses, guided by the brilliant advocacy of their chief counsel, Hayden C. Covington, won all except twelve[15] of eighty-seven cases they brought to the Supreme Court on appeal.[16] Probably the most celebrated among these cases was *West Virginia Board of*

---

[9]*Pierce* v. *Society of Sisters*, 268 U.S. 510 (1925). But states cannot be *compelled* to provide public funds to church-related schools. (*Brusca* v. *State Board of Education of Missouri*, 405 U.S. 1064 [1972]).

[10]*Garber* v. *Kansas*, 389 U.S. 51 (1967), *certiorari* denied.

[11]*Wisconsin* v. *Yoder*, 406 U.S. 205 (1972). But *cf. United States* v. *Lee*, 102 S. Ct. 1051 (1982).

[12]*Girouard* v. *United States*, 328 U.S. 61.

[13]See *United States* v. *Seeger*, 380 U.S. 163 (1965) and *Welsh* v. *United States*, 398 U.S. 333 (1970).

[14]*Gillette* v. *United States* and *Negre* v. *Larsen*, 401 U.S. 437 (1971), a unanimous holding save for Justice Douglas's dissent on free exercise grounds, in which he urged an "implied First Amendment right" of "conscience."

[15]One area is the state's right to limit the sale and distribution of merchandise and solicitation of funds at certain outings (in which another evangelistic sect, the Hare Krishna, sustained 9:0 and 5:4 losses in 1981 in *Heffron* v. *International Society for Hare Krishna Consciousness*, 452 U.S. 640).

[16]Stone once said that the Jehovah's Witnesses "ought to have an endowment in view of the aid which they give in solving the legal problems of civil liberties." As quoted by A. T. Mason, *Harlan Fiske Stone: Pillar of the Law* (New York: Viking Press, 1956), p. 599.

Education v. *Barnette*,[17] in which the Court, overruling a decision of less than three years standing,[18] struck down a state requirement that all public school children must salute the flag, over the Witnesses' objection that such a requirement would compel them to "behold a graven image." Speaking for a 6:3 majority, Justice Jackson's memorable words clearly focus the basic issue:

> *If there is any fixed star in our constitutional constellation, it is that no official, high or petty, can prescribe what shall be orthodox in politics, nationalism, religion, or other matters of opinion, or force citizens to confess by word or act their faith therein.*[19]

SEPARATION OF CHURCH AND STATE

"Free exercise of religion" is relatively uncomplicated compared to the involved and emotion-charged area of separation of church and state, where extreme positions are the rule rather than the exception. Consequently, the Court has found it enormously difficult to draw a line between those who hold that the Constitution forbids *any and all aid* to, and recognition of, religion by government, and those who believe that at least *some* such governmental action is not only constitutional but eminently desirable and a government "duty." Were the verbiage of the First Amendment, and were history, a reliable guide, the problem might have been solved. But the verbiage is subject to differing interpretation and analysis, and history, as is true so often, is a guide only in the eyes of those who wish to utilize it for their own

---

[17]319 U.S. 624 (1943). Note Justice Frankfurter's poignant dissenting opinion in the case.

[18]*Minersville School District* v. *Gobitis*, 310 U.S. 586 (1940).

[19]*West Virginia Board of Education*, loc. cit., at 642. The holding in the case was reconfirmed in 1973 in *Central School District #1* v. *Russo*, 411 U.S. 930 (this time on freedom-of-speech grounds). In 1979 the Court let stand a lower tribunal's decision that a worker may refuse on religious grounds to pay union dues (*International Association of Machinists and Aerospace Workers* v. *Anderson*, 440 U.S. 960). See also the related "separation" cases of *National Labor Relations Board* v. *Bishop of Chicago*, 440 U.S. 490 (1979) and *St. Martin's Lutheran Church* v. *South Dakota*, 451 U.S. 772 (1981), in which the Court ruled 5:4 and 9:0, respectively, that a sectarian institution may not be required to bargain collectively with a union, nor may religious schools that are truly *integrated* into a church's structure, and have no separate entity, be compelled to pay federal unemployment taxes for their employees. See also *Larkin* v. *Grendel's Den*, 454 U.S. 116 (1982), in which the Supreme Court struck down 8:1 a Massachusetts law allowing churches to control whether nearby restaurants may have liquor licenses.

evaluation. Thus both sides of the controversy cite Madison as proof for either position. Yet all that can really be said with conviction about the Madisonian position is that he wanted to make resolutely certain that Congress (and by implication the several states) would never pass a law establishing or respecting a state religion or state church. Hence the Supreme Court has found any attempt to draw a line the proverbial "can of worms." But tried it has, by giving repeated voice to what it has viewed as the Jefferson-Madison "wall of separation" between church and state.

The Child Benefit Theory. In the 1947 *New Jersey Bus Case,* the majority ruled that the "wall of separation" had *not* been breached by New Jersey's provision of free bus transportation to parochial school children as well as to those attending the township's public schools, *because the grants benefitted the child rather than the church.* Justice Black expressed the doctrine for the 5:4 Supreme Court as follows:

> The *"establishment of religion"* clause of the First Amendment means at least this: Neither a state nor the Federal Government can set up a church. Neither can pass laws which aid one religion, aid all religions, or prefer one religion over another. Neither can force nor influence a person to go or remain away from church against his will or force him to profess a belief or disbelief in any religion. No person can be punished for entertaining or professing religious beliefs or disbeliefs, for church attendance or nonattendance. No tax in any amount, large or small, can be levied to support any religious activities or institutions, whatever they may be called, or whatever form they may adopt to teach or practice religion. Neither a state nor the Federal Government can, openly or secretly, participate in the affairs of any religious organizations or groups and vice versa. In the words of Jefferson, the clause against establishment of religion by law was intended to erect a "wall of separation between Church and States."[20]

---

[20]*Everson* v. *Board of Education of Ewing Township,* 330 U.S. 1 at 15–16. Yet some fifteen years later, taking the occasion of *Engel* v. *Vitale, infra,* Justice Douglas, one of the *Everson* majority of five, announced from the bench on Opinion Monday, that he *now* believed *Everson* to have been decided wrongly. But it still stands, and will likely continue to stand—indeed, the Court refused to hear an appeal in a New Jersey case again in 1971 on the very same issue (*West Morris Regional Board of Education* v. *Sills,* 404 U.S. 986).

This is a memorable and oft-quoted position, yet whether or not it has been followed by the Court in practice depends upon one's point of view. The *New Jersey Bus Case* decision is itself a case in point.

Moreover, the Court has either upheld, or refused to review, sundry practices and legislation, frequently under the concept of the "child benefit" theory. Thus the court sanctioned Louisiana's, New York's and Pennsylvania's expenditures of public funds to furnish or loan nonsectarian textbooks to children of parochial and other private schools as well as to those in public schools[21] (but it has also upheld the precise contrary);[22] federal grants for lunches in all schools; the use of sectarian chaplains in the armed forces generally, and of a Presbyterian minister for the Nebraska legislature, in particular;[23] the practice of public school "released time," when carried on outside public school buildings[24] (the Court did strike down released-time practiced in public school buildings[25]); and blanket tax exemption for any and all religious institutions and their property unless they engage in business for profit[26]—or use it as a front for tax fraud.[27] Yet the Court has also upheld—by declining to review—state legislation and state court interpretations *banning* free bus transportation to other

---

[21]*Cochran* v. *Louisiana*, 281 U.S. 370 (1930); *Board of Education* v. *Allen*, 392 U.S. 236 (1968); *Meek* v. *Pittenger*, 421 U.S. 349 (1975); and *Wolman* v. *Walter*, 433 U.S. 229 (1977). It is interesting to note that in *Allen*, Justice Black, the author of the *Everson* decision, dissented vigorously, pointing to what he perceived as a crucial difference between the educational function of books and buses. On the other hand, the Court refused to sanction such book loans to *racially segregated* public schools (*Norwood* v. *Harrison*, 413 U.S. 455, 1973). And it declined to review a decision invalidating a Missouri law that had authorized textbook loans to pupils at church-related schools (*Reynolds* v. *Paster*, 419 U.S. 1111, 1975).

[22]*Carlson* v. *Dickman*, 371 U.S. 242 (1961) and *Dickman* v. *School District, Oregon City*, 371 U.S. 823 (1962), certiorari denied.

[23]*Marsh* v. *Chambers*, 463 U.S. 783 (1983).

[24]*Zorach* v. *Clauson*, 343 U.S. 306 (1952). Faced with a golden opportunity to reconsider *Zorach* in 1976, the Court pointedly refused to do so (*Smith* v. *Smith*, 423 U.S. 1073, certiorari denied).

[25]*McCollum* v. *Board of Education*, 333 U.S. 203 (1948).

[26]See the 1970 *Walz* decision upholding that principle as to tax exemption (*Walz* v. *Tax Commissioners of New York City*, 397 U.S. 664) and the 1972 *Diffenderfer* one as to the taxability of that part of any church property used commercially (*Diffenderfer* v. *Central Baptist Church of Miami*, 404 U.S. 412).

[27]*The Rev. Sun Myung Moon* v. *United States*, 52 LW 3828 (1984).

than public school children[28] and subventions to parochial school children.[29] Evidently, the Supreme Court has endeavored to follow a doctrine that constitutes a blend between judicial self-restraint or deference to state legislatures and between permitting certain so-called "auxiliary" or "indirect" services to religion, reasoning that such marginal aid does not breach the "wall of separation." To state that issue is, of course, to invite immediate dispute.

Prayers and Bible Reading. In the early 1960s, however, the Warren Court seemed to embark upon a new path of strictness in interpreting the separation clause—either on its own terminology or by commingling it with the free exercise of religion phrase. Two cases decided in 1962 and 1963, respectively, illustrate the new policy, if such it was. Few if any decisions—and none in the realm of religion—have caused such an outcry, whatever the motivation by the critics, as the two 6:1 and 8:1 decisions in the *New York Prayer Case*[30] and the *Abington Township Bible Reading* and *Baltimore City Lord's Prayer Cases.*[31] Since the latter decisions were basically extensions of the former, we shall concentrate upon the New York case.

At issue was a rather general, twenty-two-word nondenominational prayer,[32] composed by the New York State Board of Regents (an agency composed of state officials). The prayer was recommended, but not required, for reading aloud by the teachers and students of the New York public schools in each classroom at the start of each school day. A group of Long Island parents, contending the recommendation to be a violation of the separation of church and state principle, brought suit against the New Hyde Park Board of Education. In his not very lengthy, not very complex, and not very diplomatically phrased majority opinion for the Court, Justice Black agreed with the complaining parents. But he did try hard to put into public focus the

---

[28]High courts in Wisconsin, Delaware, New York, Iowa, Alaska, Missouri, New Mexico, Oklahoma, and Washington have held parochial student bus benefit laws unconstitutional. See, among others, *Rhoades* v. *Washington*, 389 U.S. 11 (1967) and *Worell* v. *Matters*, 389 U.S. 846 (1967).

[29]See, for example, the Vermont parochial student fees case of *Anderson* v. *Swart*, 366 U.S. 925 (1961).

[30]*Engel* v. *Vitale*, 370 U.S. 421 (1962). Justices Frankfurter and White did not participate.

[31]*Abington Township* v. *Schempp* and *Murray* v. *Curlett*, 374 U.S. 203 (1963).

[32]"Almighty God, we acknowledge our dependence upon Thee, and we beg Thy blessings upon us, our parents, our teachers, and our country."

manifold and probably insoluble problems of personal commitments that continue to bedevil the religion-constitutional controversy:

> [*T*]*he constitutional prohibition against laws respecting an establishment of religion must at least mean that in this country it is no part of the business of government to compose official prayers for any group of the American people to recite as part of a religious program carried on by government...It is neither sacrilegious nor antireligious to say that each separate government in this country should stay out of the business of writing or sanctioning official prayers and leave that purely religious function to the people themselves and to those [to whom] the people choose to look for religious guidance.*[33]

Barely one year later, in another 8:1 decision, this time written by Justice Clark (with considerably less bluntness, and much more of an eye toward soothing the public), the Supreme Court extended the *Engel* doctrine to embrace the *state-required* daily public school reading of ten verses without comment from the Holy Bible in Pennsylvania,[34] and the long-standing Baltimore practice of daily devotional Bible reading and Lord's Prayer recitation.[35] Combining the two cases, the Clark opinion—significantly pointing out en route that there is an almost inevitable overlapping between the nonestablishment and free exercise clauses of the First Amendment—concluded on this essential note:

> *The place of religion in our society is an exalted one, achieved through a long tradition of reliance on the home, the church and the inviolable citadel of the individual heart and mind. We have come to recognize through bitter experience that it is not within the power of government to invade that citadel, whether its purpose or effect be to aid or oppose, to advance or retard.* In the relationship between man and religion, the State is firmly committed to a position of neutrality.[36]

---

[33]*Engel* v. *Vitale, loc. cit.,* at 425.

[34]*Abington Township* v. *Schempp, loc. cit.*

[35]*Murray* v. *Curlett, loc. cit.*

[36]*Abington Township* v. *Schempp* and *Murray* v. *Curlett, loc. cit.* (Italics added.) But in 1974 the Court upheld a lower tribunal's decision sanctioning the inclusion of prayers in a public school commencement program (*West* v. *Mt. Lebanon School District,* 419 U.S. 967). On the other hand, the Court upheld another lower court's ban on compulsory chapel services at the national service academies (*Laird* v. *Anderson,* 409 U.S. 1076, 1972). And in late 1980 it struck down *per curiam*

Yet far from soothing the uproar caused by the *Engel* decision of one year earlier, the new Supreme Court pronouncement only seemed to increase the threat of retaliatory legislative action. (It did, however, receive some significant church support, particularly among liberal Protestant and Jewish clergy, and featured lengthy concurring opinions by the Roman Catholic Justice Brennan and the Jewish Justice Goldberg.) Deliberate violations of the *Engel* and *Schempp* decisions were not only rampant but were often encouraged by government officials on the state and local levels. By 1986 some 385 proposed constitutional amendments designed to reverse the Court's school prayer and Bible decisions had been introduced in Congress alone—a handful of these narrowly failing passage in Congress. The late 1970s and the 1980s saw a new approach: attempts to curb the appellate jurisdiction of the Supreme Court and the lower federal courts in *Engel* and *Schempp* type cases. Two passed the Senate in 1979 (by votes of 49:37 and 51:40), but the House failed to concur. In 1981, in what was more or less mere gesture, Congress voted to forbid the Department of Justice to use any appropriate funds to fight the implementation of voluntary prayer and meditation in public schools. A hotly debated bill that would have deprived the federal judiciary of jurisdiction over state-court approved voluntary prayer legislation fell to an extended filibuster in 1982. The controversy is very much alive at this writing (1986), but such legislation is unlikely to pass—as are proposed constitutional amendments designed to do what simple legislation could not. Congress did enact the 1984 Equal Access Act, enabling student religious groups to hold religious meetings in secondary public schools (the statute was being challenged in the Supreme Court in 1986). It also passed a largely symbolic law in the same presidential election year, providing for "individual prayer" by students attending public schools.

Notwithstanding the history of strong Court opposition and congressional legislative frustrations, numerous states remained undaunted on the prayer-in-public-schools front. Thus, in 1978 and again in 1982, New Jersey enacted a compulsory "silent meditation" bill, mandating a brief period of silent meditation at the opening of every school day "for quiet and private contemplation or introspection," to be conducted by the teacher "in each public classroom."

(5:4) a 1978 Kentucky statute that required the posting of a copy of the Ten Commandments in every public school classroom in the state (*Stone* v. *Graham*, 449 U.S. 39).

That law had not reached the Supreme Court by 1986, but it had fallen below 2:1. A Louisiana statute permitting "voluntary prayer" daily had been struck down by the Court in 1983; and New Mexico's "One Minute of Silence" law had been declared unconstitutional in 1983.[37] Then Alabama entered the fray prominently with both "*viva voce*" and "silent" prayer statutes. The former, which permitted public school teachers to lead prayers, lost at the bar of the Supreme Court in 1984.[38] The latter also fell one year later, in a major 6:3 decision, which declared the law to lack "a clear secular purpose"; impermissibly to "endorse religion as a favorite practice"; that its sole purpose was, in opinion-author Stevens's language, the "fostering of religious activity in the classroom."[39] It seems that simple "moments of silence" laws might surmount constitutional challenges but *not* "silent meditation or prayer" ones, such as Alabama's.

Financial Aid to Parochial Schools. The enactment in 1965 of the Federal Aid to Elementary and Secondary Schools Act was tailor-made for additional Court involvement in the vexatious church-and-state sphere, facilitated by a successful suit by interested federal taxpayers to obtain the heretofore elusive standing to sue on the constitutional question.[40] Tangentially, the basic issue of primary support of parochial schools from public funds came before the Court in a series of highly important cases in 1971.[41] The catalysts were Pennsylvania and Rhode Island laws providing *direct public fund aid* to "purchase secular services" from sectarian schools, including the payment of parochial school teachers for teaching "secular" subjects in the parochial schools. Speaking through Chief Justice Burger with only Justice White in partial dissent, the Court struck down the statutes as constituting a constitutionally impermissible "excessive entanglement between Government and religion." Endeavoring to explain the basic dimensions of the new "no excessive entanglement" line, Burger concluded:

[37]*Treen* v. *Karen B.*, 455 U.S. 913 and *New Mexico* v. *Burciaga*, 464 U.S. 982, respectively.

[38]*Wallace* v. *Jaffree*, 52 LW 373.

[39]Ibid., 53 LW 4665 (1985).

[40]*Flast* v. *Cohen*, 392 U.S. 83 (1968), a ruling that amended the long-standing contrary precedent of *Frothingham* v. *Mellon*, 262 U.S. 447 (1923). Among the winning side's counsel at the bar of the Supreme Court was Senator Sam J. Ervin (D.-N.C.), an ardent supporter of strict separation of church and state.

[41]*Lemon* v. *Kurtzman* and *Earley* v. *Dicenso*, 403 U.S. 602 (1971).

The merits and benefits of these schools . . . are not the issue before us in these cases. The sole question is whether state aid to these schools can be squared with the dictates of the Religious Clauses. Under our system the choice has been made that government is to be entirely excluded from the area of religious instruction and churches excluded from the affairs of government.[42]

It will come as no surprise, however, that the partisans of state aid to parochial schools would by no means be deterred, and they *have* continued to vie with one another for speedy enactments of new legislation, notwithstanding the Supreme Court's past stance. New cases were bound to reach the highest tribunal, especially since sundry changes in the Court's membership had begun to take place as of 1969.[43] When a bevy of them from New York and Pennsylvania did arrive on the Court's last day in 1973, a variety of schemes to provide financial aid to private secondary schools, *including* sundry types of tax relief and tuition reimbursement, were declared unconstitutional by votes ranging from 8:1 to 6:3.[44] Writing for the Court's solid majority, Justice Powell ruled that the *effect* of the various programs was "to advance religion in that [they] subsidized directly the religious activities of sectarian elementary and secondary schools,"[45] thus violating the Constitution's strictures against the commingling of church and state. Throughout the opinion, *the* governing trifold constitutional yardstick for the separation-establishment issue was stressed and restressed—namely, that any law in affecting church-

---

[42]Ibid., at 625. (Emphasis added.) A similar fate (8:1), based upon similar reasoning, befell an Ohio law that attempted to provide direct aid payments to parents of children in parochial schools in order to reimburse them for tuition payments (*Essex* v. *Wolman*, 409 U.S. 808, 1972). Still, in a rather strangely reasoned 1973 follow-up decision to *Lemon*, the Court, by a vote of 5:3, authorized Pennsylvania to reimburse sectarian schools for such "secular education services" as they had performed prior to the *Lemon* denouement (*Lemon* v. *Kurtzman*, 411 U.S. 192).

[43]Chief Justice Burger for Chief Justice Warren (1969); Justice Blackmun for Justice Fortas (1970); Justice Powell for Justice Black (1972); Justice Rehnquist for Justice Harlan (1972); and, later (1975), Justice Stevens for Justice Douglas.

[44]*Levitt* v. *Committee for Public Education and Religious Liberty*, 413 U.S. 472; *Committee for Public Education and Religious Liberty* v. *Nyquist*, 413 U.S. 756; and *Sloan* v. *Lemon*, 413 U.S. 825.

[45]*Nyquist, loc. cit.*, at 774. The impermissible thrust of the *Nyquist* case was reaffirmed in a 1979 summary holding (*Byrne* v. *Public Funds for Public Schools*, 442 U.S. 907). But it was muddied one year later, 5:4, in *Committee of Public Education and Religious Liberty* v. *Regan*, 444 U.S. 646 (1980).

state relations must have, *first,* a secular legislative purpose; *second,* its principal or primary effect must neither advance nor inhibit religion; and *third,* it must not foster an "excessive entanglement" with religion.

Not to be denied, Pennsylvania—undismayed, undaunted, and stubborn—enacted "new" aid to parochial and other private schools, comprising such services as counseling, testing, remedial classes in speech and hearing therapy, and funds for instructional equipment like charts, maps, records, films, tape recorders, and projectors, plus an additional textbook loan program. Predictably, when the all but inevitable challenges to the constitutionality of these measures reached the Supreme Court in 1975, all of them, save the textbook loan program, fell 6:3. Justice Stewart again zeroed in on the constitutional *effect* of the multiple legislation upon the mandated separation between church and state, and ruled it an "impermissible establishment of religion."[46]

Yet there was scant doubt that the Court would again find itself confronted with delicate and difficult decision making in this emotion-charged issue. Indeed, not only did its 1976 docket contain a number of pertinent cases, but one of them, to the astonishment and dismay of a number of close students of the Court's established posture on the matter, seemed to open a small crack in the "wall" of separation. In a 5:4 decision, featuring a welter of opinions but *no* majority agreement, the Supreme Court upheld Maryland's program of financial aid for church-related *colleges.* For the first time in history, the Court thus approved a system of *general purpose* subsidies from the state, designed to benefit church-related educational institutions. Over fervent, often biting dissents by Justices Brennan, Stewart, Marshall, and Stevens—who viewed the subsidies as involving "the disease of entanglement"—five justices, Blackmun, Powell, Burger, White, and Rehnquist, saw no constitutional violation for a variety of reasons. In the eyes of the majority, the decisive justification seemed to be the somewhat less than totally persuasive rationale that the "character" of the colleges, their "ability to separate their secular and religious functions," and the lower "impressionability" of college students (as contrasted with secondary- and primary-level students) thus lessened dangers of indoctrination, and hence *ipso facto* sufficed to meet the trifold requirements of nonreligious purpose, nonreligous ef-

---

[46]*Meek* v. *Pittenger,* 421 U.S. 349, at 366.

fect, and avoidance of excessive entanglement.[47] And one year later, in a welter of opinions ranging from 8:1 to 4:5—with all but Justices Blackmun and Stewart joining in the entire range of plurality decisions—the five-way split Court, while disallowing some aid to Ohio's parochial schools (e.g., wall charts, slide projectors, and field trips), okayed such broad state aid as diagnostic services, therapeutic services, and standardized tests and scoring services.[48]

Yet while reimbursement by New York for nonmandated recordkeeping and testing services for parochial schools was disallowed by a 6:3 vote of the justices six months later,[49] another badly split (5:4) Court in 1980 upheld New York's reimbursements to *all* schools for *state-mandated* tests and supporting procedures.[50] And *pace* what had seemed to be the Court's decisive 6:3 "no" on tax relief and tuition reimbursement in the 1973 *Nyquist* group of cases, a decade later it upheld in an astonishing 5:4 distinction (or was it a reversal?) a Minnesota statute that allowed *tax deductions* from state income taxes for the cost of school tuition and fees up to $700 per child annually, for private as well as public schools—the overwhelming benefits, rebounding to the former, of course.[51] That a narrow but now relatively predictable majority appeared to have embraced a demonstrably broader "accommodationist" approach became rather obvious in 1984 when the Court, in an opinion by Chief Justice Burger, upheld as a "historical symbol" rather than a "religious endorsement" Pawtucket, Rhode Island's public financial support of an annual Christmas display in a private park, centering on a life-sized crèche or Nativity scene. Over the outraged dissenting opinion by Justice Brennan, joined by his colleagues Marshall, Blackmun, and Stevens, the Chief Justice observed that total separation is neither "possible" nor "required"; that there must be accommodation between church and state.[52] A few months later, with Justice Powell not sitting, the justices voted 4:4 to uphold lower court rulings, based on the rationale

---

[47]*Roemer* v. *Maryland Public Works Board*, 426 U.S. 736 (1976). A Missouri practice statutorily sanctioning tuition grants to students attending public *and* private (including parochial-affiliated) colleges was unsuccessfully challenged in the Supreme Court, with Justice Brennan dissenting from that tribunal's refusal to review the case (*American United* v. *Rogers*, 429 U.S. 1029 [1976]).

[48]*Wolman* v. *Walter*, 433 U.S. 229 (1977).

[49]*New York* v. *Cathedral Academy*, 434 U.S. 125 (1977).

[50]*Committee for Public Education and Religious Liberty* v. *Regan*, 444 U.S. 646.

[51]*Mueller* v. *Allen*, 463 U.S. 388 (1983).

[52]*Lynch* v. *Donnelly*, 465 U.S. 668 (1984).

of the Rhode Island decision, that forced the New York community of Scarsdale to provide public land for a privately sponsored Christmas nativity scene each year.[53] The devotees of separation were dismayed, fully anticipating increasing commingling permissiveness by the Court.

Toward the end of its 1984–85 term, the Court clearly seemed to shift gears once again when, with Justice Powell in the role of "key switcher," the Court 5:4 struck down "shared time" and/or "secular purchase" practices that saw the financing of *public* school teachers on *parochial* school premises—and, in the case of New York, the utilization of federal Title I of the Federal Aid to Primary and Secondary Schools Act funds.[54] With seven new church-state cases on its 1985–86 docket, the Court would obviously have considerably more to say in the matter in the near future.

Freedom of Expression

Justice can hardly be done to this vast and complex topic in a series of volumes, let alone a few pages. Hence we will raise some essential questions in a general way, and then concentrate upon that area of freedom of expression that has proved to be the most contentious and most significant since the 1940s.

GENERALLY

Freedom of expression signifies the freedom to communicate—and, since 1976, including even purely "commercial speech."[55] In other words, it comprehends the ability to express oneself orally or in writing—in the press, through books, movies, or plays[56]—without *prior* restraint. Actually, considerably more is meant by freedom of expression than simply communicating through speech or the press; includ-

---

[53]*Village of Scarsdale* v. *McCreary*, 53 LW 4331 (1985).

[54]*Grand Rapids* v. *Ball*, 53 LW 5005 and *Aguilar* v. *Felton*, 53 LW 5013 (1985), respectively.

[55]*Virginia State Board of Pharmacy* v. *Virginia Citizens Consumer Council*, 425 U.S. 748.

[56]*Southeastern Promotions, Ltd.* v. *Conrad*, 420 U.S. 546 (1975), held, for the first time, that theatrical productions were entitled to the same kind of constitutional protection against advance censorship and prohibitions long enjoyed by newspapers, books, and movies.

ed within the concept of freedom of expression is a host of other basic liberties, such as the right to picket (a mode of communication as much as speaking and printing); the right of assembly and petition; now apparently even that of *spending* by and for a candidate for federal elective office (but *not* in the form of unlimited *contributions*).[57] Also, freedom of expression has been related to the right of banks and business corporations to make contributions or expenditures for the purpose of influencing votes on referendum proposals "other than one materially affecting any of the property, business or assets of the corporation";[58] to that of public utilities to advertise, or even insert views on controversial issues in customer bills;[59] and, as of mid-1976, to the constitutional right of federal and state government workers not to be dismissed for mere patronage reasons![60]

No matter how sweeping and unequivocal these guarantees of freedom of expression may be, they are not absolute—despite Justice Black's fervent contentions to the contrary. Under our systems of government, the majority is obliged to safeguard and respect the rights of the minority, but it does not have to acquiesce in the "tyranny of the minority." Thus, as various courts have held repeatedly, picketing and sundry street demonstrations, for example, may be an expression of freedom of speech. But, as even Black, under certain conditions, repeatedly made clear, illegal picketing and trespassing and breach of the peace are not acts of freedom of expression; nor is the burning of draft cards; nor the sale to children of sexually suggestive "girlie" and similar magazines; nor undressing in public, or walking about in the nude; nor the featuring of nude dancers in a bar and other "bacchanalian revelries"; nor homosexual acts by consenting adults in private (!), or even confessed homosexuals, as in the case of a high school teacher who was dismissed on grounds of "immorality" for being ho-

---

[57]*Buckley* v. *Valeo*, 424 U.S. 1 (1976) and *F.E.C.* v. *National Conservative Political Action Committee*, 53 LW 4293 (1985). See also *California Medical Association* v. *Federal Election Commission*, 453 U.S. 182 (1981).

[58]*First National Bank of Boston* v. *Bellotti*, 435 U.S. 765 (1978). (The Court was badly split here, 5:4.)

[59]*Consolidated Edison Co.* v. *Public Utility Commission*, 447 U.S. 530 (1980) and *Central Hudson Gas and Electric Corp.* v. *Public Service Commission*, 447 U.S. 557 (1980). But *cf. Citizens Against Rent Control* v. *Berkeley*, 50 LW 4071 (1981).

[60]*Elrod* v. *Burns*, 427 U.S. 346 (1976). (Extended to patronage *hiring* in 1979.) The prohibition on dismissals purely for patronage reasons was redefined and broadened in 1980 in *Branti* v. *Finkel*, 445 U.S. 507. To be sustained, a "policy-making, confidential employee" status must now be demonstrated by the dismissing governmental unit or agency.

mosexual; nor the violation of a school board's or police department's order to cut excessively long hair; nor journalists' refusal to testify regarding confidential sources or materials in either criminal or civil cases; nor a prohibition against sex-designated employment advertisements in newspapers; nor one against placing unstamped material in private mail boxes; nor sleeping in parks near the White House (including the putting up of 60 tents for the homeless).[61]

Yet the First Amendment does protect symbolic and related, basic free-expression activities such as wearing black armbands to a high school class in an anti-Vietnam war protest; publicly denouncing the United States flag (see also *Smith* v. *Goguen*, 415 U.S. 566 1974); the wearing, in a play, of the uniform of the United States armed forces even if the tenor of the play is unfavorable to the armed forces; the public sporting of a jacket with the words "fuck the draft" emblazoned upon it (see also *Papish* v. *Board of Curators*, 410 U.S. 667 1973); showing "stag" movies in private; having a device in an adult book store that allows a customer to view a live nude dancer; peaceful

---

[61]The several demonstration cases are illustrated by such as *Thornhill* v. *Alabama*, 310 U.S. 88 (1940); *Giboney* v. *Empire Storage and Ice Co.*, 335 U.S. 490 (1949); *Adderley* v. *Florida*, 385 U.S. 39 (1967); *Walker* v. *Birmingham*, 338 U.S. 307 (1967); *Lloyd* v. *Tanner*, 407 U.S. 551 (1972); and *Hudgens* v. *N.L.R.B.* 424 U.S. 507 (1976); *Carey* v. *Brown*, 447 U.S. 455 (1980); and *NAACP* v. *Claiborne Hardware*, 102 S. Ct. 3409 (1982). The draft card reference is to *United States* v. *O'Brien*, 391 U.S. 367 (1968); that on obscenity to *Ginsberg* v. *New York*, 390 U.S. 629 (1968); and *New York* v. *Ferber*, 458 U.S. 747 (1982) (see also *Ginzburg* v. *United States*, 383 U.S. 463 [1966]; *Miller* v. *California*, 413 U.S. 15 [1973]; *Paris Adult Theatre* v. *Slaton*, 413 U.S. 49 [1973]; *Jenkins* v. *Georgia*, 418 U.S. 153 [1974]); and *F.C.C.* v. *Pacifica Foundation*, 438 U.S. (1978); that on nude dancers to *California* v. *LaRue*, 409 U.S. 109 (1972), reconfirmed 7:2 in 1981 in *New York State Liquor Authority* v. *Bellanca*, 49 LW 3950—but see the contrary ruling in *New York* v. *Onofre*, 49 LW 3854 (1981); those on homosexuals to *Doe* v. *Commonwealth Attorney for the City of Richmond*, 425 U.S. 901 (1976) and *Gaylord* v. *Tacoma School District*, 434 U.S. 879 (1977), respectively; that on sex-designated newspaper ads to *Pittsburgh Press Co.* v. *Pittsburgh Committee on Human Relations*, 413 U.S. 376 (1973); that on undressing in public to *Nelson* v. *Iowa*, 401 U.S. 923 (1971); that on long hair, *Olff* v. *East Side Union High School District*, 404 U.S. 1042 (1972), and *Kelley* v. *Johnson*, 425 U.S. 238 (1976); that on unstamped matter in private mailboxes, *United States Postal Service* v. *Council of Greenburgh Civil Association*, 453 U.S. 114 (1981); that regarding an alleged First Amendment right to protect confidential sources against court and jury questioning, *Branzburg* v. *Hayes*, 408 U.S. 655 (1972) and *Tribune Publishing Co.* v. *Caldero*, 434 U.S. 930 (1977); and that proscribing sleeping and putting up tents in parks near the White House, *Clark* v. *Community for Non-Creative Violence*, 52 LW 4986 (1984).

assembly protest on the grounds of the Capitol in Washington, D.C. and on the sidewalks surrounding the U.S. Supreme Court; newspaper publishing, within a state, of ads for legal out-of-state abortion services; the posting by homeowners of "for sale" or "sold" signs in front of their homes; the on-campus conducting by campus-based organizations in public universities of religious services; the right of the press normally to be free from judicial "gag" orders that are unreasonable (in contrast to those that are considered reasonable by the judiciary); and the advertising by lawyers of their fees in a brief, factual manner.[62] Yelling "fire" in a crowded theater, to use the famed Holmesian illustration, is an exercise of freedom of speech (as well as a duty of citizenship) if there is a fire; but if the call is false, it represents not freedom of speech but license.[63] *Actual* overt incitement to the overthrow of the United States government by force and violence, accompanied by the language of incitement, is not freedom of expression;[64] the *theoretical* advocacy of such overthrow, on the other hand, is now considered such a freedom.[65] Calling someone

---

[62]The armband case is *Tinker* v. *Des Moines Independent Community School District*, 393 U.S. 503 (1969); the flag-denouncing one is *Street* v. *New York*, 394 U.S. 576 (1969); the uniform case is *Schacht* v. *United States*, 398 U.S. 58 (1970); the public display of vulgar language case is *Cohen* v. *California*, 403 U.S. 15 (1971); that on "stag" movies is *Stanley* v. *Georgia*, 394 U.S. 557 (1969); that on university campus religious organizations, *Widmar* v. *Vincent*, 454 U.S. 263 (1981), but not in public high or elementary schools, *Brandon* v. *Board of Education*, 50 454 U.S. 1123 (1981)—but Congress enacted the Equal Access Act of 1984, in fact so extending it; and that on Capitol grounds demonstrations, *Chief of Capitol Police* v. *Jeannette Rankin Brigade*, 409 U.S. 972 (1972) and *United States* v. *Grace*, 461 U.S. 171 (1983); that on the coin-operated machine to see nude dancers, *Schad* v. *Borough of Mount Ephraim*, 452 U.S. 61 (1981); *Tinker* was reaffirmed in 1972 in *Board of Education* v. *James*, 409 U.S. 1042. The case dealing with out-of-state abortion ads is *Bigelow* v. *Virginia*, 421 U.S. 809 (1975); the "freedom from judges' gag" victory for the press is *Nebraska Press Association* v. *Stuart*, 424 U.S. 539 (1976), its loss, *Leach* v. *Sawicki*, 434 U.S. 1014 (1978), *certiorari* denied, but *cf. Gannett* v. *DePasquale*, 443 U.S. 368 (1979), *Richmond Newspapers* v. *Virginia*, 448 U.S. 555 (1980), *Chandler* v. *Florida*, 449 U.S. 560 (1981), *Globe Newspaper Co.* v. *Superior Court*, 457 U.S. 596 (1982); and *Press Enterprise Co.* v. *Superior Court*, 464 U.S. 501 (1984); that regarding the posting of a "sold" or "for sale" sign, *Linmark Associates* v. *Willingboro*, 431 U.S. 85 (1977); and that relating to lawyers' right to advertise, *Bates* v. *Arizona State Bar*, 433 U.S. 350 (1977), as expanded in *In re R.M.J.*, 455 U.S. 191 (1982).

[63]*Schenck* v. *United States*, 249 U.S. 47 (1919).

[64]*Scales* v. *United States*, 367 U.S. 203 (1961).

[65]*Noto* v. *United States*, 367 U.S. 290 (1961).

"goddamn racketeer" and "dirty Fascist" is not freedom of speech;[66] calling a convicted thief "thief" or "crook" presumably is—at least until the individual has paid his or her debts to society. And a newspaper cannot be *required* to print replies from political candidates attacked in its columns,[67] although it *is* subject to libel laws by ordinary citizens.[68]

It is plain that the rights protected in this area of freedom of expression are certainly not absolute; hence, common as well as statutory law has imposed a number of limitations over a period of years. To the courts in general, and to the Supreme Court in particular, has fallen the task of drawing a line between the individual's cherished right of freedom of expression and that of society to safeguard its body politic against excesses. Not only *where* to draw that line, but *how* it shall be drawn, and *who* shall draw it, are problems that call for a Solomon. Amidst both cheers and jeers the Supreme Court has taken on the task.

Line-Drawing: Gamesmanship or Solution?

It is well to keep the "double standard" and "preferred freedoms" in mind as we look at some of the several "tests" devised by the Court. It is as impossible as it would be unwise to speak of any one definitive,

---

[66]*Chaplinsky* v. *New Hampshire*, 315 U.S. 568 (1952). But unless statutes like the New Hampshire one involved in that case are *very* carefully and *very* specifically drawn, they will not survive First Amendment claims, as Georgia found out in a 1972 decision (*Gooding* v. *Wilson*, 405 U.S. 518).

[67]*Miami Herald Publication Co.* v. *Tornillo*, 418 U.S. 241 (1974).

[68]Eg., *Gertz* v. *Robert Welch*, 418 U.S. 323 (1974) and *Time, Inc.* v. *Firestone*, 424 U.S. 448 (1976). But a different standard obtains vis-à-vis *bona fide* public officials, where the "actual malice" test governs. (See *The New York Times* v. *Sullivan*, 376 U.S. 254 [1964] and *Ginzburg* v. *Goldwater*, 396 U.S. 1049 [1970] for the application of the " malice " test in two different cases that led to *different* results. See also its important invocation in the "reporters' state-of-mind" case of 1979 in *Herbert* v. *Lando*, 441 U.S. 153, and that same year's narrowing of the "public figure" test in *Hutchinson* v. *Proxmire* and *Wolston* v. *Readers Digest Assn., Inc.*, 443 U.S. 111 and 157, respectively.) Similarly, see the intriguing case of *Doubleday* v. *Bindrin* and *Mitchell* v. *Bindrin*, 444 U.S. 984 (1970). For an apparent narrowing of the "malice" test, see the Court's 5:4 holding in 1985 in *Dun & Bradstreet* v. *Greenmoss*, 105 S. Ct. 2939, ruling that the First Amendment does not protect against punitive damage awards *unless* the libelous statements involve "matters of public concern." On the other hand, in what was clearly a major victory for the news media, it ruled 5:4 in 1986 that people suing news organizations for libel must overcome the difficult burden of proving that the published statements about them are false. (*Philadelphia Newspapers* v. *Hepps*, decided April 21.)

current, exclusive "test" or "line," but we may outline the major ones which the Court has embraced from time to time, depending upon personnel and circumstances.

Clear and Present Danger Test. The first such test is the best known: the famous *"clear and present danger"* test, authored in 1919 by Justices Holmes and Brandeis in *Schenck v. United States.*[69] In that case, the Court unanimously upheld the constitutionality of the Espionage Act of 1917 against the charge that its application to Charles T. Schenck's distribution of anti-draft leaflets to potential draftees was a violation of the First Amendment freedoms of expression. In emotion-charged, intemperate language, Schenck had urged the young men involved to resist the draft. Justice Holmes explained his new line or test in the following memorable passage:

> *We admit that in many places and in ordinary times the defendants in saying all that was said . . . would have been within their constitutional rights. But the character of every act* depends upon the circumstances *in which it was done. . . . The most stringent protection of free speech would not protect a man in* falsely *shouting fire in a theater and causing a panic. It does not even protect a man from an injunction against uttering words that have all the effects of force. . . . The question in every case is whether the* words used are used in such circumstances and are of such a nature as to create a clear and present danger that they will bring about the substantive evils that Congress has a right to prevent. *It is a question of proximity and degree.*[70]

One week after *Schenck,* with Holmes again speaking for the unanimous Court, two more convictions under the Act were upheld, again based on the clear and present danger doctrine.[71] (Brandeis preferred to categorize it as "a rule of reason." Correctly applied, he believed, it

---

[69]249 U.S. 47. Some students of the field would credit Judge Learned Hand with an important assist, if not the initial idea, in the creation of the doctrine. (See Robert S. Lancaster, "Judge Hand's Free Speech Problem," 10 *Vanderbilt Law Review* 301, February 1957.)

[70]Ibid., at 52. (Italics added.)

[71]*Frohwerk v. United States,* 249 U.S. 204 (1919) and *Debs v. United States,* 249 U.S. 211 (1919). Frohwerk had inserted several articles in a Missouri German-language newspaper, challenging the purposes of the war as well as the merits and constitutionality of the draft. Debs was charged with an attempt to cause insubordination in the army and to obstruct recruiting.

would preserve the right of free speech both from "suppression by tyrannous, well-meaning majorities, and from abuse by irresponsible, fanatical minorities.")

But, as if to demonstrate the difficulty of the line, barely six months later a majority of the Supreme Court, in a 7:2 decision in the case of *Abrams* v. *United States*,[72] allegedly used the clear and present danger test in sustaining the application of the Sedition Act of 1918. After World War I, twenty-nine-year-old Jacob Abrams and five young self-styled anarchist-Socialist associates—all Russian aliens, one a woman—distributed some English- and Yiddish-language leaflets from rooftops on New York's Lower East Side. The leaflets urged the "workers of the world" to resist the Allied and American military intervention against the Bolsheviks in the Vladivostok and Murmansk areas of Russia. They bitterly denounced President Wilson for his decision to intervene, and called for a general strike to prevent shipment of munitions to the anti-Soviet forces. The English leaflets closed with the following postscript: "It is absurd to call us pro-German. We hate and despise German militarism more than do your hypocritical tyrants. We have more reasons for denouncing German militarism than has the coward in the White House."[73] Visiting United States District Court Judge Henry DeLamar Clayton of Alabama sentenced three of the defendants to the maximum of twenty, one to fifteen (the girl), and one to three years in the federal penitentiary. (The jury acquitted one.) Their sentences were commuted in 1921 by President Harding on condition that they would all embark at once for Russia at their own expense—which they did. Justices Holmes and Brandeis, the authors of the clear and present danger doctrine, had joined in an impassioned dissenting opinion by the former, based upon the grounds that the "surreptitious publishing of a silly leaflet" by an unknown man (Abrams) did not constitute a "present danger of immediate evil." Wrote Holmes in an oft-quoted statement:

> *...I think that we should be eternally vigilant against attempts to check the expression of opinions that we loathe and believe to be fraught with death,* unless they so imminently threaten immediate

---

[72]250 U.S. 616 (1919).

[73]As quoted by Zechariah Chafee, Jr., in his classic *Freedom of Speech in the United States*, 6th printing (Cambridge: Harvard University Press, 1967), p. 110. Chapter 3 in this epic work on freedom of expression fully describes the circumstances surrounding the *Abrams* case (pp. 108–140).

interference with the lawful and pressing purpose of the law that an immediate check is required to save the country. . . .[74]

Bad Tendency Test.   Although a clear majority of the Court had thus sidetracked or narrowed the clear and present danger doctrine, the Court sustained its first *official* modification six years later in the famous case of *Gitlow* v. *New York.*[75] Here a 7:2 majority held that Benjamin Gitlow's verbal and written expressions constituted a *"bad tendency"* to "corrupt public morals, incite to crime, and disturb the public peace." In other words, the Court's majority in upholding Gitlow's conviction under New York's Criminal Anarchy statute dodged the clear and present danger doctrine—perhaps "watered it down" would be a more accurate description—by adopting the *"bad tendency"* test: that is, a "bad tendency" to bring about a danger—a "kill-the-serpent-in-the-egg" test that had initially been given its casual terminology in the 1920 case of *Schaefer* v. *United States.*[76] Clearly, the new test effectively shifted the balance between the individual and the state in the latter's favor.

The Imminence Test.   Two years after *Gitlow,* in *Whitney* v. *California,*[77] Justice Brandeis, with the staunch support of his colleague Holmes, attempted not only to resurrect the clear and present danger doctrine, but to expand or liberalize it, by joining to it the test of *"imminence"*—that is, that the danger must not only be "clear and present" but also "imminent" in order to justify suppressive and punitive state action. Both jurists did agree with the decision of their colleagues on the bench in upholding Miss Whitney's conviction under California's 1919 Criminal Syndicalism Act (which would be declared unconstitutional in 1968) because of evidence that appeared to point to the existence of a conspiracy to violate the law. However, in their concurring opinion, Brandeis and Holmes rejected the majority's interpretation of another section of the Act, which not only made it a crime to advocate or teach or practice "criminal syndicalism," but that was also directed at "association with those who proposed to preach it." Thus, in his restatement of the clear and present danger test, Justice Brandeis gave posterity the following admonition:

---

[74]*Loc. cit.,* at 630 (Italics added.)
[75]268 U.S. 652 (1925). See pp. 117–118 in this text.
[76]251 U.S. 466.
[77]274 U.S. 357 (1927).

Fear of serious injury cannot alone justify suppression of free speech and assembly . . . there must be reasonable ground to fear that serious evil will result if free speech is practiced. . . . There must be reasonable ground to believe that the danger apprehended is imminent. There must be reasonable ground to believe that the evil to be prevented is a serious one. . . . In order to support a finding of clear and present danger it must be shown either that immediate serious violence was to be expected or was advocated, or that the past conduct furnished reason to believe that advocacy was then contemplated . . . no danger flowing from speech can be deemed clear and present, unless the incidence of the evil apprehended is so imminent that it may befall before there is opportunity for full discussion. . . .[78]

It was this general philosophy that the Supreme Court practiced at the end of the 1930s and for much of the 1940s. During that period its view that there should be "more exacting judicial scrutiny" of First Amendment freedoms was at its apogee. It was then that the Court recognized beyond doubt a constitutionally protected area of "preferred freedom," in line with the famous footnote by Justice Stone in *United States* v. *Carolene Products Co.*,[79] calling for a special niche for "legislation which restricts the political processes."[80]

But the picture began to change when Fred M. Vinson assumed the chief justiceship upon the death of Harlan F. Stone in 1946. And when both Justices Murphy and Rutledge died unexpectedly in the summer of 1949, their replacement by Justices Tom C. Clark and Sherman Minton heralded an almost instant departure from the "preferred freedom" doctrine and the "imminence" test. Especially in the delicate and contentious matters of Communist threat and national security, the "clear and present danger" doctrine began to be transformed into what some observers viewed as the *"grave and probable"* test; and by others, perhaps facetiously, as the *"possible and remote" doctrine.* The Vinson Court (1946–1953) commenced to reserve the clear and present danger test and its "imminence" appendage for other aspects of freedom of expression—for example, street-corner oratory and press freedom—while fairly consistently applying the "bad tendency" test to the national security field. However, once Chief Justice Warren had established his leadership in the latter area,

---

[78]Ibid., at 376–378. (Italics added.)
[79]304 U.S. 144 (1938).
[80]Ibid.

roughly midway in his sixteen-year term (1953–1969), the Court returned to the "clear and present danger" plus imminence test for the national security realm as well, including the overruling of *Whitney* in *Brandenburg* v. *Ohio*.[81] With the advent of the "Burger Court" in 1969—Warren Earl Burger having replaced Earl Warren in the center chair—a renewed change in direction seemed likely. Yet, at its end in 1986, there had been no return to the Vinson approach, nor had there been any tendency to move toward Justice Black's *absolutist* posture on free speech.[82] The Burger Court had evinced a generous interpretation of the First Amendment's free expression mandates, notwithstanding some possible narrowing or "balancing" in the obscenity and press sectors.[83]

THE COURT AND NATIONAL SECURITY

Understandably, there is no area where the Court has trod more carefully, and where it has been more mindful of public opinion or consensus, than the realm of the Communist cold war threat and national security. Recognizing the threat as well as the problem, the Court has gone out of its way to save congressional statutes and intent, while at the same time insisting that procedures adopted in the execution of the various statutes must be fair to individuals concerned. Moreover, it has not been remiss in curbing Congress by *statutory interpretation*, and, in the case of the Warren Court, by occasional declarations of unconstitutionality.[84] It has thus pursued a wavering line, but a relatively predictable one, clearly mindful of its role as a law court as well as a political and governmental institution. Some illustrations will demonstrate the point.

Congressional Investigating Committees. Nothing is dearer to the collective heart of Congress than its power of investigation. That it must have this power in order to legislate intelligently, to inform the public, and to oversee the administrative branch is as obvious as it is

---

[81]395 U.S. 444 (1969).

[82]A case could be made for treating Black's approach as a fourth "test" or "line"; but it never commanded majority support on the Court and is not likely to do so.

[83]See p. 155 of this text for some illustrations. For an extensive up-to-date treatment of freedom of expression, see Chapter V, "The Precious Freedom of Expression," in my *Freedom and the Court: Civil Rights and Liberties in the United States*, 4th ed. (New York: Oxford University Press, 1982).

[84]See pp. 166 of this text.

historically demonstrable—and the Supreme Court has repeatedly so held.[85] But that this enormous power also readily lends itself to abuses is equally clear, and the Supreme Court has so held as well.[86] Again, the matter has been particularly sticky in the multiple instances of investigations of subversive activities, particularly in connection with the refusal of witnesses to respond to questions by invoking the *First* rather than the Fifth Amendment.

Matters seemed to come to a head in 1957, when the Court was confronted with the case of *Watkins* v. *United States.*[87] In this case the issue was John T. Watkins's refusal, on *First* Amendment freedoms grounds, to answer some questions put to him by the House Committee on Un-American Activities concerning certain of his associates. The Court, 6:1, held specifically that the Committee had failed to "spell out" its jurisdiction and the purpose of its investigation with "sufficient particularity." The chief justice went further to point out that there *are* limits to the authority of Congress to inquire; that there exists no general authority to expose the private affairs of individuals merely "for the sake of exposure"; that Congress is not a law enforcement or trial agency; and that, in the words of Warren's expansive opinion and *obiter dicta,* "no inquiry is an end in itself; it must be related to and in furtherance of a legitimate task of Congress."[88] These general constitutional limitations were on the very same day also applied to *state* legislative investigations via the Fourteenth Amendment in *Sweezy* v. *New Hampshire.*[89]

Congressional and public reaction was predictably vehement and condemnatory, and various pieces of legislation designed to deprive the federal judiciary of jurisdiction over investigative procedures were introduced in Congress at once. The legislation, which was tied in

---

[85]See, among others, *Anderson* v. *Dunn*, 6 Wheaton 204 (1821); *In re Chapman*, 166 U.S. 661 (1897); *McGrain* v. *Daugherty*, 273 U.S. 135 (1927); *Braden* v. *United States*, 365 U.S. 431 (1961); and *Stamler* v. *Willis*, 393 U.S. 217 (1968), which upheld the constitutionality of the House Committee on Un-American Activities. (The committee was abolished in 1975, and its functions transferred to the Judiciary Committee. Its Senate counterpart, the Judiciary Committee's Subcommittee on Internal Security, was disbanded in 1977).

[86]See, among others, *Kilbourn* v. *Thompson*, 103 U.S. 168 (1880); *Marshall* v. *Gordon*, 243 U.S. 521 (1917); *United States* v. *Rumely*, 345 U.S. 41 (1953); *Watkins* v. *United States*, 354 U.S. 178 (1957); and *De Gregory* v. *Attorney General*, 383 U.S. 825 (1966).

[87]354 U.S. 178.

[88]Ibid., at 187.

[89]354 U.S. 234 (1957).

with other highly restrictive barriers to the Supreme Court's appellate jurisdiction,[90] failed to be enacted. However, that failure was in no small measure due to what (despite denials and explanations of distinguishing facts) would clearly seem to have been a strategic retreat by the Court in the form of two 5:4 decisions,[91] announced on the same day in 1959 and followed by two others by the same close vote two years later.[92] The Court majority took pains to distinguish these several decisions from *Watkins* and *Sweezy*, but there was a strong feeling that the majority had read and heeded "the political signs." On the other hand, the Court has continued to reiterate time and again that it will sanction neither patently unconstitutional investigative procedure nor lack of proper authorization to investigate.[93]

Tests of Anti-Communist Legislation

Most controversial of all aspects of the national security field and judicial review has been the delicate task of the Supreme Court in interpreting cases dealing with the major anti-Communist statutes —especially the Smith Act of 1940 and the Internal Security (McCarran) Act of 1950, both designed to curb and prevent activities to further the internal Communist activity. A third statute, the hastily enacted Communist Control Act of 1954, which was more or less ignored by the Justice Department as a basis for prosecution, had not been judicially tested by early 1986 in any constitutional sense, although it had figured tangentially in two cases some two decades earlier.[94]

The Smith Act.   The first test, appropriately of the Smith Act, came in the celebrated 1951 case of *Dennis* v. *United States*.[95] Here

---

[90]See the intriguing struggles surrounding the proposed "Jenner-Butler Bill," well described in Walter F. Murphy, *Congress and the Court* (Chicago: University of Chicago Press, 1962).

[91]*Barenblatt* v. *United States*, 360 U.S. 109 and *Uphaus* v. *Wyman*, 360 U.S. 72.

[92]*Braden* v. *United States*, 365 U.S. 431 (1961) and *Wilkinson* v. *United States*, 365 U.S. 399 (1961).

[93]E.g., *Russell* v. *United States*, 369 U.S. 749 (1962) and *De Gregory* v. *Attorney General of New Hampshire*, 383 U.S. 825 (1966).

[94]*Pennsylvania* v. *Nelson*, 350 U.S. 497 (1956) and *Communist Party* v. *Catherwood*, 367 U.S. 389 (1961). In the latter case the Court ruled 9:0 that the Communist Party could not be barred from state unemployment systems.

[95]341 U.S. 494.

the Supreme Court, in a 6:2 decision, upheld the Act's constitutionality against charges that it infringed on First Amendment rights of
freedom of expression and due process of law under the Fifth Amendment. In federal Judge Harold F. Medina's trial court, eleven top
leaders of the American Communist Party had been indicted and
found guilty of a conspiracy to teach and advocate the overthrow of
the United States government by force and violence, and of conspiring
to organize the Communist Party to teach and advocate the same. In
sustaining the Smith Act, Chief Justice Vinson's majority opinion
invoked what he viewed as the "clear and present danger" doctrine in
relation to the *conspiratorial nature* of the defendants' activities. But
in so doing, he joned to the test that of "probability," adopting the following excerpt from Chief Judge Learned Hand's opinion in upholding the conviction of the defendants when their case had reached his
United States Court of Appeals from the trial court below:

> . . . [*Courts*] *in each case. . . must ask whether the gravity of the evil,*
> discounted by its improbability, *justifies such invasion of free speech*
> *as is necessary to avoid the danger.*[96]

The chief justice continued that

> [*t*]*he formation by* [*the convicted persons*] *of such a highly*
> *organized conspiracy, with rigidly disciplined members subject to*
> *call when the leaders. . . felt that the time had come for action,*
> *coupled with the inflammable nature of world conditions, similar*
> *uprisings in other countries, and the touch-and-go nature of our re-*
> *lations with countries with whom* [*the convicted persons*] *were in*
> *the very least ideologically attuned, convince us that their convic-*
> *tions were justified on this score.*[97]

Yet there were two passionate dissenting opinions by Justices
Black and Douglas. They *denied* the existence of a danger either
"clear and present" enough to justify the limitation of freedom of expression; charged that the majority had, in effect, resurrected the bad
tendency test of *Gitlow;*[98] and argued for "full and free discussion
even of ideas we hate." Justice Douglas belittled the alleged internal
strength and threat of the Communist movement, pointing out that in

---

[96]*Dennis* v. *United States*, 183 F. 2d 201 (1950), at 212.
[97]*Dennis* v. *United States*, 341 U.S. 494 (1951), at 510–511.
[98]*Gitlow* v. *New York*, 268 U.S. 652 (1925).

America "they are miserable merchants of unwanted ideas: their wares remain unsold."[99] Justice Black concluded his dissent with the following observation:

> *Public opinion being what it now is [1951], few will protest the conviction of these Communist petitioners. There is hope, however, that in calmer times, when present pressures, passion and fears subside, this or some later Court will restore the First Amendment liberties to the high preferred place where they belong in a free society.*[100]

Justice Black's expression of hope seemed to attain at least partial vindication six years later (after the federal government had obtained 145 indictments and eighty-nine convictions under the Smith Act). In June 1957—a month that featured several broadly libertarian decisions by the Supreme Court, including the above-discussed *Watkins*[101]—a six-man majority, with but Justice Clark dissenting, handed down a series of significant amendative interpretations of the Smith Act in *Yates* v. *United States*,[102] thus henceforth drastically limiting its application. Writing for the majority, Justice Harlan narrowed the meaning of the term "to organize"—a term that Congress, in retaliation, broadened again in 1962—and attempted to draw an important legal distinction between the *statement of a philosophical belief* and the *advocacy of an illegal action*. The Smith Act still stood, but the federal government would now no longer be able to punish members of the Communist Party for *expressing a mere belief* in the violent overthrow of the government. It would have to prove that individuals on trial for violating the Smith Act actually intended to overthrow the government by force and violence now or in the future, or to persuade others to do so, and the language employed must be "calculated to incite to action...to *do* something, now or in the future, rather than merely believe in something"—thus reintroducing the clarity, if not the "imminence," requirement.

---

[99]*Dennis* v. *United States*, 341 U.S. 494 (1951), at 589.

[100]Ibid., at 581.

[101]*Watkins* v. *United States*, 354 U.S. 178; *Sweezy* v. *New Hampshire*, 354 U.S. 234; *Jencks* v. *United States*, 353 U.S. 657; *Konigsburg* v. *State Bar of California*, 353 U.S. 252; *Schware* v. *Board of Bar Examiners*, 353 U.S. 232.

[102]354 U.S. 298.

Almost as if to rectify the anticipated adverse public reaction to the *Yates* decision, however, the Court in 1961 upheld 5:4 the so-called membership clause of the Smith Act, ruling through Justice Harlan that a person who was a "knowing, active" member of a subversive group, and who personally had "a specific intent to bring about violence," was convictable under the statute.[103] But in a companion case, with the opinion also authored by Harlan, the Court held unanimously that *here* the government had not validly met the above requirements of a carefully drawn distinction between "knowing" membership and mere "passive" membership in a subversive group, and must thus release the prisoner.[104]

On the other hand, as if to demonstrate the vexatious balancing problems anew, the Supreme Court, in its first significant ruling involving the McCarran Act of 1950—and in one of the lengthiest opinions in Court history, written by Justice Frankfurter—held 5:4, also in 1961, that its registration requirements did not violate the First Amendment by their forced disclosure of Communist Party members' names.[105] With characteristic caution, and deference to legislative action, the Court deliberately failed to reach any of the other constitutional questions involved here, including the difficult matter of compulsory self-incrimination under the Fifth Amendment.

The McCarran Act. The Court's hand was forced little more than two years later when, in 1963, the United States Court of Appeals for the District of Columbia *did* meet the registration issue squarely in *reversing* the federal trial court conviction of the American Communist Party for having failed to register under the McCarran Act. The party's constitutional argument was that since the Smith Act treats membership in the Communist Party as a criminal conspiracy, compelled registration would be self-incriminating. Accepting this reasoning, the Court of Appeals ruled unanimously that since "mere association with the party incriminates," statutory registration would force self-incrimination in the face of Fifth Amendment guarantees against it. The United States government appealed this decision to the Supreme Court—which refused to review it, thus letting stand, without comment, the government's defeat on the issue

---

[103]*Scales* v. *United States*, 367 U.S. 203.

[104]*Noto* v. *United States*, 367 U.S. 290.

[105]*Communist Party* v. *Subversive Activities Control Board*, 367 U.S. 1.

below.[106] But two weeks later, on the last Opinion Monday of its 1963–1964 term, the Court did squarely come to constitutional grips with another section of the McCarran Act that it had purposely ignored in its 1961 decision—that section which denied passports to members of the Communist Party and its fronts. In a 6:3 decision delivered by Justice Goldberg—who had replaced Justice Frankfurter in 1962—the Court ruled that Section 6 of Title I "too broadly and indiscriminately restricts the right to travel and thereby [unconstitutionally] restricts the liberty guaranteed by the Fifth Amendment."[107] (That the right to travel is not absolute, however, would be articulated (7:2) by the Court seventeen years later.[108])

Still, there remained the question of whether *individual* members of the Communist Party, rather than the party itself, could be compelled to register under the Act. "No,"[109] came the Court's unanimous reply late in 1965! In fact, all that saved the membership provision from a declaration of unconstitutionality on self-incrimination grounds was the Court's somewhat strained judgment that an individual member could conceivably *agree* to incriminate himself.[110]

Undoubtedly, future turmoil and legal clashes continue to loom for the troublesome national security sector, which almost necessarily represents such a vexatious public policy puzzle. But it is one that the judiciary has been increasingly willing to adjudicate—within limits.[111] In the final analysis, even in the realm of the precious freedom of expression, it is simply not possible to get entirely away from the concept of "balancing" liberty and authority, freedom and responsibility—a concept scathingly denounced by Justice Black throughout his lengthy and noble career.[112] But when "balancing" is called for, and in the absence of a "danger clear, present, and imminent," we must presume the scale to be weighted on the side of the individual.

---

[106]*United States* v. *Communist Party of the United States*, 377 U.S. 968.

[107]*Aptheker* v. *Secretary of State*, 378 U.S. 500 (1964), at 514.

[108]*Haig* v. *Agee*, 453 U.S. 280 (1981).

[109]*Albertson* v. *Subversive Activities Control Board*, 382 U.S. 70.

[110]Ibid., at 81.

[111]In addition to the cases discussed specifically on pp. 115 ff. *supra*, see such landmark decisions as *United States* v. *The Washington Post* and *The New York Times* v. *United States*, 403 U.S. 713 (1971) and, of course, *United States* v. *Nixon*, 417 U.S. 683 (1974).

[112]See his *A Constitutional Faith* (New York: Alfred A. Knopf, 1968).

Racial, Sexual, and Political Equality

The subjects of racial, sexual, and political equality today are so vast and so inextricably related that, in effect, they cannot be separated. However, for the sake of explication, we shall give distinct thumbnail considerations of political and sexual equality and a more extensive analysis of racial equality.

POLITICAL EQUALITY

Minority Suffrage. Progress along the road to universal suffrage in this country (as well as in others) was met with many obstacles. After the initial discriminations against Quakers, Catholics, and Jews had subsided, it took a civil war to gain theoretical suffrage for the Negro; until 1920 to gain it for women; and until 1972 for eighteen-year-olds. The chief struggle has centered in black Americans' quest for that political equality to which all citizens are entitled under the Constitution—yet which, to all intents and purposes, did not exist for most blacks until 1965, notwithstanding the Fifteenth Amendment. Success first came in the 1920s, but it was not actually consummated legally until the Court's famous 1944 decision in *Smith* v. *Allwright*,[113] which by an 8:1 vote declared the "white primary" to be unconstitutional as a violation of the Fifteenth Amendment. The federal Civil Rights Acts of 1957, 1960, 1964, and 1968 represented important steps in the struggle to make black suffrage a reality. And the outrages perpetrated upon marchers led by Dr. Martin Luther King, Jr., in Selma, Alabama, served as the catalyst for enactment of the tough and generally successful Voting Rights Act of 1965, which outlawed such tools of voting discrimination as literacy tests, "understanding" clauses, and other subtler widespread practices. The passage of this act was justly hailed by President Johnson as "a proud moment for this nation." Although total black suffrage may still not be an accomplished fact, the tools for its attainment now demonstrably exist—and so do those for blacks seeking and holding any public office. Black suffrage is now a fact of political life, especially given the significant expansions of the 1965 statute in 1970, 1975 (for seven years), and particularly its twenty-five-year prolongation and liberalization in 1982. The 1964 ratification of the Twenty-Fourth Amend-

---

[113]321 U.S. 649.

ment banning the poll tax for *federal* elections coupled with the 6:3 decision in 1966 in *Harper* v. *Virginia Board of Elections,* banning it in *state* elections,[114] and the fallout from a crucial 1972 Supreme Court 6:1 ruling[115] that struck down "durational" registration requirements in state and local elections by suggesting that "thirty days appear to be an ample period of time" for states to register new arrivals to vote, also materially advanced the cause of black suffrage. Millions of blacks were added to the voting rolls forthwith, with blacks reaching *registration* parity with whites in mid-1984 at 73 percent of those eligible. The difference between black and white voting *turnout* had shrunk to 6 percent by 1985. And not only did some 6,100 blacks hold elective public office after the November 1984 elections in forty-six states and the District of Columbia (including *all* southern and border states), but over 2,600 did so in the eleven states of the Confederacy. Nationwide, by mid-1985 there were 286 black mayors (6 of those in America's ten largest cities), 90 state senators, and 302 representatives. The Old Confederacy states saw a 3,000-plus percent increase over the two decades after 1965, with the largest number of black *elected* officials in the heart of the formerly segregated South Alabama and Mississippi, with 444 and 375, respectively. There were also 373 black judges (14 of them on the highest state court) and 293 law enforcement officials nationwide.[116]

Representation. Another related aspect of the matter of political equality is the long battle of urban voters to gain their fair share of representation. Any literature on the subject before 1962 would have had to note that the long-standing practice of discrimination against urban and suburban voters, created and perpetuated by deliberate legislative malapportionment on the part of rurally dominated state

---

[114]383 U.S. 663.

[115]*Dunn* v. *Blumstein,* 405 U.S. 330, a Tennessee case. However, a year later the Court upheld 6:3 the fifty-day *pre-election* registration requirement for state and local elections in Arizona and Georgia (*Marston* v. *Lewis* and *Burns* v. *Fortson,* 410 U.S. 679). (Ditto, 5:4, a New York state eight- to eleven-month *pre-primary* registration requirement.)

[116]See "Population Characteristics," *Current Population Reports,* U.S. Department of Commerce, U.S. Bureau of the Census, December 1978, pp. 1 and 3; the annual reports by the Voter Education Project (John Lewis, Executive Director); those by the U.S. Bureau of Labor Statistics; the *Statistical Abstract of the United States; The New York Times,* December 26, 1980, p. A-18, *et. seq., The New York Times Magazine,* September 27, 1981, p. 104; *The New York Times,* September 1, 1985, p. 32; and *The Washington Post,* June 6, 1985, p. A5.

legislatures—sometimes as high or as low as 1,000:1 (Vermont[117]) and 99:1 (Georgia)—would continue indefinitely, for the Supreme Court had consistently refused to accept the matter for adjudication on the grounds that this was a "political question."[118] But thanks to persistent litigants and a gradual change in the thinking of a Court majority, the year 1962 wrought a revolutionary change. In the aforementioned, momentous decision of *Baker* v. *Carr*,[119] in which the issue was the sixty-year-long refusal of Tennessee state legislators to redistrict in the face of state constitutional commands to do so regularly, a 6:2 majority of the Supreme Court held that the distribution of seats in state legislatures was subject to the constitutional scrutiny of the federal courts under the equal protection clause of the Fourteenth Amendment. Justice Frankfurter's sixty-eight-page dissenting opinion (his last signed opinion prior to his retirement because of ill health), joined by Justice Harlan, urged the retention of the "political question" status quo, crying out against involvement in the "political thicket" and becoming entangled in a "mathematical quagmire."[120]

That his appeal to "sear the conscience of the people's representatives" was instead now a lost cause, at long last, became rapidly clear with several successive, highly significant extensions of *Baker*. First, one year later, down went the notorious Georgia County Unit system—a blatant practice of discrimination against urban areas such as Atlanta—with Justice Douglas holding for the 8:1 majority that "*one person, one vote . . .* is the only conception of political equality under historical standards."[121] Less than a year thereafter the Supreme Court addressed itself to the gerrymandering of *congressional* districts. Ruling 6:3 (or 7:2 depending upon one's analysis of Justice Clark's partly concurring and partly dissenting opinion), the Court, speaking through Justice Black, lectured Georgia and the country:

> *While it may not be possible to draw Congressional districts with mathematical precision, that is no excuse for ignoring our Constitution's plain objective of making equal representation for equal num-*

---

[117]Burlington (pop. 35,531) and Stratton (pop. 36) *each* were given one representative in the Vermont House.

[118]See *Colegrove* v. *Green*, 328 U.S. 549 (1946) and *South* v. *Peters*, 339 U.S. 276 (1950).

[119]369 U.S. 186.

[120]Ibid., at 270.

[121]*Gray* v. *Sanders*, 372 U.S. 368 (1963), at 381. (Italics added.)

bers of people the fundamental goal for the [national] House of Representatives. That is the high standard of justice and common sense which the founders set for us.[122]

Then, in 1964, came the most far-reaching follow-up of the *Baker* decision when the Court, in a series of six state cases, held 6:3 in the lead Alabama case of *Reynolds* v. *Sims*[123] that since apportionment is to be on a "one person, one vote" basis, *both* state legislative houses must reflect a representation formula of being "substantially equal in population." Wrote Chief Justice Warren for his Court: "Legislators represent people, not trees or acres. Legislators are elected by voters, not farms or cities or economic interests. . . . To the extent that a citizen's right to vote is debased, he is that much less a citizen. The weight of a citizen's vote cannot be made to depend on where he lives." A 1967 decision (8:1) took a direct, although still very inconclusive slap against the age-old vice of the gerrymander.[124] Soon came, in a 6:2 decision, the extension of the *Reynolds* principle to units of *local* government.[125] And in 1969 the Court broadened the 1964 congressional districting decision by striking down New York's and Missouri's planned districting that varied in population represented from but 14 and 6 percent, respectively, ruling that states must justify *any numerical* variance between districts, *no matter how small*, in order to meet constitutional requirements.[126] But the "Burger Court" of the 1970s and early 1980s gave signs that it would henceforth be inclined to be at least somewhat more flexible, that is, less strict, on the general issue with the *states*, provided the variances and/or deviations do not clearly violate the basic guidelines of the 1960s.[127] Yet it continued to be very tough with *Congress:* thus it disallowed 5:4 a New Jersey district deviation of less than 1/7th of 1 percent in 1984![128]

---

[122]*Wesberry* v. *Sanders*, 376 U.S. 1 (1964) at 18.

[123]*Reynolds* v. *Sims*, 377 U.S. 533 (1964) and five companion cases (377 U.S. 633–713). Warren's statement is at 562 and 567.

[124]*Rockefeller* v. *Wells*, 389 U.S. 421 (1967). The Court had the issue before it in early 1986.

[125]*Avery* v. *Midland County, Texas*, 390 U.S. 474 (1968).

[126]*Wells* v. *Rockefeller*, 394 U.S. 542 and *Kirkpatrick* v. *Preisler*, 394 U.S. 526.

[127]E.g., *Gordon* v. *Lance*, 403 U.S. 1 (1971)—upholding, 7:2, a Virginia requirement of a 60 percent vote approval to incur bonded indebtedness or increase taxes of political subdivisions; *Whitcomb* v. *Chavis*, 403 U.S. 124 (1971)—validating, 6:3, an Indiana multi-member election district; and *Abate* v. *Mundt* 403 U.S. 182 (1971)—sanctioning, 7:2, total voting equalities in five New York towns of 11.9

The redistricting decisions were heatedly criticized in some quarters and, after *Reynolds*, were sporadically threatened with various forms of congressional counteraction led by Senator Everett McKinley Dirkson (R.-Ill.), who came close in 1967 when a "delayer" bill passed both houses but died in the Senate after its Conference Committee stage. Nevertheless, there is no doubt whatever that, collectively, these landmark decisions (again with the exception of the *Reynolds* case) not only found a more or less friendly reception, but engendered an almost unbelievable flurry of activity toward compliance by the states. Indeed, *all* states had taken some form of redistricting action by 1972—a very different response from the reaction evoked by the initial segregation-integration decisions.

RACIAL EQUALITY

The abolition of slavery, the Civil War, and the adoption of the Fourteenth Amendment introduced and/or intensified major interracial problems between black and white in the United States. Because of the predominant concentration of blacks in southern and border

---

percent, because the arrangements there were "based on the long tradition of overlapping function and dual personnel in Rockland County government to favor particular political interests or geographic areas." (The *Abate* opinion was written by Justice Marshall, Justices Brennan and Douglas dissenting. Going further, in 1973 the Court sanctioned several deviations in state districting to the tune of 16.4 percent (!) in Virginia; 9.9 percent in Texas; and 7.8 percent in Connecticut [*City of Virginia Beach* v. *Howell*, 410 U.S. 315; *White* v. *Regester*, 412 U.S. 755 and *Gaffney* v. *Cummings*, 412 U.S. 735, respectively]). In *White* the Court, for the first time, sustained an attack on multi-member districts as tending "unconstitutionally to minimize the strength of racial groups." But compare *City of Mobile* v. *Bolden*, 446 U.S. 55 (1980); *Rogers* v. *Lodge*, 458 U.S. 613 (1984); and *Mississippi Republican Committee* v. *Brooks*, 53 LW 3361 (1984). The Court also made allowances for "weighted" voting in special-purpose districts, e.g., 6:3, a water storage one (*Salyer Land Company* v. *Lake Tulare Water Storage District*, 410 U.S. 719 [1975] and for voting restricted to property owners in another water district (*Ball* v. *James*, 49 LW 4459 [1981]). But it held to its very strict mathematical equality standards on *congressional* districts, disallowing a 4 percent deviation in the same year of 1973 (*White* v. *Weiser*, 412 U.S. 783). And, obviously, there are limits on permissible state deviations, as North Dakota found out when in 1975 it attempted to institute multi-member senatorial districts with 20 percent differentials (*Chapman* v. *Meier*, 420 U.S. 1). Later that year the Court did allow an eight-member appointive central school board arrangement, based on two members each from four elected town school boards (*Rosenthal* v. *Board of Education*, 420 U.S. 980).

[128]*Karcher* v. *Daggett*, 462 U.S. 725 (1984).

states,[129] particularly in the former where in certain areas blacks still outnumber whites, the core of the attendant difficulties in race relations has been concentrated there. However, as the northern ghetto riots of the mid- and late 1960s and the emotional issue of busing of students have demonstrated only too clearly, the "racial problem," like the "farm problem," is neither exclusively regional nor is it just *one* nice, easily identifiable, monolithic problem. Whereas in 1900 almost 90 percent of America's blacks lived in the fifteen states below the Mason-Dixon line, by 1978 the figure had "stabilized at about 53 percent," reversing the trend of past decades, with more blacks moving *to* rather than *out* of the South.[130] By early 1986 there were 28.7 million blacks in the United States, constituting 12.2 percent of the population.

History and Progress

Representative Types of Discrimination. Discrimination against blacks long took place on both the public and private levels, although the increasing sweep of legislative remedies officially relegated it to the private sphere—one not easy to define. Thus *public* authorities, chiefly at the state and local level, enacted measures either simply *permitting* or even *requiring* segregation of: buses, streetcars, taxicabs, railroads, waiting rooms, comfort stations, drinking fountains, state and local schools, state colleges and universities, hospitals, sporting events, beaches, bath houses, swimming pools, parks, golf courses, courthouse cafeterias, libraries, jails, housing, theaters, hotels, cemeteries, restaurants, and other similar facilities—public, quasi-public, or private in nature—and interracial marriages were simply proscribed. *Private* groups and/or individuals acted to deny blacks access to social clubs, fraternities and sororities, private schools, private colleges and universities, churches, funeral parlors, cemeteries, hospitals, hotels, housing, restaurants, movies, bowling alleys, swimming pools, bath houses, sporting events, comfort stations, drinking fountains, barber and beauty shops, employment agencies, and em-

---

[129]There are eleven southern states: Virginia, North Carolina, South Carolina, Georgia, Florida, Alabama, Louisiana, Mississippi, Texas, Arkansas, and Tennessee. Six are commonly classified as border states: Maryland, Delaware, West Virginia, Kentucky, Oklahoma, and Missouri.

[130]Report of the U.S. Bureau of the Census, quoted in *The New York Times*, July 28, 1975, p. 9c, and "Geographical Mobility: March 1975 to March 1977," a March 1978 release by the Bureau. See also "Blacks Returning to Southern Cities," *The New York Times*, July 4, 1981, p. 4.

ployment. Little, if anything, was covert about either public or private discrimination as it used to be practiced—it was simply a way of life.

The Doctrine of "Separate but Equal."   There was little blacks could do initially to combat *private* discrimination, but they commenced to battle the *public* variety in the courts soon after the Reconstruction era had ended with the Hayes Compromise of 1877. They relied principally upon the Fourteenth Amendment's "due process of law" and "equal protection of the laws" clauses, ultimate success coming chiefly as a result of a firm reliance upon the latter. Initially, however, the efforts of the black community seemed doomed to failure, for in 1896 the United States Supreme Court handed down its famous "separate but equal" doctrine in the historic case of *Plessy* v. *Ferguson*.[131] At issue was a Louisiana law commanding segregation of all *intra*state railway carriers, but at the same time requiring these to provide "equal but separate accommodations for the white and colored races." Its 7:1 decision, written for the Court by Justice Henry B. Brown, a Yale graduate from Michigan, upheld the statute as a reasonable exercise of the state's police power against the challenge by Homer Plessy (who, incidentally, was 7/8 white) that it violated the "equal protection of the laws" clause of Amendment Fourteen. The often-quoted lone dissent, at once angry and eloquent, of former Kentucky slaveholder Justice John Marshall Harlan, "Our Constitution is colorblind and neither knows nor tolerates classes among citizens,"[132] drew no support: Harlan's brothers on the Court all joined in the majority opinion's key contention that "if the civil and political rights of both races be equal, one cannot be inferior to the other civilly or politically." And, continued the then generally popular Brown opinion, if the "enforced separation of the two races stamps the colored race with the badge of inferiority. . . [it is] solely because the colored race chooses to put that construction upon [the statute]."[133]

The "separate but equal" doctrine remained the permissive law of the land until 1954,[134] with segregation continuing to be practiced in the public as well as the private sector in more than one-third of the

----

[131]163 U.S. 537.

[132]Ibid., at 559.

[133]Ibid., at 544, 551.

[134]*Brown* v. *Board of Education of Topeka*, 347 U.S. 483, and *Bolling* v. *Sharpe*, 347 U.S. 497 (1954).

states and the District of Columbia. But, as the years went by, the "separate but equal" doctrine inevitably came under increasing legal attack. Time and again, the Supreme Court struck down certain state practices as not being "equal" in facilities—without, however, going so far as to hold the doctrine itself to be unconstitutional. Yet its days were patently numbered.

The "Doctrine" Beleaguered. Concentrating at the graduate level of *higher education,* the Court began in the late 1930s to order specific state universities either to admit individually qualified blacks who had been denied such admission and had appealed to the highest tribunal, or else to provide *truly* "equal facilities"—probably literally impossible. State law schools in Missouri and Oklahoma were the first to be so ordered,[135] followed by the University of Oklahoma Graduate School.[136] But in 1950, in a Texas law school case, the Supreme Court found the so-called equal Texas law school for blacks to be "clearly inferior," hence constituting a denial of the equal protection of the Texas law to its black citizens.[137] At the end of the 1950s, the Court had made resolutely clear that state-operated colleges and universities could no longer limit admissions on the basis of race or color; and by 1963, blacks, no matter how few, attended one or more graduate or professional institutions of higher learning in *every* state of the heretofore segregated South. To achieve that, however, necessitated the federal-troop-enforced, bloodshed-accompanied admission of James Meredith to the University of Mississippi in the fall of 1962; the similarly troop-enforced, but peaceful, entry of three blacks to campuses of the University of Alabama in 1963; and the admission of Harvey Gantt to Clemson University in South Carolina, also in 1963.

Yet the executive and legislative branches of the federal government, as well as its judiciary, had increasingly become involved in segregation battles in other areas: President Roosevelt created the first

---

[135]*Missouri* ex rel *Gaines* v. *Canada,* 305 U.S. 337 (1938) and *Sipuel* v. *Board of Regents of the University of Oklahoma,* 332 U.S. 631 (1948). The first black to be ordered court-admitted actually was Donald Murray in 1936 (to the University of Maryland School of Law) by the Maryland Court of Appeals (*Pearson* v. *Murray,* 169 Md. 478).

[136]*McLaurin* v. *Oklahoma State Regents for Higher Education,* 339 U.S. 637 (1950). (Oklahoma had admitted McLaurin but compelled him to sit away from the students, eat at a separate table in the cafeteria, and study at a special desk in the library).

[137]*Sweatt* v. *Painter,* 339 U.S. 629.

FEPC (Fair Employment Practices Committee) in 1941; in 1948 President Truman outlawed segregation in the armed forces by executive order and established a Fair Employment Board; the Court, in a heavily attacked decision in 1948, held restrictive housing covenants legal but unenforceable in any court in the land;[138] President Eisenhower, following the lead of his Missouri predecessor, created a Committee on Government Contract Compliance in 1953; in 1957 Congress passed its first Civil Rights Act since Reconstruction days (later followed by acts of 1960, 1964, and 1968); Presidents Kennedy and Johnson banned discrimination in federally constructed or financially supported housing; and the Supreme Court, in a host of decisions, struck down numerous state laws requiring or permitting segregation in sundry public or quasi-public facilities.[139] Strictly *private* facilities remained unaffected for the time being, in the absence of state or local public "equal accommodations," "equal opportunity," or other anti-discrimination statutes—which did exist in half of the states by the late 1940s (and were adopted by most of the states, although not by all, as the years went by). But the judiciary rejected as patently unconstitutional dodges the various widespread attempts to render public facilities "private" by leasing them to private entrepreneurs.[140]

Public transportation facilities similarly had to bow to executive and judicial mandates to discontinue compulsory segregation. As early as 1946, Virginia's statute as applied to interstate buses fell.[141] After a few series of preliminary and specific "cease and desist" orders, the Interstate Commerce Commission in 1955 issued a blanket order forbidding all racial segregation in interstate buses and trains, including public waiting-room facilities. The lower judiciary attacked state segregation laws on public *intra*state carriers; and as of

---

[138]*Shelley* v. *Kraemer*, 334 U.S. 1 (1948) and *Hurd* v. *Hodge*, 334 U.S. 24 (1948). See also *Barrows* v. *Jackson*, 346 U.S. 249 (1953). In 1968 Congress enacted a federal ban against discrimination in the sale, rental, and advertising of housing, which the court sustained in *Jones* v. *Alfred H. Mayer Co.*, 392 U.S. 409 (1968); see pp. 142 and 147, *infra*.

[139]For example, *Holmes* v. *City of Atlanta*, 350 U.S. 879 (1955); *City of Petersburg* v. *Alsup*, 353 U.S. 922 (1957); *State Athletic Commission* v. *Dorsey*, 359 U.S. 533 (1959); *Burton* v. *Wilmington Parking Authority*, 365 U.S. 715 (1961); *Watson* v. *Memphis*, 373 U.S. 526 (1963); *Moses H. Cone Memorial Hospital* v. *Simkins*, 376 U.S. 938 (1964); *Lee* v. *Washington*, 390 U.S. 333 (1968).

[140]For example, *Derrington* v. *Plummer*, 240 F. 2d 922 (1957); *Griffin* v. *Prince Edward County School Board*, 377 U.S. 218 (1964); *Louisiana* v. *Pointdexter*, 389 U.S. 571 (1968).

[141]*Morgan* v. *Virginia*, 328 U.S. 373.

1960 the Supreme Court began to strike down as violative of the Fourteenth Amendment all mandated or permitted racial segregation in air, railroad, and bus terminals, together with their waiting rooms and restaurants, be they publicly *or* privately operated.[142] The tough Civil Rights Act of 1964 was designed to strike a death blow at almost all discriminatory aspects and areas of "public accommodations" and "equal employment" opportunities. And, having in 1964 declared unconstitutional a Florida law forbidding cohabitation between whites and blacks while permitting it among whites *or* among blacks,[143] the Court in a unanimous opinion tackled in 1967 the larger issue of the miscegenation problem per se: it threw out Virginia's anti-racial intermarriage law on equal protection grounds.[144]

The 1954 Desegregation Decisions. Most, if not all, of the actions just outlined briefly resulted directly, or indirectly, from *Brown* v. *Board of Education of Topeka*, the most significant judicial decision in the segregation-integration field since *Plessy* v. *Ferguson*[145] in 1896. In *Brown*, the Court, in the words of Alpheus T. Mason, "initiated the greatest social revolution of this generation."[146] On May 17, 1954, a unanimous Court[147]—including natives from Alabama (Black), Kentucky (Reed), and Texas (Clark),[148] the three southerners who, in Chief Justice Warren's words almost two decades later,[149]

---

[142]See *Boynton* v. *Virginia*, 364 U.S. 454 (1960); *Turner* v. *Memphis*, 369 U.S. 350 (1962); and *Bailey* v. *Patterson*, 369 U.S. 31 (1962).

[143]*McLaughlin* v. *Florida*, 379 U.S. 184 (1964), a 9:0 decision.

[144]*Loving* v. *Virginia*, 388 U.S. 1.

[145]163 U.S. 537.

[146]*The Supreme Court: Palladium of Freedom* (Ann Arbor: University of Michigan Press, 1962), p. 170, referring to *Brown* (347 U.S. 483).

[147]Justice Frankfurter, one of the key architects of that unanimity, noted in a letter to his colleague Reed, that the decision would probably have had four dissenters had it been handed down just one term earlier (and one of them would have been Reed). Letter exhibited at Harvard Law School Memorial Exhibit on the occasion of "F.F.'s" 95th birthday, October 21, 1977.

[148]Chief Justice Warren and Associate Justices Frankfurter, Douglas, Jackson, Burton, and Minton were the other six—nonsouthern—members of the Court. It has been fairly reliably established now that the last two "holdouts" against unanimity were Jackson and Reed, with the latter not acquiescing until the very last moment.

[149]Seminar with Chief Justice Earl Warren, University of Virginia, Charlottesville, Va., April 25, 1973. He elaborated: "These three men couldn't go back to their homes for ten years after the decision in the case." (Ibid., p. 10).

"deserve the credit for the Court's unanimity"—after deliberating roughly two years, struck down the "separate but equal" doctrine.[150] Speaking for himself and his eight associate justices in a single, brief opinion,[151] Chief Justice Warren called public education "the very foundation of good citizenship" and "a principal instrument in awakening the child." Noting the findings of psychologists and sociologists, the chief justice, in observations heavily criticized later, declared that in segregated, separated facilities[152] "a sense of inferiority affects the motivations of a child to learn." He then turned to the heart of the constitutional issue and pronounced compulsory segregation in public schools unconstitutional (contrary to widespread misconceptions he did *not* say anything about "integration" per se):

> ...*in the field of public education the doctrine of "separate but equal" has no place. Separate educational facilities are inherently unequal*...*[Plaintiffs] are, by reason of the segregation complained of, deprived of the equal protection of the laws guaranteed by the Fourteenth Amendment*....[153]

Quite aware of the crushing effect this decision would have upon the South and its long-standing traditions, and of the many genuine difficulties involved in compliance, the Court delayed issuing an enforcement order of its decision for one year. But, on May 31, 1955,

---

[150]*Brown* v. *Board of Education of Topeka*, 347 U.S. 483 and *Bolling* v. *Sharpe*, 347 U.S. 497.

[151]*Brown* v. *Board of Education of Topeka, loc. cit.*, at 494. Warren told a University of Virginia Student Legal Forum meeting that he purposely kept the opinion short "so that any layman interested in the problem could read the entire opinion...of which I wrote every blessed word....In drafting it I sought to use low-key, unemotional language" (Charlottesville, Va., April 18, 1973). He kept its text secret, locked in his safe, until he read it aloud from the bench in full on that historic Monday in 1954. (See Chief Justice Warren's full-length obituary in *The New York Times*, July 11, 1974, p. 35a). For a superb account of the decision's history and dénouement, see Kluger, *Simple Justice*, p. 47, fn. 127.

[152]Historical candor commands notice, however, that the 39th Congress, which framed and passed the 14th Amendment, denied almost to a man that the Amendment's "equal protection of the laws" clause required the desegregation of public facilities. Indeed, that Congress not only racially segregated the District of Columbia's public schools but its own Senate gallery. See, among others, Ch. 15, "The Rule of Law," and Ch. 23, "Conclusion," in Raoul Berger, *Government by Judiciary: The Transformation of the Fourteenth Amendment* (Boston: Harvard University Press, 1977).

[153]347 U.S. 483, at 495–97.

having invited the views of interested authorities (of whom but a few submitted suggestions), it ordered the end of compulsory racial segregation in all public schools, charging local authorities with responsibility for compliance under the scrutiny of the appropriate United States district court. It directed these tribunals to order "a prompt and reasonable start," but willingly kept the door open for consideration of specific local problems. Nevertheless, the Court left no doubt that it expected full and relatively prompt compliance "with all deliberate speed"[154]—a formula evidently suggested by Justice Frankfurter who allegedly found it in a 1911 Holmes opinion dealing with monetary matters between states.[155] Holmes had identified it there as "language of the English Chancery."

Compliance. Although ten years later no state remained completely untouched by public school desegregation as a result of the two *Brown* decisions (Mississippi succumbed in August 1964), compliance in all but the border states was slow or even token. In stark contrast to the ready compliance in the *Redistricting Cases,*[156] every conceivable stratagem was employed to delay and frustrate efforts to comply with the *Brown* decisions. Thus in 1957 federal troops had to be sent to Little Rock, Arkansas, to overcome Governor Orval Faubus's interference with judicial enforcement orders.[157] In the decade between 1954 and 1964 following the first *Brown* decision, almost 200 state segregation laws were enacted, all designed to frustrate implementation of the hated judgments. Many legal and sometimes physical battles were still ahead. Customs that have stood for generations, no matter what their moral implications, are not altered readily, Rarely, if ever, had the Supreme Court found itself under such heavy and prolonged attack by so large and vocal a segment of the population with such significant political strength. Yet the highest tribunal, in a

---

[154]Ibid., 349 U.S. 294 (1955).

[155]*Virginia* v. *West Virginia,* 222 U.S. 17, at 20.

[156]See p. 173 of this text.

[157]See *Cooper* v. *Aaron,* 358 U.S. 1 (1958). Five years later, President Kennedy deployed 25,000 federal troops to overcome Mississippi Governor Ross Barnett's obstruction of the Court-ordered admission of a black, James Meredith, to the University of Mississippi at Oxford. And a few months thereafter the President again had to use troops, this time to beat the defiance of a federal court order by Governor George C. Wallace of Alabama to the admission of two black graduate students to the University of Alabama at Tuscaloosa. (Ten years later Wallace "crowned" the first black Homecoming Queen at the same university!)

unanimous opinion by Justice Goldberg, made quite clear again in 1963 that its decision in *Brown*

> ...*never contemplated that the concept of "deliberate speed" would countenance indefinite delay in elimination of racial barriers in schools, let alone other public facilities not involving the same physical problems or comparable conditions.... The basic guarantees of our Constitution are warrants for the here and now.*[158]

The Civil Rights Act of 1964, with its tough Title VI provisions for withholding funds from noncomplying school districts, provided tools for acceleration in enforcement. And the Court made increasingly and resolutely clear that it was simply not going to stand for any more irrelevant delays, emphasizing its determination with the statement in a unanimous 1968 decision assailing "freedom of choice" plans that "delays are no longer tolerable."[159] The other shoe fell in October 1969 when the Court, speaking crisply *per curiam*, ended the "all deliberate speed" guideline once and for all (it had lasted for fourteen years): it ruled 8:0 that all school districts must end segregation "at once" and operate "unitary" integrated schools "now and hereafter."[160]

A Nationwide Problem.   As the 1960s had come upon the scene, what had been fully anticipated became a fact. The North, which all too frequently had gloated in the face of the Southern predicament, suddenly found that it, too, was deeply involved in the segregation-integration controversy. Here it was not a matter of *legal* inequality or *publicly* mandated discrimination, for that no longer existed in the North. What did exist, however, was racial discrimination in employment practices, in access to private housing, in private accommodations, and, largely because of the housing and income disparity so prevalent in the urban areas of the North and West, *de facto* segregation in public schools. Many of these practices had been blunted by the various antidiscrimination statutes present in almost forty states by the early 1960s, and stood to be further reduced by the Civil Rights

---

[158]*Watson* v. *Memphis*, 373 U.S. 526.

[159]*Green* v. *School Board of New Kent County*, 391 U.S. 430 at 439. See also the three 1967 decisions of: *United States* v. *Wallace*, 389 U.S. 215; *Bibb County, Alabama* v. *United States*, 389 U.S. 215; and *Caddo Parish, Louisiana, School Board* v. *United States*, 389 U.S. 840.

[160]*Alexander* v. *Holmes County, Mississippi, Board of Education*, 396 U.S. 19 at 20.

Acts of 1964 and 1968 (the latter especially in private housing) but much remained to be done—against the backdrop of ever increasingly militant action by restive black communities throughout the land, especially in urban ghettos.

This action, which began with boycotts and picketing, "sit-ins," "pray-ins," "stand-ins" "wade-ins," "stall-ins," and a host of similar demonstrations,[161]—often highly effective economically—regrettably turned to sporadic violence, rioting, and bloodshed, beginning in August 1965 in the Watts section of Los Angeles.[162] By the end of 1969 some 260 cities had experienced riots, resulting in more than 280 deaths—43 of these in the horrible 1967 riots in Detroit, 34 in those of Watts—thousands of injured, tens of thousands of arrests, and billions of dollars in property damage.

Enter Busing

The Holmes County, Mississippi, decision ending the "all deliberate speed" guideline to desegregation in late 1969, seemed to be a response, at least in the educational sector. It was during that period that, acting on the first school desegregation suit filed in the *North*, United States District Court Judge Julius J. Hoffman (later of "Chicago Seven" fame) ordered a suburban Chicago school district to desegregate its facilities and student bodies "forthwith."[163] At that point approximately 38 percent of the black students in the South attended desegregated schools, which compared favorably with black students in the North, whose attendance in desegregated schools averaged 35 percent. But how, given some of the verities of geography, could these orders, coming with increasing frequency nationwide, be implement-

---

[161]This phase of the struggle commenced with the sit-in demonstration staged by four black students from North Carolina Agricultural and Technical College at a Woolworth's lunch counter in Greensboro on February 1, 1960. (Twenty years later they returned to celebrate its anniversary and to reenact that event.)

[162]The Watts riots lasted six days and resulted in thirty-four deaths, 1,032 injuries, the arrest of 3,952 persons, and $40 million in property damage (more than 600 buildings were damaged, 200 totally destroyed). The Detroit riots of 1967 were even worse. That bloodiest uprising in the country in half a century lasted five days, resulted in forty-three deaths, 347 injuries, 3,800 arrests, 5,000 made homeless, 1,300 buildings reduced to rubble, and $500 million in damages. See my *Freedom and the Court: Civil Rights and Liberties in the United States*, 4th ed. (New York: Oxford University Press, 1982), p. 311.

[163]*United States* v. *School District 151 of Cook County, Ill.*, 301 F. Supp. 201.

ed? The response from courts, some legislatures, and a good many boards of education created one of the most volatile, most emotion-charged, most politically tinged of contemporary issues: enforced *busing* of children to achieve desegregation—a device that, according to Chief Justice Warren, the Court never considered in its implementation conference of 1954–1955.[164]

Racial Quotas. The fat was in the fire. A series of cases came up, headed by one for the Charlotte-Mecklenburg, North Carolina, metropolitan school district, in which a group of parents contended that the "color-blind" ruling of the Supreme Court in the *Brown* case meant that assignments of students would have to be made on just such a "color-blind" basis, and that, accordingly, busing to achieve integration was patently unconstitutional. In April 1971, speaking for his unanimous Court, Chief Justice Burger—in what must have suprised not only a large segment of the country but, specifically, the land's most highly placed opponent to busing, President Nixon—specifically upheld not only *busing* but also *racial quotas,* pairing or grouping of schools, and gerrymandering of attendance zones as well as other devices designed to "remove all vestiges of state imposed segregation. . . . *Desegregation plans cannot be limited to the walk-in school,*" he declared.[165] The Court's controversial decision stopped short of ordering the elimination of all-black schools or of requiring racial balance in the schools. (And, at that point, it made clear that the instant decision did *not* apply to northern-style *de facto* segregation, based on neighborhood patterns.[166]) But it said that the existence of all-black schools created a presumption of discrimination and held that federal district judges—to whom it gave enormously broad dis-

---

[164]Responding to a question by a University of Virginia student of Charlottesville, Va. (See fn. 149 of this text, April 18, 1973.)

[165]*Swann* v. *Charlotte-Mecklenburg Board of Education,* 402 U.S. 1, at 15, 30. (Italics added.) For some interesting background analysis, heavily critical of the Chief Justice's role, see Bernard Schwartz, *Swann's Way: The School Busing Case and the Supreme Court* (New York: Oxford University Press, 1986).

[166]On the other hand, the Court voted 6½:1½ in 1973 that the Denver system, featuring "substantial pockets of demonstrable segregation," was subject—like all other Northern school districts henceforth—to "rigorous desegregation standards," even though racial separation—as was eminently true of Denver—was predominantly, although not exclusively, a product of *social patterns* rather than purely formal law (*Keyes* v. *School District #1 of Denver,* 413 U.S. 189).

cretion—may indeed use racial quotas[167] as a guide in fashioning de-segregation decrees.

On the busing issue, the chief justice, in a nod to that large element of the populace favoring the neighborhood school concept, admitted that "all things being equal, with no history of discrimination, it might well be desirable to assign pupils to schools nearest their homes. But all things are not equal," he continued, "in a system that has been deliberately constructed and maintained to enforce racial segregation."[168] Yet the long-standing Court unanimity of two decades on the segregation issue ended in 1972, when the four Nixon appointees dissented from what they considered and characterized as an effort to *require racial balance* rather than desegregation—which they charged the majority of five to have approved.[169] Rarely has the Court been unanimous on the issue since.

Reaction to Busing. Both public and private reaction was generally adverse. The President and Congress were clearly displeased, and a host of state legislatures endeavored to prohibit busing by statute and even by constitutional amendment. The candidacy of Governor George C. Wallace of Alabama in both the 1972 and 1976 presidential sweepstakes received a huge boost—not only in the South, but in the North, and particularly in the urban centers, such as Boston, where anti-busing sentiment reached its zenith in 1975–1976. Consistently having defied, or at least but mildly obeyed, U.S. district court orders to bus its children, the Boston community, led by South Boston (heavily white ethnic), was confronted with a series of drastic

---

[167]This notwithstanding the on-its-face prohibition by Sec. 2000e-6 of Title IV of the Civil Rights Act of 1964, which *specifically* would seem to *forbid* racial quota assignments. But the chief justice brushed that argument aside, invoking the Court's "historic equitable remedial powers" with respect to the full attainment of the spirit as well as the letter of the "equal protection of the laws" clause of the Fourteenth Amendment. For other uses of racial quotas, now in connection with reapportionment under the Voting Rights Act of 1965, as amended, see the contentious 1977 multiple-opinion plurality holding in *United Jewish Organizations of Williamsburg* v. *Carey*, 430 U.S. 144. For Civil Rights Act of 1964 litigation, see the *De Funis* and *Bakke* higher education cases (see pp. 189–193 of this text); the *Weber* employment case (pp. 193–194 of this text); the *Fullilove* minority business enterprises "set-aside" quota case (pp. 194–196 of this text); and the *Stotts* and *Wygant* seniority cases (pp. 196–198 of this text).

[168]*Swann* v. *Charlotte-Mecklenburg Board of Education*, at 28.

[169]*Wright* v. *Council of the City of Emporia*, 407 U.S. 451.

ultimata by Judge W. Arthur Garrity, Jr. Rejecting or downplaying these, the Boston School Committee, an elected, popular body, subsequently found itself deprived of many of its powers in 1975, and some of its schools placed in the hands of a court-appointed receiver. The proverbial fat was in the fire—with the busing issue becoming (along with abortion) the *key* concern of the Massachusetts presidential primary races. The strife-torn public school system continued in effect to be administratively directed by Judge Garrity until late 1985—whose stern desegregation order was denied review,[170] and thus upheld, by the U.S. Supreme Court, which did so again in 1976 and once more in 1977.[171]

The Boston reaction—and that in similarly affected cities, such as Cleveland, Ohio, where Judge Frank J. Battisti took even sterner measures—matched in intensity of feeling that which had greeted collateral federal district court decisions in Richmond, Detroit, and Los Angeles. The latter decisions, however, went further by ordering cross-district busing between the core city (usually heavily black) and the surrounding suburbs (almost always predominantly white). Thus in 1972 Judge Robert R. Merhige, Jr.—in a 325-page opinion(!)—had ordered the merger of the public schools in the City of Richmond, Virginia (then with a black school enrollment of 70 percent) with those of suburban Chesterfield and Henrico counties (almost 91 percent white).[172] The uproar caused by that decision was matched only by a similar one handed down for the Detroit area. One discernible result was a decisive Wallace victory in the 1972 Florida Democratic presidential primary. Here Wallace had fashioned his campaign almost exclusively upon the busing issue, as he did, more or less, in Massachusetts in 1976. A welter of bills was subsequently introduced in Congress to forbid or delay busing. President Nixon, in a special television broadcast to the nation, asked for legislation to bring about a "moratorium" on busing—which Congress gave him by enacting a delay in the implementation of court desegregation orders that required the busing or transfer of students "for the purposes of achieving

---

[170]*Hennigan* v. *Morgan*, 421 U.S. 963 (1975). The Garrity order ultimately included the establishment of a permanent Department of Implementation (administration of racial segregation) with an annual budget of $473,559 as of 1977 (*The New York Times*, June 26, 1977, Sec. 4, p. 12e).

[171]*White* v. *Morgan*, 426 U.S. 935 and *McDonough* v. *Morgan*, 429 U.S. 1042, respectively.

[172]*Bradley* v. *School Board of the City of Richmond*, 338 F. Supp.

a balance among students with respect to race," either until all appeals had been exhausted or until January 1, 1974.

Several constitutional amendments to prohibit busing were introduced, and Wallace won the Michigan primary, predominantly on the busing issue. In the interim, the orders by the federal district court judges were appealed, and Judge Merhige's order, for one, was reversed 5:1 by the United States Court of Appeals for the Fourth Circuit in 1972.[173] "Affirmed by an equally divided Court," was the Supreme Court's response when the case reached it in 1973. Although Virginia's Justice Powell did not participate in that case,[174] one year later he joined the majority opinion of the 5:4 Court, written by Chief Justice Burger, that absolved Detroit from bowing to a lower court cross-country busing order because there was no proof of *deliberate* racial discrimination in drawing school district boundaries. The four dissenting justices—White, Marshall, Douglas, and Brennan—saw, in Marshall's words, "a giant step backwards."[175] But the vast majority of the country seemed to support the Court majority. Thereafter, the Court severally reiterated its insistence that normally, albeit not inevitably, proof of *intent* was needed to demonstrate an alleged constitutional violation in such racial discrimination cases.[176] In another case, evidently perceiving valid proof of such discrimination, the Court let stand 4:3 a lower federal court-ordered desegregation plan for Wilmington, Delaware, to merge that city's heavily black school district with those of eleven surrounding counties in order to achieve a better "racial balance."[177] The Court reconfirmed this holding by denying *certiorari* 6:3 in 1980, with the three dissenters (Justices Stewart, Powell, and Rehnquist) characterizing the order as "more Draconian than any other approved by this Court."[178] A similar order to Louisville, Kentucky, was also upheld, this one 7:1.[179] But the

---

[173]*School Board of the City of Richmond* v. *Bradley*, 462 F. 2d 1058.

[174]*Bradley* v. *State Board of Education of the Commonwealth of Virginia*, 411 U.S. 913.

[175]*Milliken* v. *Bradley I* 418 U.S. 717 (1974). Detroit commenced a peaceful inner-city busing program pursuant to a federal district judge's order on remand of the aforegone case.

[176]E.g., *Metropolitan School District of Perry* v. *Buckley*, 429 U.S. 1068 (1977).

[177]*Delaware State Board of Education* v. *Evans*, 429 U.S. 1068 (1977).

[178]Ibid., 447 U.S. 916.

[179]*Hollenback* v. *Haycraft*, 434 U.S. 930 (1977).

Court said "no" to a drastic Atlanta, Georgia, regional integration plan.[180]

Busing Legislation. Increasingly becoming an issue in presidential election politics, forced busing grew apace as a major national controversy. A defusing appeared on the horizon, however, when, just prior to its adjournment in July 1976, the Court ruled 6:2 in a Pasadena, California, case (Justices Brennan and Marshall in dissent) that if the school authorities initially comply with a court-ordered busing plan and thereby achieve a racially neutral student assignment plan, the Court cannot then require the school authorities to readjust busing zones each subsequent year in an effort to maintain the same initial racial mix in the face of changing population patterns. This rule applies, the Court held in an opinion by Justice Rehnquist, even where the school system is not yet "unitary" in all respects—for instance, where there has not been full compliance regarding such things as hiring of teachers.[181] Concurrently, the Court unanimously declined to review, and thus in effect upheld, a lower federal appellate court ruling that school authorities in Chattanooga, Tennessee, need not redraft a desegregation plan to reflect population shifts that had taken place after busing and other desegregation measures had been duly and constitutionally adopted.[182]

Indeed, while making clear in 1977 that federal tribunals may order school districts to provide far-reaching, broader-than-ever, and costly *remedial* education programs—such as remedial reading classes, teaching training, counseling, and career-guidance[183]—the Court also made clear, in an important system-wide desegregation case involving Dayton, Ohio, that before courts issue such orders —which the Supreme Court approved for Dayton in 1979[184]— they would have to "tailor" the remedy to the nature and scope of the illegal act. In other words, the highest tribunal at once expanded and

---

[180]*Armour v. Nix*, 446 U.S. 930 (1980).

[181]*Pasadena City Board of Education v. Spangler*, 427 U.S. 424 (1976).

[182]*Mapp v. Board of Education of Chattanooga*, 427 U.S. 911 (1976).

[183]*Milliken v. Bradley II*, 433 U.S. 267 (1977).

[184]*Dayton Board of Education v. Brinkman*, 429 U.S. 1060 (1977) and 443 U.S. 526 (1979). Ditto *Columbus Board of Education v. Penick*, 443 U.S. 449 (1979). See also *Austin Independent School District v. United States*, 429 U.S. 990 (1976) and 443 U.S. 915 (1979); the 1980 Cleveland, Ohio, case (*Cleveland Board of Education v. Reed*, 445 U.S. 935); and that same year's *Estes v. Dallas*, 444 U.S. 437).

limited the lower judiciary's equity powers: In reiterating the *Swann* rationale of wide decree-making desegregation authority,[185] the Supreme Court ordered that such decrees, to be constitutional, must be based on specific findings regarding legal violations. And that, although the Court would be sympathetic in its perception, the findings cannot exceed the scope of the violation at issue; there must be proof of past or continuing discrimination.

The Court reiterated that important requirement in two 1982 holdings that brought diverse results: In the first, it struck down 5:4 a 1978 state of Washington voter initiative that limited busing to neighborhood schools because the measure provided too many exceptions allowing busing for other purposes. But in the second, with only Justice Marshall in dissent, it upheld 8:1 a California 1979 initiative that limited the state's power to order involuntary busing to the *federal* standards of *intentional* discrimination.[186]

In 1977, 1978, 1979, 1980, 1981, and 1982 Congress added riders to Health, Education and Welfare (HEW) (later Health and Human Services)–Labor appropriations legislation, intended to strike at enforced racial busing. But it is readily evident that mere legislation will not decisively affect the judiciary's perceived equity powers under the "equal protection of the laws" clause of Amendment Fourteen. It would probably require a constitutional amendment and, while many have been introduced and debated, none had passed either house of Congress by early 1986.

On other fronts the pace of governmental pressure to remedy race and sex discrimination quickened perceptibly. Generous applications and interpretations of the Civil Rights Acts of 1964 and 1968 by the Department of Health, Education and Welfare and the Department of Labor, augmented by executive orders from both the Johnson and Nixon-Ford administrations, resulted in stiff mandates to many sectors of American business, labor, and education. When the Carter administration took over in January 1977, these orders and pressures were increased significantly, being applied both vigorously and strictly at all levels. Using the threat of withholding federal contracts and grants of a host of types, the federal government insisted on specific goals and guidelines concerning minority employment, admission,

---

[185]See fn. 165 and text, pp. 183–184 of this text.
[186]*Washington* v. *Seattle School District*, 458 U.S. 457 and *Crawford* v. *Board of Education*, 458 U.S. 527, respectively.

and recognition in personnel practices,[187] generally based on Titles VI, VII, and IX of the Civil Rights Act of 1964, as amended, and as applied by the executive agencies charged with their interpretative enforcement. Although they would seem to have been expressly forbidden by the same federal statute, quotas (usually referred to as "goals" or "guidelines") were in effect demanded from such diverse sectors as the construction industry, telephone services, and federally aided colleges and universities. Many states followed suit with their own requirements. Inevitably, these policies raised serious questions, not only of illegal "quotas," but also of "reverse discrimination," support of "separatism," and "compensatory" and "preferential" treatment—the latter also expressly forbidden by the Civil Rights Act of 1964.[188] Here, too, the Court ultimately drew another set of delicate, difficult lines. However, when it initially had an opportunity to do so in connection with the preferential admissions policies of the University of Washington in the *De Funis* case of 1974, it pointedly refused. In a narrowly decided (5:4) unsigned opinion, it declared the issue to be "moot," since Marco De Funis had been admitted to the law school as a result of an order by a lower court, the reversal of which was stayed on appeal by Justice Douglas in his capacity as Circuit Justice for the Ninth U.S. Circuit.

Initially denied admission by the University, De Funis had filed suit because, as a result of the application of preferential criteria, thirty-seven "minority" applicants had been admitted, of whom thirty-six had predicted first-year averages *lower* than that of

---

[187]A 6:3 Court majority thus ruled in 1976 that blacks who were denied jobs in violation of Title VII of the Civil Rights Act of 1964 must be awarded retroactive seniority once they succeeded in obtaining those jobs (*Franks* v. *Bowman*, 424 U.S. 747). But compare the 1977 *Teamster* cases, in which the Court ruled 7:2 that unless a seniority plan *intentionally* discriminates among workers it is not illegal under the 1964 statute. Thus, "neutral" seniority systems can legally perpetuate employment practices that favor white males *if* these systems were operative before the enactment of the Civil Rights Act of 1964 (*Teamsters* v. *United States*, 431 U.S. 324 and *T.I.M.E.-D.C., Inc.* v. *United States*, 431 U.S. 324). See, similarly, *California Brewers Association* v. *Bryant*, 444 U.S. 598 (1980). In 1982 the Court came full cycle by ruling 5:4 that the *T.I.M.E.-D.C.* principle applies to seniority systems established before as well as after the passage of the Civil Rights Act (*American Tobacco Co.* v. *Patterson*, 456 U.S. 63; and in 1984 it made clear that the C.R.A. "affirmatively protects bona fide seniority systems, including those with discriminatory effect on minorities" (*Firefighters Local Union* v. *Stotts*, 52 LW 4767).

[188]Title VII, Sec. 703 (j).

De Funis, a "non-minority" (white Jewish) applicant. Obviously, the Supreme Court was not eager to reach the merits of the case—hence its "mooting." But Justice Douglas, in his lone dissenting opinion on those merits, flayed what he called the "arbitrariness" of admissions policies generally, and warned that the "Equal Protection Clause commands the elimination of racial barriers, not their creation, in order to satisfy our theory as to how society ought to be organized. The purpose of the University of Washington cannot be to produce black lawyers for blacks, Polish lawyers for Poles, Jewish lawyers for Jews, Irish lawyers for the Irish. It should be to produce good lawyers for Americans and not to have First Amendment barriers against anyone."[189] It would be four years before the Court readdressed the volatile issue in the *Bakke* case, and subsequently in such landmark cases as *Weber, Fullilove, Stotts,* and *Wygant.*[190]

Meanwhile, in a significant 7:2 decision two years later, involving a challenge to an examination for applicants to the District of Columbia police force—an examination that blacks failed in higher proportion than whites—the Court ruled that not only was it necessary to prove "a racially discriminatory purpose," but that a statute or an official act is not unconstitutional just because it places a "substantially disproportionate" burden on one race.[191] This posture may have signalled a qualification of a tough, unanimous 1971 holding, in which the Court had ruled that the 1964 Title VII statute bars the administration of examinations that do not "relate" to qualifications to perform work, and that the employer bore the burden of proof.[192]

Indeed, the Court subsequently unanimously rejected review of an unusual challenge of the Georgia bar exam, which blacks have traditionally failed more than whites.[193] Just prior to the end of its 1975–1976 term, it held, in 7:2 and 9:0 decisions, in opinions written by its only black member, Justice Marshall, that the Civil Rights Act of 1866 as well as Title VII of that of 1964 prohibits employers from discriminating against whites on the basis of their race in and to the

---

[189]*De Funis* v. *Odegaard*, 416 U.S. 312, at 320 ff.

[190]*Regents of the University of California* v. *Bakke*, 438 U.S. 265 (1978); *Steelworkers* v. *Weber*, 443 U.S. 193 (1979); *Fullilove* v. *Klutznick*, 448 U.S. 448 (1980); and *Firefighters Local Union* v. *Stotts*, 52 LW 4767 (1984). See the discussion on the following pages.

[191]*Washington* v. *Davis*, 426 U.S. 229 (1976). (See also pp. 183–184 and 192–196 of this text.)

[192]*Griggs* v. *Duke Power Co.*, 401 U.S. 424.

[193]*Tyler* v. *Vickey*, 426 U.S. 940 (1976).

same extent they prohibit racial discrimination against blacks.[194] And early in 1978, the Court upheld 5:2 the employment of the National Teacher Examination as having a valid relationship between high scores and professional skills, although it disqualified more than four times as many blacks as whites.[195] There was but little doubt that additional litigation on the "reverse discrimination" front would ensue as a consequence of these employment front decisions—plus that of the long-awaited *Bakke* decision that came down in June of that year.[196]

The Bakke Case. Eagerly awaited by the general citizenry, the long-in-coming ruling on the "reverse discrimination" front proved to be historic in the sense that, in its own fashion, it came to grips with the basic problem of "affirmative action," which the mooted *De Funis* decision[197] had strived hard, and successfully, to avoid four years earlier. In effect, there were neither clear-cut "winners" nor clear-cut "losers" in the Court's *Bakke* holding—and that may well be precisely what the justices intended. Still, disappointment by friends, foes, and neutrals was widespread, for very little was in fact finally settled by *Bakke*, given the seriously divided, verbose opinions—a stark contrast to the brief, unanimous decision in the seminal *Brown I and II* cases[198] a quarter of a century earlier. Still, the multiple six-opinion, 154-page judgments did spell out some basics, although the case neither settled, nor did it pretend to settle, the ongoing controversy at issue which lingers to this day.

Essentially and summarily, three identifiable groups of justices rendered at least three different opinions, with the two controlling ones fashioned by the swing vote of the key Justice in the case, Lewis F. Powell, Jr. In one of these (joined by Justices Stevens, Stewart, Rehnquist, and Chief Justice Burger), Powell's 5:4 opinion affirmed the California judiciary's decision ordering the University of California's Medical School at Davis to admit Allan Bakke, a white applicant who had twice been rejected by Davis—notwithstanding the university's frank admission that he was more highly qualified than the 16 minority group admittees who had entered the medical school under a

---

[194]*McDonald* v. *Santa Fe Transportation Co.*, 427 U.S. 273 (1976).

[195]*National Education Association* v. *South Carolina*, 434 U.S. 1026.

[196]*Regents of the University of California* v. *Bakke*, 438 U.S. 265 (1978).

[197]*De Funis* v. *Odegaard*, 416 U.S. 312 (1974), discussed on p. 189 of this text.

[198]347 U.S. 483 (1954) and 349 U.S. 294 (1955), respectively.

special program that had set aside, on an admission quota basis, sixteen of the 100 openings at the school for minorities. Justice Powell held the university's action to be an unconstitutional violation of the "equal protection of the laws" clause of the Fourteenth Amendment, whereas the other four justices regarded any racial quota systems utilized by government-supported programs (e.g., higher education) to be an obvious violation of the explicit language of Title VI of the Civil Rights Act of 1964. The four dissenters—Justices Brennan, White, Marshall, and Blackmun—on the other hand, saw neither a constitutional nor a statutory infraction, and called for the permissive use of race as a justifiable "compensatory" action to redress past wrongs generally. (No racial discrimination against blacks or any other minorities had ever been charged against the University of California at Davis.) While refusing to join these four in so expansive a constitutional stance, Justice Powell nevertheless teamed with them in holding that the California courts had been wrong in ruling that race could *never* be a factor in admissions decisions (the state's judiciary had adjudged such a practice to be *both* illegal and unconstitutional); that a state university had a "substantial interest" in a diverse student body "that legitimately may be served by a properly devised admissions program [he pointed to Harvard] involving the competitive consideration of race and ethnic origin."

What the Supreme Court did then was to disallow (5:4) specific, rigid, racial quotas like those established by California, and to uphold (5:4) the use of "race" as a tool of affirmative action programs in the absence of Davis-like quota arrangements. But it rejected (4:5) the interpretation by the Stevens, Stewart, Rehnquist, and Berger group that believed the use of race in programs benefitting from federal financial assistance to be illegal; and the Court also rejected (4:5), at least by implication, the position of the opposing group (Brennan, White, Marshall, and Blackmun) that the "affirmative action" use of race was not constitutionally proscribed at all. In a sense, then, *The Wall Street Journal* was justified in headlining the *Bakke* verdict as "The Decision Everyone Won"[199]—although, *de minimis*, that statement needs both explication and qualification.

In fine, the Court's long-awaited decision left intact the bulk of affirmative action programs that gave special consideration to statutorily identified minority groups (and women), while running up a

---

[199]June 29, 1978, p. 1.

caveat flag on obvious, rigid, racial quotas—and, by implication, probably affecting other quotas as well. Yet the so controversial matter at issue in *Bakke*—confined, as it was, to higher education, hardly settled the overall "reverse discrimination" problem; this was readily evinced by the string of cases that were winding their way through the judicial structure in the late 1970s en route to the highest court in the land, headed by the potentially seminal *Weber quota* case involving employment in the steel industry.

At issue in *Weber* was a "voluntary" affirmative action plan devised by the Kaiser Aluminum and Chemical Corporation and the United Steel Workers Union for the former's Gramercy, Louisiana, plant, under which one-half of the available positions in a voluntary on-the-job training program had been reserved for blacks. Finding himself excluded solely because he was white, Brian Weber filed suit in federal court alleging a *prima facie* violation of Title VII of the Civil Rights Act of 1964 that categorically bans any racial discrimination in employment, no matter whether the individual's race be black or white, and which specifically states that its provisions are not to be interpreted

> to require any employer...to grant preferential treatment to any individual or to any group because of the race...of such individual or group.

Moreover, the congressional history of the statute's enactment made crystal clear that Congress meant precisely what it said, and that the Civil Rights Act's proponents had so assured the doubters during the exciting eighty-three days of floor debate in 1964. *Ergo*, based upon the language of Title VII and the congressional debates, enshrined in the *Congressional Record*, both the U.S. District Court and the U.S. Court of Appeals upheld Weber's contentions and ruled the affirmative action plan at issue to be illegal under Title VII.

But in an astonishing decision, handed down in 1979, the Supreme Court reversed the courts below in a 5:2 holding, Justices Powell and Stevens abstaining. Writing for the majority, Justice Brennan (joined by Justices Stewart, White, and Marshall and, with reservations, by Justice Blackmun) frankly conceded that the rulings by the lower federal courts had followed the *letter* of the Civil Rights Act of 1964, but that they had failed to follow its "spirit." He contended that Congress's primary concern had been with "the plight of the Negro in our economy," and that it would be "ironic indeed" if

Title VII would be used to prohibit "all voluntary, private, race-conscious efforts to abolish traditional patterns" of discrimination.[200]

Chief Justice Burger and Justice Rehnquist dissented vehemently, charging that the majority had engaged in the crassest kind of judicial activism *cum* legislating; that it had in fact "totally rewritten a crucial part" of the law. As a member of Congress, admonished the Chief Justice, he would have readily sided with the views expressed by the majority, but as a judge he had no business in writing legislation. "Congress," he wrote with feeling," expressly *prohibited* the discrimination against Brian Weber" that the five-member majority now approved. In what may well constitute one of the angriest dissenting opinions in recent times, Justice Rehnquist accused the majority of acting like Harry Houdini, the escape artist. Congress sought to require racial equality in government, Rehnquist contended, and "there is perhaps no device more destructive to the notion of equality than...the quota. Whether described as 'benign discrimination' or 'affirmative action,' the racial quota is nonetheless a creator of castes, a two-edged sword that must demean one in order to prefer the other." He concluded:

> With today's holding, the Court introduces...a tolerance for the very evil that the law was intended to eradicate, without offering even a clue as to what the limits on that tolerance may be.... The Court has sown the wind. Later courts will face the impossible task of reaping the whirlwind.[201]

When the Court faced its initial post-*Weber* opportunity to do so in a *Weber*-like case involving the *public* (rather than the *private*) sector, it denied *certiorari* and thereby upheld a test-manipulation that pushed six nonpassing blacks into a passing posture to the detriments of whites. Chief Justice Burger and Justice White joined in Justice Rehnquist's biting dissent from the denial.[202]

Fullilove. Since the *Weber* majority held that, notwithstanding prohibitory statutory language, racial quotas were neither illegal nor unconstitutional if adopted on a "voluntary" and "temporary" basis, the Court's six-opinion "reverse-discrimination" decision in *Fullilove*

---

[200]*Steelworkers* v. *Weber* 442, U.S. 193 (1979).

[201]Ibid., at 255.

[202]*Bushey* v. *New York State Civil Service Commission*, 53 LW 3497 (1985).

v. *Klutznick*[203] one year later did not come as a major surprise. At issue in the latter case was the constitutionality of a 1977 congressional law that, in a floor amendment, adopted without prior hearings, had set aside 10 percent of a $4 billion public-works program for "minority business enterprises," defined in the statute as companies in which blacks, Hispanic-Americans, Oriental-Americans, American Indians, Eskimos, or Aleuts controlled at least a 50 percent interest. What was surprising was that the controlling plurality opinion was written by the chief justice, who had so sternly dissented in *Weber*.[204] But speaking, too, for Justices White and Powell (with the latter also filing a separate concurring opinion)[205]—and joined on far more permissive grounds in another concurrence by Justice Marshall, who in turn was joined by Justices Brennan and Blackmun[206]—Chief Justice Burger found warrant for his ruling that the program did "not violate the equal protection component of the Due Process Clause of the Fifth Amendment"[207] in the power of Congress "to enforce by appropriate legislation" the equal protection guarantees of the Fourteenth Amendment.[208] Rejecting the contention by the nonminority business enterprises that Congress is obligated to act in a "color-blind" fashion, and is in fact forbidden to employ racial quotas under the Constitution's mandates, Burger referred repeatedly to what he viewed as the temporary nature of the "narrowly tailored" program, one designed by the national legislature to remedy long-standing past wrongs.[209]

There were three vocal dissenters, their leading opinion being written by Justice Stewart, who had joined the majority in *Weber* but had been on the other side in *Bakke*. This dissenting opinion was also signed by Justice Rehnquist, who consistently opposed racial quotas in all three cases. The other dissent was filed by Justice Stevens, who did not sit in *Weber*, but whose views were in accord with Rehnquist in *Bakke* as well as now in *Fullilove*. Bristling with anger, Stewart accused his colleagues on the other side of the decision of having rendered a "racist" decision,[210] an adjective he veritably spit out while

---

[203]448 U.S 448 (1980).

[204]*United Steelworkers of America* v. *Weber*, 443 U.S. 193 (1979).

[205]*Fullilove* v. *Klutznick*, at 495.

[206]Ibid., at 517.

[207]Ibid., at 473.

[208]Ibid., at 476.

[209]Ibid., at 482.

[210]Ibid., at 532.

reading his dissent in full from the bench on that 1980 July Opinion Day. Styling the "set-aside law" an "invidious discrimination by government," he pleaded that the Constitution permits no discrimination of any kind between the races, musing that "our statute books will once again have to contain laws that reflect the odious practice of delineating the qualities that make one person a Negro and make another white;" that the

> Fourteenth Amendment was adopted to ensure that every person must be treated equally by each State regardless of the color of his skin...that the law would honor no preference based on lineage.[211]

and he concluded:

> Today the Court derails this achievement and places its imprimatur on the creation once again by government of privileges based on birth.[212]

In his even more scathing dissenting opinion, which he also read aloud from the bench on the day of the decision, Justice Stevens charged that the "minority set-aside law" represents a "perverse form of reparation," a "slapdash" law that rewards some who may not need rewarding and hurts others who may not deserve hurting.[213] Suggesting that such a law could be used simply as a patronage tool by its authors, he warned that it could breed more resentment and prejudice than it corrects,[214] and he asked what percentage of "oriental blood or what degree of Spanish-speaking skill is required for membership in the preferred class?"[215] Sarcastically, he said that now the government must devise its version of the Nazi laws that defined who is a Jew.[216]

Stotts. After having upheld several racial quota affirmative action arrangements,[217] the Court, to the pleasant surprise of some

---

[211]Ibid., at 531.

[212]Ibid., at 213.

[213]Ibid., at 537–39.

[214]Ibid., at 545.

[215]Ibid., at 552, fn. 30.

[216]Ibid., at 534.

[217]E.g., *Guardian Association* v. *Civil Service Commission of City of New York,* 463 U.S. 582 (1983) and *Bratton* v. *City of Detroit,* 464 U.S. 1040 (1984), certiorari denied.

observers and to the contrary of others, appeared to shift gears in a case reaching it from Memphis, Tennessee, in 1984. A lower federal court had forced the layoff or demotion of senior white firefighters in that city in order to protect black hiring and promotion gains achieved under a court-approved affirmative action plan in 1980. The latter required that at least 50 percent of all new employees be black until two-fifths of the department was black. Responding to long-term pressure that generated the arrangement, Memphis increased the proportion of black firefighters from 4 percent in 1974 to 11½ percent in 1980.

As a result of 1981 budget crunch, however, the city announced that it would abide by a "last-hired-but-first-fired" seniority system negotiated with the union. It thus began to lay off those who had most recently been hired, a group that included many of the new black firefighters. But a federal district court denied the city's right to reduce the proportion of blacks in the department and, as a result, three whites lost their jobs to three blacks who had less seniority. Both the city of Memphis and the Union appealed to the United States Supreme Court.

In a 6:3 opinion, written by Justice White—who had been on the "other" side in *Bakke, Weber,* and *Fullilove*—the Court held that Title VII of the Civil Rights Act of 1964 clearly "protects bona fide seniority systems," unless the plans are *intentionally discriminatory* or black workers can demonstrate that they were *individually* victimized by hiring discrimination.[218] Joined in dissenting by Justices Brennan and Marshall, Justice Blackmun—perhaps loathe to reach the merits of the case—contented himself by voting to throw out the controversy as being legally irrelevant to those involved because the layoff orders had since been rescinded.

Wygant. The Court continued to receive affirmative action/ reverse discrimination cases and, two years after *Stotts,* it handed down a decision in which it seemed to say both "yes" *and* "no" to racial preferences, while evidently promising to return to the fray in yet other cases then still on its 1985–86 docket. In the former, *Wygant* v. *Jackson Board of Education* (decided on May 19, 1986), the Court held unconstitutional a Michigan school board's plan for laying off teachers that gave preference to members of minority groups. Under that plan the school district had sought to protect minority hiring gains by laying off white teachers ahead of blacks who had *less*

---

[218]*Firefighters Local Union* v. *Stotts,* 52 LW 4767 (1984).

seniority. But the six-opinion 5:4 holding, written by Justice Powell, was so diverse in reasoning that it seemed to provide a bit of triumph for both foes *and* friends of affirmative action. The Reagan Administration could take solace from the majority's view that the mere fact of discrimination in American life is not in and of itself a constitutionally sufficient reason for resorting to the type of affirmative action remedy propounded by the Jackson school board. On the other hand, the supporters of affirmative action *per se* could and did find much satisfaction in Justice O'Connor's concurring opinion, which appeared to be *the* controlling one in terms of the practice's future.

The Court's junior Justice, and only woman, professed to see a forging of "a degree of unanimity" in rejecting a central contention of the Administration, namely, that affirmative action is appropriate only as a device to remedy discrimination *against specific individual victims*. But as Justice O'Connor saw the gravamen of the issue, "a carefully constructed affirmative-action program...need not be limited to the remedying of specific instances of identified discrimination," and that the Court would be prepared to approve such a course. The Jackson school board, however, had not "narrowly tailored" its plan, as Justice Powell put it, and he suggested that, while such race-based *firing* schemes were too harsh on the innocent, the Court might well look more favorably upon some *hiring* plans—thus signaling a case-by-case approach. While rejecting the four dissenters' willingness to find constitutional authority even in such firing schemes, Powell acknowledged that "in order to remedy the effects of prior discrimination, it may be necessary to take race into account"—even if that meant that "innocent persons may be called upon to bear some of the burdens of the remedy." The last word obviously had not yet been spoken on the wrenching issue.

The *Bakke, Weber, Fullilove, Stotts,* and *Wygant* rulings once again underscore not only the wrench of the quest for equal justice under law but also the omnipresent question of the judicial role—of how to draw that line between judicial restraint and judicial activism, between the judiciary's presumed role of finding rather than of making the law and its other assumed role of being the country's "conscience."[219]

As for the issue of "reverse discrimination"—with several new cases on the Court's 1985–1986 docket that again promise renewed controversy—the words of Philip B. Kurland, one of the country's

---

[219]See my *The Judicial Process*, 4th ed. (New York: Oxford University Press, 1980), Chapters VII, VIII, and IX.

foremost experts on constitutional law and history, are worth keeping in mind. In his view, the entire syndrome will almost certainly be with us for years to come, given what he regards as the "fundamental shift of constitutional limitations from protection of individual rights to protection of class rights...[and the measurement of equality] from equality of opportunity to equality of condition or result."[220]

SEXUAL EQUALITY[221]

In a host of ways, although superficially differing in kind, degree, and genesis, discrimination on the basis of sex—that is, gender-based discrimination—is part and parcel of the past American dilemma. Gender-based discrimination, like racially-based discrimination, is now constitutionally impermissible. However, although there has long been a "women's movement," the issue of invidious discrimination in the realm of gender did not impress itself upon the public conscience until the desegregation movement evolved close to its crescendo in the 1960s. And, as was true of racial discrimination, the judiciary again was called upon to articulate and to mandate egalitarianism and equal opportunity in the realm of sex, based upon the implicit and explicit commands of the "equal protection of the laws" and the "due process of law" clauses of the Constitution.

A difference in the Supreme Court's approach to the problem, however, has surfaced in its unwillingness to accord "suspect" category status to gender-based legislative classifications. Although four justices have evinced a desire to place sex on the same footing as race, and thus to consider both on the "suspect" plane, a clear majority has so far preferred "close" or "very close" scrutiny. It is conceivable that the defeat of the Equal Rights Amendment (ERA) may bring a change in the judicial attitude, but that remains to be seen. Meanwhile—as references to court cases in the gender-based sector of public law throughout the foregone pages have indicated—the Court has followed an approach that appears to vary between the "rationality" test for legislation (e.g., see *Reed* v. *Reed*, in Table 4-1) and that of a "compelling state interest" (e.g., see *Frontiero* v. *Richardson*). In *both* instances the allegations by women of invidious gender-based discrimination prevailed unanimously in the first and 8:1 in the second case. And, broadening the grounds for law suits by women con-

---

[220]"The Private I: Some Reflections on Equality and the Constitution," X, *The University of Chicago Record* 4 (July 19, 1976).

[221]The following materials on sexual equality are adapted from my book *Freedom and the Court*, pp. 392–95, with the permission of the Oxford University Press.

TABLE 4–1 Representative Decisions by the United States Supreme Court in Recent Gender-Based Discrimination Cases

Case	Year Decided	Issue and Disposition	Vote	Dissents
Reed v. *Reed*, 404 U.S. 71	1971	State of Idaho gave preference to males in intestate administration. Declared a violation of the equal protection clause of the Fourteenth Amendment.	9:0	None
Frontiero v. *Richardson*, 411 U.S. 677	1973	Federal law that automatically qualified male service personnel for spousal benefits but that required female personnel to show proof of dependency. Declared unconstitutional infringement of due process clause of the Fifth Amendment.	8:1	Rehnquist
Kahn v. *Shevin*, 416 U.S. 351	1974	Florida law granting widows but not widowers $500 property-tax exemption. Declared constitutional because a woman's loss of spouse imposed greater financial disability usually than a man's loss of spouse.	6:3	Douglas Brennan Marshall
Geduldig v. *Aiello*, 417 U.S. 484	1974	State of California disability insurance payments to private employees not covered by workmen's compensation, *excluding* normal pregnancies, among other disabilities. Upheld as a rational choice by state.	6:3	Douglas Brennan Marshall
Schlesinger v. *Ballard*, 419 U.S. 498	1975	Federal law on mandatory Navy discharges: women guaranteed 13 years of service; men automatically discharged after failing twice to be promoted. Upheld as rational because women have less opportunity for promotion.	5:4	Douglas Brennan Marshall White
Taylor v. *Louisiana*, 419 U.S. 522	1975	Louisiana statutory and constitutional provisions excluding women from juries unless they manifest a desire to serve via a written request. Declared unconstitutional as violation of equal protection clause of the Fourteenth Amendment.	8:1	Rehnquist
Stanton v. *Stanton*, 421 U.S. 7	1975	Utah law that provides for lower age of majority for girls than for boys in connection with parental obligation to pay child support. Struck down as irrational legislative judgment.	8:1	Rehnquist

Case	Year	Description	Vote	Dissenting
General Electric Co. v. Gilbert, 429 U.S. 125	1976	Private employer's disability plan excluding pregnancies from coverage. Upheld as not invidiously discriminatory under "due process of law" clause of the Fifth Amendment.	6:3	Brennan Marshall Stevens
Craig v. Boren, 429 U.S. 190	1976	Oklahoma statute prohibiting sale of 3.2 percent beer to males under 21 years of age but to females only under 18. Held to be invidiously discriminatory under equal protection clause of the Fourteenth Amendment.	7:2	Burger Rehnquist
Califano v. Webster, 430 U.S. 313	1977	Section of federal Social Security Act providing that wives may exclude three more of their lower earning years in computing average wage for retirement benefits than husbands may. Upheld as "benign," not illogical, and thus not constitutionally defective.	9:0	None
City of Los Angeles Department of Water v. Manhart, 435 U.S. 702	1978	Municipal regulation that required female employees to pay 15 percent more into pension fund than male employees because women expect statistically to live longer than men. Declared unconstitutional as violation of "equal protection of the laws" clause of Amendment Fourteen.	6:2	Burger Rehnquist
Orr v. Orr, 440 U.S. 268	1979	Alabama law providing that husbands but not wives are liable to pay post-divorce alimony. Struck down as violation of equal protection clause of Fourteenth Amendment.	6:3	Burger Powell Rehnquist
Califano v. Westcott, 443 U.S. 76	1979	Section of federal Social Security Act providing benefits to needy dependent children only because of father's unemployment, not because of mother's. Struck down as violation of the due process clause of the Fifth Amendment.	9:0	None
Wengler v. Druggists Mutual Insurance Co., 446 U.S. 142	1980	Section of Missouri's workmen's compensation law that requires a husband to prove actual dependence on his spouse's earnings but does not require wife to prove such dependence. Declared unconstitutional as violation of the equal protection clause of the Fourteenth Amendment.	8:1	Rehnquist
Michael M. v. Superior Court, 450 U.S. 464	1981	California statutory rape law punishing males, but not females, for sexual intercourse with an underage partner of the opposite sex upheld as not irrational since "only women may become pregnant."	5:4	Brennan White Marshall Stevens

TABLE 4–1 Continued

Case	Year Decided	Issue and Disposition	Vote	Dissents
McCarty v. McCarty, 453 U.S. 210	1981	Congressional statute to preserve military pensions as the service member's personal entitlement, not subject to being shared with anyone else, upheld as preventing such benefits from becoming part of a property settlement in a divorce.	6:3	Rehnquist Brennan Stewart
Kirchberg v. Feenstra, 450 U.S. 455	1981	Louisiana law giving husband the unilateral right to dispose of property jointly owned by husband and wife. Declared unconstitutional as invidious discrimination by gender.	9:0	None
Mississippi Univ. for Women v. Hogan, 458 U.S. 718	1982	May a state statute exclude males from enrolling in a state-supported professional nursing school? Despite 100 years of such unchallenged practice, the answer is "no" as violative of the equal protection guarantees of the Fourteenth Amendment.	5:4	Burger Blackmun Powell Rehnquist
Arizona v. Norris, 464 U.S. 808	1983	Title VII of the Civil Rights Act of 1964, which outlaws employment discrimination on the basis of both race and sex, requires employees to be treated as individuals rather than as members of a group (here women's level of pensions).	5:4	Burger Blackmun Powell Rehnquist
Roberts v. U.S. Jaycees, 465 U.S. 555	1984	Gender discrimination may be interdicted as a "compelling state interest" even in heretofore accepted all-male organizations, such as the Jaycees, since theirs is a "large and broadly unselective" membership.	7:0	None

Case	Year		Vote	Dissent
Hishon v. *King & Spaulding,* 52 LW 4627	1984	Title VII of the Civil Rights Act of 1964, barring gender discrimination, applies even to partnerships in law firms, thus reaching the question of impermissible discrimination in the promotion of junior rank lawyers to the status of partner.	9:0	None
Grove City College v. *Bell,* 52 LW 4283	1984	(a) Title IX of the Federal Education Act of 1972, subjects noncompliant educational institutions to federal fund cutoff, since any aid to students constitutes aid to their institutions. However, (b) ''any educational program or activity receiving financial aid'' under the statute means *only* the *specific program* of a college or university, *not* the *entire* institution.	6:3	Brennan Marshall Stevens

cerned with equal pay issues, the Court ruled 5:4 in a 1981 case of potentially far-reaching significance that the Civil Rights Act of 1964, which prohibits discrimination in employment on the basis of sex as well as race, is not limited to claims of "equal pay for equal work" —but may extend to a standard of "comparable" work or worth.[222]

As the accompanying table on selected key gender-based discrimination decisions readily indicates, there remains little doubt that great strides—judicially punctuated and embraced—have been made along the road toward the eradication not only of invidious discrimination but also of the arguably non-invidious kind. The latter category evolved from some of the actions taken and decisions rendered as a result of congressional enactment of what became generally known as "Title IX." That visible section of the Education Amendments of 1972 bars, with certain exceptions, discrimination on the basis of sex in any education program receiving federal assistance. The resultant welter of regulations issued by the Department of Health, Education and Welfare (now Health and Human Services) did much to remedy past wrongs; but it also did much to drive coaches of the so-called "contact" sports, especially of the revenue-producing kind, up the proverbial wall. They appear to have survived, however.

The controversial enactment of the draft-registration statute of 1980, which specifically *excluded* women, created predictable controversy by friend and foe of sexual equality alike, all of which tended to blur lines between otherwise predictable supporters and opponents of legislative classification by gender. A major class-action suit was filed almost instantly in federal court by a group of *male* registrants, alleging invidious sex discrimination. *Either*, so the argument went, the exclusion of women constitutes a violation of *their* Fifth Amendment constitutional rights of due process of law ("equal protection" *per se* not being applicable because it is confined to *state* infractions under the Fourteenth Amendment), *or* it constitutes a violation of the rights of *males* because they are being "singled out."

The Court's answer came in 1981: It ruled 6:3 that the registration provisions excluding women do *not* violate the Fifth Amendment; that Congress acted well within its constitutional authority to raise and regulate armies and navies, noting that Congress's judgment is "particularly appropriate" in defense and military affairs.[223] Three years later it held 6:2 that a controversial law, which required male

---

[222]*County of Washington* v. *Alberta Gunther*, 452 U.S. 161.
[223]*Rostker* v. *Goldberg*, 453 U.S. 57.

college students to register for the draft if they wish to obtain federal financial aid, was constitutional as "a plainly rational means to improve compliance with the registration requirements" (that had been flouted by a sizeable number of putative registrants).[224]

A host of gender discrimination cases on the Court's 1986 docket—and on those of a plethora of lower federal tribunals—points to continuing litigation and trailblazing on the frontier of the equal protection of the laws.

The State Action Problem

Since much alleged discrimination falls into categories of *private* discrimination, one of the most vexatious and fascinating problems has become the question of where, when, and how to draw the line between *state* (that is, public) action and *private* action. Briefly, the line is drawn at the point where the state becomes involved; then its action is subject to the strictures of Section I of the Fourteenth Amendment which states that:

> No State shall make or enforce any law which shall abridge the privileges or immunities of citizens of the United States; nor shall any State deprive any person of life, liberty, or property, without due process of law; nor deny to any person within its jurisdiction the equal protection of the laws.

Since the Supreme Court held long ago in the *Civil Rights* cases of 1883 that only a state, and not a private individual, is forbidden by the Constitution to discriminate,[225] private individuals are thus presumably free to discriminate if they choose, provided only that they receive no assistance from the state in their discrimination—and, of course, that they do not violate any state laws. This in turn raises the delicate question of *what is and what is not "state action."* It becomes a matter of balancing, and of drawing lines between liberty and equality; between, one might add, the alleged private right to discriminate—so long as no law is violated—and the public right to be constitutionally protected against illegal discrimination.

The Court had held in 1948 and 1953 that (as noted earlier) *private* discriminatory, restrictive housing covenants (in the absence of the steadily spreading legislation on the subject) are *not* state action,

---

[224]*Selective Service System* v. *Minnesota Public Interest Resource Group*, 52 LW 5140.

[225]109 U.S. 3.

but were any court to enforce these, such action *would* be state action.[226] Then in 1967 the Court declared unconstitutional, 5:4, California's anti-open housing initiative (Proposition 14), which had enabled property owners to "decline to sell, lease, or rent" property "in their absolute discretion," because its narrow majority regarded the action by the voters as proscribed "state action."[227] However, four years later the Court upheld 5:3 the right of local communities in that state to veto proposed public housing projects by special referendum votes.[228] And it came full cycle in the *private* housing sector when, following the enactment of the 1968 Civil Rights Act with its limited housing provisions, it ruled 7:2 that under an almost forgotten civil rights law of 1866 (enacted under Amendment Thirteen) racial discrimination in the purchase, lease, sale, holding, and conveyance of any real and personal property is expressly forbidden.[229] In effect, the housing sections of the 1968 law were thus rendered moot, save for the law's enforcement powers. Under the same rediscovered authority, the Court ruled 5:3 in 1969 that a swimming pool and park owned by the residents of a suburban community could *not* exclude a black family that had moved into the neighborhood, because it had obtained a share in both pool and park by leasing one of the community's shareholder's homes.[230]

Nor, as the unanimous Court held in 1973, could a "recreation association" that draws all of its members from *whites* living within

---

[226]*Shelley* v. *Kraemer*, 334 U.S. 1 (1948); *Hurd* v. *Hodge*, 334 U.S. 24 (1948); and *Barrows* v. *Jackson*, 346 U.S. 249 (1953).

[227]*Reitman* v. *Mulkey*, 387 U.S. 369. See also *Hunter* v. *Erickson* (1969). But compare *Eastlake* v. *Forest City Enterprises*, 426 U.S. 668 (1976).

[228]*James* v. *Valtierra* and *Schaeffer* v. *Valtierra*, 402 U.S. 137. Justice Black, writing the majority opinion, distinguished the earlier ruling from the present by pointing out that the former related to racial discrimination "and this one does not....Provisions for referendums demonstrate devotion to democracy, not to bias, discrimination, or prejudice." See also the *Arlington Heights Zoning* case of 1977 for a significant new interpretation in the face of allegations of "apparent" versus "intended" racial discrimination in low and moderate income housing (*Village of Arlington Heights* v. *Metropolitan Housing Development Corporation*, 429 U.S. 252). But note the follow-up decision, ibid., 434 U.S. 1025 (1978), distinguishing the earlier holding on statutory interpretation grounds.

[229]*Jones* v. *Alfred H. Mayer Co.*, 392 U.S. 409 (1968). In 1976 the Court ruled 8:0 that federal courts can order the creation of low-cost public housing for minorities in a city's white suburbs to relieve racial segregation in housing within the city (here Chicago) *if* the government has been found to contribute to the latter's segregation through its public housing programs (*Hills* v. *Gautreaux*, 425 U.S. 284).

[230]*Sullivan* v. *Little Hunting Park, Inc.*, 395 U.S. 229.

three-quarters of a mile of its swimming pool, bar *non*-whites living in that area from using its facilities. (The Court refused to recognize the association as a "private club on any level.")[231]

What of the rights of a private entrepreneur to refuse to provide service? In the event of sit-ins, may he or she ask the police to eject the intruders? What of the right of peaceable assembly versus breach of the peace or trespass? The Court tried on several occasions to find answers to some of these problems. In an important series of 1963 cases, it reversed the conviction of numerous lunch counter sit-ins and other demonstrators in several southern states, because in the cases at issue the state and local authorities involved had *required* segregation either by statute or official policy or announced custom.[232] And barely ten days prior to the enactment of the Civil Rights Act of 1964, the Court—without reaching the fundamental constitutional issue of the presence or absence of "state action" in the trespass conviction of forty-two persons who demanded nondiscriminatory service at privately owned places of business in three states without official segregation policies—*reversed* their conviction 6:3 on various statutory and associated grounds.[233]

It is an interesting tribute to the herein repeatedly expressed caution against oversimplifications and snap judgments regarding the judicial posture and philosophy of the justices, to note that one of the three dissenters was Justice Black, who, wishing to meet the constitutional issue, albeit in *dissent*, noted that "this Court has never said in the school segregation decisions or any before or since, that the prejudice of individuals could be laid to the state."[234] From the bench, on the last day of the Court's 1963–1964 term, this great champion of the individual said sarcastically that the idea that the Fourteenth Amendment *itself* prohibited segregation in public accommodations made "the last six months' struggle in Congress a work of supererogation."[235] Like his long-time jurisprudential "adversary," the then-retired Justice Frankfurter, Hugo Black then once again admonished his country and his world that:

---

[231] *Tillman* v. *Wheaton-Haven Recreation Association*, 410 U.S. 431, at 437. The Court again based its rationale on the 1866 statute noted above.

[232] *Peterson* v. *Greenville*, 373 U.S. 244 and *Lombard* v. *Louisiana*, 373 U.S. 267.

[233] *Griffin* v. *Maryland*, 378 U.S. 130 (1964); *Robinson* v. *Florida*, 378 U.S. 153 (1964); and *Barr* v. *City of Columbia*, 378 U.S. 146 (1964).

[234] Comment from the bench, June 22, 1964.

[235] As quoted in *The New York Times*, June 23, 1964, p. 16.

The worst citizen no less than the best *is entitled to equal protection of the laws of his state and of his nation.*[236]

Many of the delicate questions of private property rights still remained unanswered. And what of such routine services by the state as licensing, probating of wills, and bona fide protective services? The answers to some of these lay with the Civil Rights Act of 1964, which, by becoming law early that July, rendered some of the questions moot, for example, denial of service in "public accommodations." Ultimately, most answers such as housing, would lie with the Supreme Court of the United States.

The first test of the 1964 Act was not long in coming, and it did not prove to be a difficult one for the Court to handle. At issue was the just-alluded-to "public accommodations" section of the act—its very heart—passed by Congress under its power over interstate commerce. It states:

> *All persons shall be entitled to full and equal enjoyment of goods, services, facilities, privileges, advantages and accommodations of any place of public accommodations as defined in this section, without discrimination or segregation on the ground of race, color, religion or national origin.*[237]

The Court's unanimous opinion upholding this crucial segment of the Civil Rights Act of 1964 was delivered by Justice Clark in December of that year. He easily disposed of two challenges to the section (involving a motel and a restaurant) by returning to and re-emphasizing the broad construction given to the federal interstate commerce power as far back as the days of Chief Justice Marshall:

> *How obstruction in commerce may be removed—what means are to be employed—is within the sound and exclusive discretion of the Congress. It is subject to only one caveat—that the means chosen by it must be reasonably adapted to the end permitted by the Constitution. We cannot say that its choice here was not adapted. The Constitution requires no more.*[238]

---

[236]*Bell* v. *Maryland,* 378 U.S. 226, at 328, dissenting opinion. (Italics supplied.)
[237]Stat. 437.
[238]*Heart of Atlanta Motel* v. *United States* and *Katzenbach* v. *McClung,* 379 U.S. 241 and 379 U.S. 294, respectively.

Of Wills and Clubs. As time went by, it became increasingly clear that the Court would continue to regard the probation of wills as a routine "non-state" action,[239] but that "non-state" status would become constitutionally proscribed "state" action if the subject had a "public character," such as attempts to bar blacks by will from a public park[240] or the banning of nonwhites by will from a private high school that was adjudged to be of a quasi-public nature.[241] On the other hand, the Court did *not* regard as proscribable "state action" the return of the aforementioned public park to the donor's heirs rather than admitting blacks to its use,[242] nor the court substitution of private for public trustees of a private educational institution,[243] nor the closing of *all* of a city's public swimming pools rather than desegregating them.[244]

By 1969 the Court had begun to reach the "private" club syndrome: It held 7:1 that even a lake recreation club in an out-of-the-way Arkansas location was covered by the public accommodations provisions of the Civil Rights Act of 1964 and must therefore admit blacks.[245] The case involved a boating and swimming facility, called Lake Nixon, located in a rural area about twelve miles west of Little Rock. The establishment advertised widely, charged but twenty-five cents for "membership," and had 100,000 "members" in a single year. The Court found an effect upon interstate commerce, since some of the club's equipment, facilities, and food—for example, a jukebox and records, canoes, and three or four snack bar items—came from outside the state and could thus be reached by the federal public accommodations legislation.

But what of a private club or lodge that admittedly discriminates on racial—or on sexual or religious—grounds? Can the Loyal Order

---

[239]*Pennsylvania* v. *Board of Directors of City Trusts of the City of Philadelphia*, 357 U.S. 570 (1958). That principle was reconfirmed in a 1975 case, *Sutt* v. *First National Bank of Kansas City*, 421 U.S. 992, which let stand a bequest to Protestant Christian hospitals in a single county to help care for native-born white patients.

[240]*Evans* v. *Newton*, 382 U.S. 296 (1966).

[241]*Brown* v. *Commonwealth of Pennsylvania*, 391 U.S. 321 (1968).

[242]*Evans* v. *Abney*, 396 U.S. 435 (1970).

[243]*Pennsylvania* v. *Board of Directors of City Trusts of the City of Philadelphia*, 353 U.S. 230 (1957).

[244]*Palmer* v. *Thompson*, 403 U.S. 217 (1971). The city voluntarily reopened its pools on a desegregated basis a few years later.

[245]*Daniel* v. *Paul*, 395 U.S. 298 (1969).

of Moose, for example, limit membership in its 2,000 lodges to white adult Caucasian males who, if married, are married to white Caucasians, and are of "good moral character," "mentally normal," and "express a belief in a supreme being"? If it is truly a private organization, receives no government aid, and pays its taxes, the answer would presumably be in the affirmative—for the liberty to associate privately, even on a discriminatory basis, would appear to outweigh egalitarian considerations.

Yet what if that organization holds a state liquor license? Does that fact qualify it for state action? The Pennsylvania Commonwealth Court had that question before it, involving the black majority leader of the Pennsylvania State House of Representatives, K. Leroy Irvis. As a guest of a member of Lodge #107 of the Loyal Order of Moose, Irvis had been refused food and an alcoholic beverage. The state tribunal held the lodge to be exempt on grounds of privacy and association.[246] But a three-judge federal district court reversed the ruling, saying that the holder of a state liquor license was indeed clothed with "state action" under the Fourteenth Amendment.[247] The Moose immediately appealed the decision to the United States Supreme Court, which, in 1972, in a 6:3 opinion written by its then-junior member, Justice Rehnquist, ruled that mere liquor regulation does *not* involve the state in the sense of discriminatory state action forbidden by the Fourteenth Amendment.[248] That August, however, the Pennsylvania Supreme Court, while carefully distinguishing its decision from the aforegone one, upheld a ruling by the Pennsylvania Human Rights Commission that Moose Lodge #107 cannot exclude black nonmember guests from its dining room and bar as long as it allows nonmember guests to be served—for by opening its facilities to guests, it becomes "a place of public accommodation."[249] The Moose took that holding to the Supreme Court, which rejected the appeal for lack of a "substantial fed-

---

[246]*Commonwealth* v. *Loyal Order of Moose*, 92 Dauph. 234 (1970).

[247]*Irvis* v. *Moose Lodge #107*, 318 F. Supp. 1246 (1970).

[248]*Moose Lodge #107* v. *Irvis*, 407 U.S. 163. The dissenting justices were Douglas, Brennan, and Marshall. This holding was reconfirmed in 1973 when the Court, 8:1, let stand a decision below that upheld the right of a New Orleans hotel to bar women from its men's grill, under a state ordinance that licenses bars but does not forbid sexual discrimination in places of public accommodation (*Millenson* v. *New Hotel Monteleone, Inc.*, 414 U.S. 1011). The latter ruling was inferentially confirmed in 1977 in *Kiwanis Club* v. *Board of Trustees*, 434 U.S. 859. But *cf. Golden* v. *Biscayne Bay Yacht Club*, 429 U.S. 872 (1976), *certiorari* denied.

[249]*Loyal Order of Moose* v. *Pennsylvania Human Rights Commission* (decided August 1, 1972).

eral question," thereby upholding the Pennsylvania ruling.[250] The fascinating elements inherent in this new clash between liberty and equality in a free democratic society under a written Constitution, subject to judicial interpretation, engaged lay as well as professional observers. It received renewed attention in 1984 when the Court rejected freedom of association claims by the all-male Jaycees, ruling 7:0 that Minnesota had a "compelling interest" in ordering them to open their membership to women, given the organization's "large and basically unselective nature."[251]

Another significant issue had been addressed in 1976: the eagerly awaited Court answer to the question whether *totally private* schools may bar black students solely because of their race. On the basis of the aforementioned Civil Rights Act of 1866, U.S. District Judge Albert V. Bryan, Jr., of Virginia, rejected the alleged right of two private Virginia secondary schools to do so. Bryan was upheld 4:3 by the U.S. Court of Appeals for the Fourth Circuit in 1975, and the highest court in the land took jurisdiction, hearing oral argument in the spring of 1976.

In an historic 7:2 decision[252]—written by Justice Stewart, who was joined by his colleagues Burger, Brennan, Marshall, Blackmun, Powell, and Stevens, the latter two concurring in the judgment solely on the basis of precedent[253]—the Supreme Court's answer was to uphold the lower courts, ruling that "private, commercially operated, non-sectarian schools" may not deny "admission to prospective students because they are Negroes." Over a strongly worded dissenting opinion by Justice White, who was joined by Justice Rehnquist, the Court majority based its holding on a section of the Civil Rights Act of 1866—an act passed to enforce the Thirteenth Amendment's ban on slavery—that accords "all persons the same rights to" make and enforce contracts as is enjoyed by white citizens. In response to the challenge that this interpretation and application of the statute violated constitutional guarantees of freedom of association, the right to privacy, and parental rights, the majority found no invasions of any of

---

[250]Ibid., 409 U.S. 1052 (1972). On a related matter, the Court in 1976 declined to review, and thereby sustained, a lower court ruling that health spas are "places of entertainment" within the meaning of the Civil Rights Act of 1964 and thus subject to the act's prohibitions (*Shape Spa for Health and Beauty* v. *Rousseve*, 425 U.S. 911).

[251]*Roberts* v. *U.S. Jaycees*, 465 U.S. 555.

[252]*Runyon* v. *McCrary*, 427 U.S. 160.

[253]*Jones* v. *Alfred H. Mayer Co.*, 392 U.S. 409 (1968).

212 ☆ CHAPTER 4

these safeguards, holding that they "do not provide easy or ready escapes" through which whites "can contravene laws enacted by Congress to enforce the Constitutional right to equality."

But Justice White's dissenting opinion viewed the legislative history and intent of the section of the 1866 statute at issue utterly differently than that of the majority: It confirms, he wrote,

> *that the statute means what it says and no more, i.e., that it outlaws any legal rule disabling any person from making or enforcing a contract, but does not prohibit private racially motivated refusals to contract.... What is conferred by [the disputed section of the law] is the right—which was enjoyed by whites—"to make contracts" with other willing parties and to enforce those contracts in court.... The statute by its terms does not require any private individual or institution to enter into a contract or perform any other act under any circumstances, and it consequently fails to supply a cause of action by respondent students against petitioned schools based on the latter's racially motivated decision not to contract with them.*

In language and philosophy reminiscent of Justices Harlan II and Frankfurter, Justice White concluded by flaying his seven colleagues for undertaking "the political task of" construing a statute...a task appropriate for the legislature, not the judiciary."[254]

Justice Stewart's majority opinion left unanswered until a future day and Court such collateral questions as the right of *sectarian* schools to discriminate on the basis of race and, conceivably, the application of the 1866 statute to private clubs. Indeed, the Court did address that fascinatingly vexatious line between liberty and equality a few years later in what became known as "The Christian Schools Cases." The Internal Revenue Service had withdrawn the schools' tax-exemption status "as a matter of public policy." In an 8:1 opinion the Supreme Court ruled that here "governmental interest [i.e., the eradication of racial discrimination in education] substantially outweighs whatever burden denial of tax benefits places on petitioners' exercise of their religious beliefs...."[255] Although he joined Chief Justice Burger's majority opinion, Justice Powell's concurrence noted a widespread concern, namely, the conviction that the "contours of

---

[254]Ibid., at 194, 195, 212.

[255]*Bob Jones University* v. *United States* and *Goldsboro Christian Schools* v. *United States*, 461 U.S. 574 (1983).

public policy should be determined by Congress, not by judges or the Internal Revenue Service."[256]

Rightly or wrongly, it is with the Court that "the buck stops," an observation with which we began this book. In the final analysis, it is the Supreme Court that articulates the defense as well as the interpretation of our basic freedoms. It is the Court that has been, and will unquestionably continue to be, the definer of values and the proclaimer of principles in our constitutional constellation. It is an institution at once legal, political, and human. As such, it can escape neither criticism nor controversy—nor should it, for it is the greatest institutional safeguard we possess—even if, under our system, it is, or certainly it ought to be, "We, the People," who shoulder the ultimate responsibility for our fate on earth.

---

[256]Ibid., at 584.

For Further Reading

There is a wealth of background reading available to the student of constitutional law, the judicial process, and civil rights and liberties. Space permits the listing of but a very few of the many important ones among these. (An asterisk (*) denotes books currently available in paperback.)

*Abraham, Henry J. *Freedom and the Court: Civil Rights and Liberties in the United States.* 4th ed. New York: Oxford University Press, 1982. Expository-analytical treatment of the problems of freedom and the role of the Supreme Court in drawing lines between individual and societal rights and responsibilities.

*Beard, Charles A. *The Supreme Court and the Constitution.* Englewood Cliffs, N.J.: Prentice-Hall, 1938. Still the most persuasive explanation in print for the authenticity of judicial review.

*Berger, Raoul. *Government by Judiciary: The Transformation of the Fourteenth Amendment.* Cambridge, Mass.: Harvard University Press, 1977. A scathing, controversial attack on the latter-day judiciary's interpretation of the original meaning of the Fourteenth Amendment, plus a trenchant analysis and critique of what Berger views as rampant judicial activism since 1953.

Beveridge, Albert J. *The Life of John Marshall*. Boston: Houghton Mifflin Co., 1916. Still one of the most significant biographical studies of a Supreme Court member to date; provides keen insight into a historical framework.

*Bickel, Alexander M. *The Supreme Court and the Idea of Progress*. New Haven, Conn.: Yale University Press, 1978. One of the most sophisticated and perceptive critiques of the judicial role, granting the need for judicial power, but concerned about its exercise within proper parameters.

Black, Hugo L. *A Constitutional Faith*. New York: Alfred A. Knopf, 1968. Written as a valedictory work, it shines with first principles and the touching faith of one of America's greatest constitutionalists.

*Cannon, Mark W. and O'Brien, David M. *Views from the Bench: The Judiciary and Constitutional Politics*. Chatham, N.J.: Chatham House, 1985. A useful anthology comprising views on the nature of the judicial process and public law from the pens of members of the U.S. Supreme Court and other tribunals.

*Cardozo, Benjamin N. *The Nature of the Judicial Process*. New .Haven, Conn.: Yale University Press, 1921. Probably the most important single work on the subject—a must. (Reprinted regularly.)

*Chafee, Zechariah, Jr. *Free Speech in the United States*. Cambridge, Mass.: Harvard University Press, 1941. Still *the* classic in the field. (Reprinted in 1967.)

*Choper, Jesse H. *Judicial Review and the National Political Process*. Chicago: University of Chicago Press, 1980. An imaginative endeavor to articulate a novel "line" between judicial activism and restraint by concurrently expanding and narrowing the parameters of judicial power.

*Corwin, Edward S. *The Higher Law Background of American Constitutional Law*. Ithaca, N.Y.: Cornell University Press, 1929. Superb analysis of the historical-theoretical foundations of the topic.

*Ely, John Hart. *Democracy and Distrust: A Theory of Judicial Review*. Cambridge, Mass.: Harvard University Press, 1980. Designed to achieve an original approach to the theory of judicial review, this sophisticated, challenging, and controversial work pinpoints "process" as the catalyst to reconcile judicial review with democratic theory.

*Fortas, Abe. *Concerning Dissent and Civil Disobedience*. New York: New American Library, 1968. Perhaps the definitive work on the subject that so informed the late 1960s. The late Supreme Court justice points out that dissenters have no monopoly on dissent and must permit dissent from their dissent.

*Frank, Jerome. *Courts on Trial: Myth and Reality in American Justice*. New York: Atheneum, 1967. A brilliant, witty, comprehensive, realistic analysis *cum* critique of the judicial process.

Harris, Robert J. *The Quest for Equality*. Baton Rouge: Louisiana State University Press, 1960. One of the few trenchant and analytical studies of the meaning and range of the equal protection clause—an "action" call.

*Jackson, Robert H. *The Supreme Court in the American System of Government*. Cambridge, Mass.: Harvard University Press, 1955. A brief but superb analysis of the Court as a legal, political, and governmental institution.

Kelly, A. H.; Harbison, W. A.; and Belz, A. H. *The American Constitution—Its Origin and Development*. 6th ed. New York: W. W. Norton and Co., 1983. One of the two or three best historical-analytical studies of constitutional development extant.

*Kluger, Richard. *Simple Justice: The History of Brown v. Board of Education and Black America's Struggle for Equality*. New York: Alfred A. Knopf, 1976. The most thoroughly researched and documented account and analysis of the famous 1954 desegregation decision, written with warmly sympathetic bent.

Lusky, Louis. *By What Right? A Commentary on the Supreme Court's Right to Revise the Constitution*. Charlottesville, Va.: The Michie Co., 1975. A trenchant critical analysis and evaluation of the Court's policy-making role by a leading veteran observer.

*McCloskey, Robert G. *The Modern Supreme Court*. Ed. by Martin Shapiro. Cambridge, Mass.: Harvard University Press, 1972. The best brief history of the Court from the Stone Court through 1971. For the pre-Stone years in the Court's history, *see* McCloskey's *The American Supreme Court*. Chicago: University of Chicago Press, 1961.

*Murphy, Walter F. *Elements of Judicial Strategy*. Chicago: University of Chicago Press, 1964. An outstanding "behavioral" exploration and analysis of the judiciary's influence upon public policy.

O'Brien, David M. *Storm Center: The Supreme Court in American Politics*. New York: W. W. Norton and Co., 1986. A vivid, authoritative account of the Court's *modus operandus*, penned by a highly qualified former Judicial Fellow at the Supreme Court.

*Myrdal, Gunnar. *An American Dilemma: The Negro Problem and Modern Democracy*. Rev. ed. New York: Harper & Row, 1962. Unquestionably still the most significant study of the problem on record.

*Pritchett, C. Herman. *The American Constitutional System.* 5th ed. New York: McGraw-Hill Book Co., 1981. An excellent, learned, highly readable evaluative account of our constitutional constellation.

*Rutland, Robert Allen. *The Birth of the Bill of Rights, 1776–1791.* Rev. ed. Boston: Northeastern University Press, 1983. An excellent description and analysis of the antecedents, framing, adoption, and application of the seminal charter of our liberty.

Silberman, Charles E. *Criminal Violence, Criminal Justice.* New York: Random House, 1978. A searching, enlightening, gloomy, rational study of crime, criminology, and punishment.

Stokes, Anson Phelps. *Church and State in the United States.* Condensed and edited by Leo Pfeffer. New York: Harper & Row, 1964. The key work on the separation of church and state, both historically and analytically—albeit from a very controversial point of view.

*Wilkinson, J. Harvie, III. *From Brown to Bakke: The Supreme Court and School Integration: 1954–1978.* New York: Oxford University Press, 1979. A sensitive, realistic, objective treatment of the historic developments informing the path between the *Brown* and *Bakke* cases. The book goes beyond judicial decisions.

*Wilson, James Q. *Thinking about Crime.* Rev. ed. New York: Random House, 1985. A hard-nosed, realistic analysis of crime, its causes, and those who are its progenitors, emphasizing that it is suicidal to blame "society" for all criminals.

APPENDIX A

Statistical Data on Supreme Court Justices

Appointing President	President's Political Party	Dates of President's Service	Name of Justice	Dates of Birth & Death	Justice's Nominal Party Allegiance on Appointment	State from Which Justice Was Apptd*	Dates of Service on Supreme Court
Washington	Federalist	1789–1797	1. Jay, John†	1745–1829	Federalist	N.Y.	1789–1795
"	"	"	2. Rutledge, John	1739–1800	"	S.C.	1789–1791‡
"	"	"	3. Cushing, William	1732–1810	"	Mass.	1789–1810
"	"	"	4. Wilson, James	1724–1798	"	Pa.	1789–1798
"	"	"	5. Blair, John	1732–1800	"	Va.	1789–1796
"	"	"	6. Iredell, James	1751–1799	"	N.C.	1790–1799
"	"	"	7. Johnson, Thomas	1732–1819	"	Md.	1791–1793
"	"	"	8. Paterson, Wm.	1745–1806	"	N.J.	1793–1806
"	"	"	9. Rutledge, John†	1739–1800	"	S.C.	1795§
"	"	"	10. Chase, Samuel	1741–1811	"	Md.	1796–1811
"	"	"	11. Ellsworth, Oliver†	1745–1807	"	Conn.	1796–1800
Adams	"	1797–1801	12. Washington, Bushrod	1762–1829	"	Va.	1798–1829
"	"	"	13. Moore, Alfred	1755–1810	"	N.C.	1799–1804
"	"	"	14. Marshall, John†	1755–1835	"	Va.	1801–1835
Jefferson	Democrat-Republican	1801–1809	15. Johnson, Wm.	1771–1834	Democrat-Republican	S.C.	1804–1834
"	"	"	16. Livingston, Henry B.	1757–1823	"	N.Y.	1806–1823
"	"	"	17. Todd, Thomas	1765–1826	"	Ky.	1807–1826
Madison	"	1809–1817	18. Duval, Gabriel	1752–1844	"	Md.	1811–1835
"	"	"	19. Story, Joseph	1779–1845	"	Mass.	1811–1845

President	Term	Party	#	Justice	State	Party	Dates	Tenure
Monroe	1817–1825	"	20.	Thompson, Smith	N.Y.	"	1768–1843	1823–1843
Adams	1825–1829	Democrat	21.	Trimble, Robert	Ky.	"	1777–1828	1826–1828
Jackson	1829–1837	Democrat	22.	McLean, John	Ohio	Democrat	1785–1861	1829–1861
"	"	"	23.	Baldwin, Henry	Pa.	"	1780–1844	1830–1844
"	"	"	24.	Wayne, James M.	Ga.	"	1790–1867	1835–1867
"	"	"	25.	Taney, Roger B.†	Md.	"	1777–1864	1836–1864
"	"	"	26.	Barbour, Philip P.	Va.	"	1783–1841	1836–1841
"	"	"	27.	Catron, John°	Tenn.	"	1778–1865	1837–1865
Van Buren	1837–1841	"	28.	McKinley, John	Ala.	"	1780–1852	1837–1852
"	"	"	29.	Daniel, Peter V.	Va.	"	1784–1860	1841–1860
Tyler	1841–1845	Whig	30.	Nelson, Samuel	N.Y.	"	1792–1873	1845–1872
Polk	1845–1849	Democrat	31.	Woodbury, Levi	N.H.	"	1789–1851	1846–1851
"	"	"	32.	Grier, Robert C.	Pa.	"	1794–1870	1846–1870
Fillmore	1850–1853	Whig	33.	Curtis, Benjamin R.	Mass.	Whig	1809–1874	1851–1857
Pierce	1853–1857	Democrat	34.	Campbell, John A.	Ala.	Democrat	1811–1889	1853–1861
Buchanan	1857–1861	"	35.	Clifford, Nathan	Me.	"	1803–1881	1858–1881
Lincoln	1861–1865	Republican	36.	Swayne, Noah H.	Ohio	Republican	1804–1884	1862–1881
"	"	"	37.	Miller, Samuel F.	Iowa	"	1816–1890	1862–1890
"	"	"	38.	Davis, David	Ill.	"	1815–1886	1862–1877
"	"	"	39.	Field, Stephen J.	Cal.	Democrat	1816–1899	1863–1897
"	"	"	40.	Chase, Salmon P.†	Ohio	Republican	1808–1873	1864–1873
Grant	1869–1877	"	41.	Strong, William	Pa.	"	1808–1895	1870–1880
"	"	"	42.	Bradley, Joseph P.	N.J.	"	1813–1892	1870–1892
"	"	"	43.	Hunt, Ward	N.Y.	"	1810–1886	1872–1882
"	"	"	44.	Waite, Morrison R.†	Ohio	"	1816–1888	1874–1888
Hayes	1877–1881	"	45.	Harlan, John M. I.	Ky.	"	1833–1911	1877–1911
"	"	"	46.	Woods, William B.	Ga.	"	1824–1887	1880–1887
Garfield	Mar.–Sept.	"	47.	Matthews, Stanley	Ohio	"	1824–1889	1881–1889

Appointing President	President's Political Party	Dates of President's Service	Name of Justice	Dates of Birth & Death	Justice's Nominal Party Allegiance on Appointment	State from Which Justice Was Apptd*	Dates of Service on Supreme Court
Arthur	"	1881–1885	48. Gray, Horace	1828–1902	"	Mass.	1881–1902
"	"	"	49. Blatchford, Samuel	1820–1893	"	N.Y.	1882–1893
Cleveland	Democrat	1885–1889	50. Lamar, Lucius Q. C.	1825–1893	Democrat	Miss.	1888–1893
"	"	"	51. Fuller, Melville W.†	1833–1910	"	Ill.	1888–1910
Harrison	Republican	1889–1893	52. Brewer, David J.	1837–1910	Republican	Kans.	1889–1910
"	"	"	53. Brown, Henry B.	1836–1913	"	Mich.	1890–1906
"	"	"	54. Shiras, George, Jr.	1832–1924	"	Pa.	1892–1903
"	"	"	55. Jackson, Howell E.	1832–1895	Democrat	Tenn.	1893–1895
Cleveland	Democrat	1893–1897	56. White, Edward D.	1845–1921	Democrat	La.	1894–1910
"	"	"	57. Peckham, Rufus W.	1838–1909	"	N.Y.	1896–1909
McKinley	Republican	1897–1901	58. McKenna, Joseph	1843–1926	Republican	Cal.	1989–1925
Roosevelt	Republican	1901–1909	59. Holmes, Oliver W., Jr.	1841–1935	"	Mass.	1902–1932
"	"	"	60. Day, William R.	1849–1923	"	Ohio	1903–1922
"	"	"	61. Moody, William H.	1853–1917	"	Mass.	1906–1910
Taft	"	1909–1913	62. Lurton, Horace	1844–1914	Democrat	Tenn.	1909–1914
"	"	"	63. Hughes, Charles E.	1862–1948	Republican	N.Y.	1910–1916
"	"	"	64. White, Edward D.‖†	1845–1921	Democrat	La.	1910–1921
"	"	"	65. Van Devanter, Willis	1859–1941	Republican	Wyo.	1911–1937
"	"	"	66. Lamar, Joseph R.	1857–1916	Democrat	Ga.	1910–1916
"	"	"	67. Pitney, Mahlon	1858–1924	Republican	N.J.	1912–1922

President	Term	#	Justice	Birth–Death	Party	State	Service
Wilson	1913–1921	68.	McReynolds, James C.	1862–1946	Democrat	Tenn.	1914–1941
"	"	69.	Brandeis, Louis D.	1856–1941	Republican¶	Mass.	1916–1939
"	"	70.	Clarke, John H.	1857–1945	Democrat	Ohio	1916–1922
Harding	1921–1923	71.	Taft, William H.†	1857–1930	Republican	Conn.	1921–1930
"	"	72.	Sutherland, George	1862–1942	"	Utah	1922–1938
"	"	73.	Butler, Pierce	1866–1939	Democrat	Minn.	1922–1939
Coolidge	1923–1929	74.	Sanford, Edward T.	1865–1930	Republican	Tenn.	1923–1930
Hoover	1929–1933	75.	Stone, Harlan F.	1872–1946	"	N.Y.	1925–1941
"	"	76.	Hughes, Charles E.†	1862–1948	"	N.Y.	1930–1941
"	"	77.	Roberts, Owen J.~	1875–1955	"	Pa.	1930–1945
"	"	78.	Cardozo, Benjamin N.	1870–1938	Democrat	N.Y.	1932–1938
Roosevelt	1933–1945	79.	Black, Hugo L.	1886–1971	"	Ala.	1937–1971
"	"	80.	Reed, Stanley F.	1884–1980	"	Ky.	1938–1957
"	"	81.	Frankfurter, Felix	1883–1965	Independent	Mass.	1939–1962
"	"	82.	Douglas, William O.	1898–1980	Democrat	Conn.	1939–1975
"	"	83.	Murphy, Frank	1893–1949	"	Mich.	1940–1949
"	"	84.	Byrnes, James F.	1879–1972	"	S.C.	1941–1942
"	"	85.	Stone, Harlan F.‖†	1872–1946	Republican	N.Y.	1941–1946
"	"	86.	Jackson, Robert H.	1892–1954	Democrat	N.Y.	1941–1954
"	"	87.	Rutledge, Wiley B.	1894–1949	"	Iowa	1943–1949
Truman	1945–1953	88.	Burton, Harold H.	1888–1965	Republican	Ohio	1945–1958
"	"	89.	Vinson, Fred M.†	1890–1953	Democrat	Ky.	1946–1953
"	"	90.	Clark, Tom C.	1899–1977	"	Tex.	1949–1967
"	"	91.	Minton, Sherman	1890–1965	"	Ind.	1949–1956
Eisenhower	1953–1961	92.	Warren, Earl†	1891–1974	Republican	Cal.	1953–1969
"	"	93.	Harlan, John M. II	1899–1971	"	N.Y.	1955–1971
"	"	94.	Brennan, Wm. J., Jr.	1906–	Democrat	N.J.	1956–

Appointing President	President's Political Party	Dates of President's Service	Name of Justice	Dates of Birth & Death	Justice's Nominal Party Allegiance on Appointment	State from Which Justice Was Apptd*	Dates of Service on Supreme Court
Eisenhower	Republican	1953–1961	95. Whittaker, Charles	1900–1973	Republican	Mo.	1957–1962
"	"	"	96. Stewart, Potter	1915–1985	"	Ohio	1958–1981
Kennedy	Democrat	1961–1963	97. White, Byron R.	1917–	Democrat	Colo.	1962–
"	"	"	98. Goldberg, Arthur	1908–	"	Ill.	1962–1965
Johnson	"	1963–1969	99. Fortas, Abe	1910–1982	"	Tenn.	1965–1969
"	"	"	100. Marshall, Thurgood	1908–	"	N.Y.	1967–
Nixon	Republican	1969–1974	101. Burger, Warren E.†	1907–	Republican	Va.	1969–1986
"	"	"	102. Blackmun, Harry A.	1908–	"	Minn.	1970–
"	"	"	103. Powell, Lewis F., Jr.	1907–	Democrat	Va.	1972–
"	"	"	104. Rehnquist, William H.	1924–	Republican	Ariz.	1972–
Ford**	"	1974–1977	105. Stevens, John Paul	1920–	"	Ill.	1975–
Reagan**	"	1981–	106. O'Connor, Sandra D.	1930–	"	Ariz.	1981–

*Not necessarily, but often, state of birth. †Chief Justice. ‡Resigned without sitting. §Unconfirmed recess appointment, rejected by Senate, December 1795. ||Promoted from Associate Justice. °Nominated by Jackson, but not confirmed until after Van Buren had assumed office. ¶Many — and with some justice — consider Brandeis a Democrat; however, he was in fact a registered Republican when nominated. **In June 1986, President Reagan announced the elevation of Associate Justice Rehnquist to the Chief Justiceship to replace the retiring Warren E. Burger, and Judge Antonin Scalia of the United States Court of Appeals to take Justice Rehnquist's slot. As these pages went to press, Senate confirmation hearings on the two nominees were in process.

APPENDIX B

The Constitution of the United States of America

We, the people of the United States, in order to form a more perfect Union, establish Justice, insure domestic Tranquility, provide for the common defence, promote the general Welfare, and secure the Blessing of Liberty to ourselves and our Posterity, do ordain and establish this CONSTITUTION for the United States of America.

Article I

Section 1.   All legislative Powers herein granted shall be vested in a Congress of the United States, which shall consist of a Senate and House of Representatives.

Section 2.   The House of Representatives shall be composed of Members chosen every second Year by the People of the several States, and the Electors in each State shall have the Qualifications requisite for Electors of the most numerous Branch of the State Legislature.

No Person shall be a Representative who shall not have attained the Age of twenty-five Years, and been seven Years a Citizen of the United States, and who shall not, when elected, be an Inhabitant of that State in which he shall be chosen.

[Representatives and direct Taxes shall be apportioned among the several States which may be included within this Union, according to their respective Numbers, which shall be determined by adding to the whole Number of free Persons, including those bound to Service for a Term of Years, and excluding Indians not taxed, three-fifths of all other persons.][1] The actual Enumeration shall be made within three Years after the first Meeting of the Congress of the United States, and within every subsequent Term of ten Years, in such Manner as they shall by Law direct. The Number of Representatives shall not exceed one for every thirty thousand, but each State shall have at Least one Representative; and until such enumeration shall be made, the State of New Hampshire shall be entitled to chuse three, Massachusetts eight, Rhode Island and Providence Plantations one, Connecticut five, New York six, New Jersey four, Pennsylvania eight, Delaware one, Maryland six, Virginia ten, North Carolina five, South Carolina five, and Georgia three.

When vacancies happen in the Representation from any State, the Executive Authority thereof shall issue Writs of Election to fill such Vacancies.

The House of Representatives shall chuse their Speaker and other Officers; and shall have the sole Power of Impeachment.

Section 3. The Senate of the United States shall be composed of two Senators from each State, chosen by the Legislature thereof,[2] for six Years; and each Senator shall have one Vote.

Immediately after they shall be assembled in Consequence of the first Election, they shall be divided as equally as may be into three Classes. The Seats of the Senators of the first Class shall be vacated at the Expiration of the second Year, of the Second Class at the Expiration of the fourth Year, and the third Class at the Expiration of the sixth Year, so that one-third may be chosen every second Year; and if Vacancies happen by Resignation, or otherwise, during the Recess of the Legislature of any State, the Executive thereof may make temporary Appointments until the next Meeting of the Legislature, which shall then fill such Vacancies.

No Person shall be a Senator who shall not have attained to the Age of thirty Years, and been nine Years a Citizen of the United States, and who shall not, when elected, be an Inhabitant of that State for which he shall be chosen.

---

[1]This provision was modified by the Sixteenth Amendment. The three-fifths reference to slaves was rendered obsolete by the Thirteenth and Fourteenth Amendments.

[2]See the Seventeenth Amendment.

The Vice President of the United States shall be President of the Senate, but shall have no Vote, unless they be equally divided.

The Senate shall chuse their other Officers, and also a President pro tempore, in the absence of the Vice President, or when he shall exercise the Office of President of the United States.

The Senate shall have the sole Power to try all Impeachments. When sitting for that Purpose, they shall be on Oath or Affirmation. When the President of the United States is tried, the Chief Justice shall preside; And no Person shall be convicted without the Concurrence of two-thirds of the Members present.

Judgment in Cases of Impeachment shall not extend further than to removal from Office, and disqualification to hold and enjoy any Office of honor, Trust or Profit under the United States; but the Party convicted shall nevertheless be liable and subject to Indictment, Trial, Judgment and Punishment, according to Law.

Section 4. The Times, Places and Manner of holding Elections for Senators and Representatives, shall be prescribed in each State by the Legislature thereof; but the Congress may at any time by Law make or alter such Regulations, except as to the Places of chusing Senators.

The Congress shall assemble at least once in every Year, and such Meeting shall be on the first Monday in December, unless they shall by Law appoint a different Day.[3]

Section 5. Each House shall be the Judge of the Elections, Returns and Qualifications of its own Members, and a Majority of each shall constitute a Quorum to do Business; but a smaller Number may adjourn from day to day, and may be authorized to compel the Attendance of absent Members, in such Manner, and under such Penalties as each House may provide.

Each House may determine the Rules of its Proceedings, punish its Members for disorderly Behavior, and, with the Concurrence of two-thirds, expel a Member.

Each House shall keep a Journal of its Proceedings and from time to time publish the same, excepting such Parts as may in their Judgment require Secrecy; and the Yeas and Nays of the Members of either House on any question shall, at the Desire of one-fifth of those Present, be entered on the Journal.

---

[3]See the Twentieth Amendment.

Neither House, during the Session of Congress, shall without the Consent of the other, adjourn for more than three days, nor to any other Place than that in which the two Houses shall be sitting.

Section 6. The Senators and Representatives shall receive a Compensation for their Services, to be ascertained by Law, and paid out of the Treasury of the United States. They shall in all Cases, except Treason, Felony, and Breach of the peace, be privileged from Arrest during their Attendance at the Session of their respective Houses, and in going to and returning from the same; and for any Speech or Debate in either House, they shall not be questioned in any other Place.

No Senator or Representative shall, during the Time for which he was elected, be appointed to any civil Office under the Authority of the United States, which shall have been created, or the Emoluments whereof shall have been increased during such time; and no Person holding any Office under the United States, shall be a Member of either House during his Continuance in Office.

Section 7. All Bills for raising Revenue shall originate in the House of Representatives; but the Senate may propose or concur with Amendments as on other Bills.

Every Bill which shall have passed the House of Representatives and the Senate, shall, before it become a Law, be presented to the President of the United States; If he approve he shall sign it, but if not he shall return it, with his Objections to that House in which it shall have originated, who shall enter the objections at large on their Journal, and proceed to reconsider it. If after such Reconsideration two-thirds of that House shall agree to pass the Bill it shall be sent, together with the Objections, to the other House, by which it shall likewise be reconsidered, and if approved by two-thirds of that House, it shall become a Law. But in all such Cases the Votes of both Houses shall be determined by Yeas and Nays, and the Names of the Persons voting to and against the Bill shall be entered on the Journal of each House respectively. If any Bill shall not be returned by the President within ten Days (Sundays excepted) after it shall have been presented to him, the Same shall be a Law, in like Manner as if he had signed it, unless the Congress by their Adjournment prevent its Return, in which Case it shall not be a Law.

Every Order, Resolution, or Vote to which the Concurrence of the Senate and House of Representatives may be necessary (except on a question of Adjournment) shall be presented to the President of the United States: and before the Same shall take Effect, shall be approved by him, or being disapproved by him, shall be repassed by two-thirds of the Senate and House of Representatives, according to the Rules and Limitations prescribed in the Case of a Bill.

Section 8. The Congress shall have Power To lay and collect Taxes, Duties, Imposts and Excises, to pay the Debts and provide for the common Defence and general Welfare of the United States; but all Duties, Imposts and Excises shall be uniform throughout the United States;

To borrow money on the Credit of the United States;

To regulate Commerce with foreign Nations, and among the several States, and with the Indian Tribes;

To establish an uniform Rule of Naturalization, and uniform Laws on the subject of Bankruptcies throughout the United States.

To coin Money, regulate the Value thereof, and of foreign Coin, and fix the Standard of Weights and Measures;

To provide for the Punishment of counterfeiting the Securities and current Coin of the United States;

To establish Post Offices and post Roads;

To promote the Progress of Science and useful arts, by securing for limited Times to Authors and Inventors the exclusive Right to their respective Writings and Discoveries;

To constitute Tribunals inferior to the supreme Court;

To define and punish Piracies and Felonies committed on the high Seas, and Offenses against the Law of Nations;

To declare War, grant Letters of Marque and Reprisal, and make Rules concerning Captures on Land and Water;

To raise and support Armies, but no Appropriation of Money to that Use shall be for a longer Term than two Years;

To provide and maintain a Navy;

To make Rules for the Government and Regulation of the land and naval Forces;

To provide for calling forth the Militia to execute the Laws of the Union, suppress Insurrections and repel Invasions;

To provide for organizing, arming, and disciplining the Militia, and for governing such Part of them as may be employed in the Service of the United States, reserving to the States respectively, the Appointment of the Officers, and the Authority of training the Militia according to the discipline prescribed by Congress;

To exercise exclusive Legislation in all Cases whatsoever, over such District (not exceeding ten Miles square) as may, by Cession of particular States, and the acceptance of Congress, become the Seat of the Government of the United States, and to exercise like Authority over all Places purchased by the Consent of the Legislature of the State in which the Same shall be, for the Erection of Forts, Magazines, Arsenals, dock-Yards, and other needful Buildings;—And

To make all Laws which shall be necessary and proper for carrying into Execution the foregoing Powers, and all other Powers vested by this Constitution in the Government of the United States, or in any Department or Officer thereof.

Section 9. The Migration or Importation of such Persons as any of the States now existing shall think proper to admit, shall not be prohibited by the Congress prior to the Year one thousand eight hundred and eight, but a tax or duty may be imposed on such importation, not exceeding ten dollars for each Person.

The privilege of the Writ of Habeas Corpus shall not be suspended, unless when in Cases of Rebellion or Invasion the public Safety may require it.

No Bill of Attainder or ex post facto Law shall be passed.

No capitation, or other direct Tax shall be laid, unless in Proportion to the Census or Enumeration herein before directed to be taken.[4]

No Tax or Duty shall be laid on Articles exported from any State.

No Preference shall be given by any Regulation of Commerce or Revenue to the Ports of one State over those of another; nor shall Vessels bound to, or from one State, be obliged to enter, clear, or pay Duties in another.

No Money shall be drawn from the Treasury, but in Consequence of Appropriations made by Law; and a regular Statement and Account of the Receipts and Expenditures of all public Money shall be published from time to time.

No Title of Nobility shall be granted by the United States: And no Person holding any Office of Profit or Trust under them, shall, without the Consent of the Congress, accept of any present, Emolument, Office, or Title, of any kind whatever, from any King, Prince, or foreign State.

Section 10. No State shall enter into any Treaty, Alliance, or Confederation; grant Letters of Marque and Reprisal; coin Money; emit Bills of Credit; make any Thing but gold and silver Coin a Tender in Payment of Debts; pass any Bill of Attainder, ex post facto Law,

---

[4]See the Sixteenth Amendment.

or Law impairing the Obligation of Contracts, or grant any Title of Nobility.

No State shall, without the Consent of the Congress, lay any Imposts or Duties on Imports or Exports, except what may be absolutely necessary for executing its inspection Laws: and the net Product of all Duties and Imposts, laid by any State on Imports or Exports, shall be for the Use of the Treasury of the United States and all such Laws shall be subject to the Revision and Control of the Congress.

No State shall, without the Consent of Congress, lay any duty of Tonnage, keep Troops, or Ships of War in time of Peace, enter into any Agreement or Compact with another State, or with a foreign Power, or engage in War, unless actually invaded, or in such imminent Danger as will not admit of delay.

Article II

Section 1.　The executive Power shall be vested in a President of the United States of America. He shall hold his Office during the Term of four Years, and, together with the Vice President, chosen for the same Term, be elected, as follows

Each State shall appoint, in such Manner as the Legislature thereof may direct, a Number of Electors, equal to the whole number of Senators and Representatives to which the State may be entitled in the Congress; but no Senator or Representative, or Person holding an Office of Trust or Profit under the United States, shall be appointed an Elector.

The Electors shall meet in their respective States, and vote by Ballot for two persons, of whom one at least shall not be an Inhabitant of the same State with themselves. And they shall make a List of all Persons voted for, and of the Number of Votes for each; which List they shall sign and certify, and transmit sealed to the Seat of the Government of the United States, directed to the President of the Senate. The President of the Senate shall, in the Presence of the Senate and House of Representatives, open all the Certificates, and the Votes shall then be counted. The Person having the greatest Number of Votes shall be the President, if such Number be a Majority of the whole Number of Electors appointed; and if there be more than one who have such Majority, and have an Equal Number of Votes, then the House of Representatives shall immediately chuse by Ballot one of them for President; and if no Person have a Majority, then from the five highest on the List the said House shall in like Manner chuse the President, but in chusing the President, the Votes shall be taken by States, the Representation from each State having one Vote; A quorum for this Purpose shall consist of a Member or Members from two-thirds of the States, and a Majority of all the States shall be necessary to a Choice. In every Case, after the Choice of the President, the Person having the greatest Number of Votes of the Electors shall be the Vice-President. But if there should remain two or more who have equal Votes, the Senate shall chuse from them by Ballot the Vice President.[5]

The Congress may determine the Time of chusing the Electors, and the Day on which they shall give their Vote; which Day shall be the same throughout the United States.

No person except a natural born Citizen, or a Citizen of the United States, at the time of the Adoption of this Constitution, shall be eligible to the Office of President; neither shall any Person be eligible to that Office who shall not have attained the Age of thirty-five Years, and been fourteen Years a Resident within the United States.

In Case of the Removal of the President from Office, or of his Death, Resignation, or Inability to discharge the Powers and Duties of the said office, the same shall devolve on the Vice President, and the Congress may by Law provide for the Case of Removal, Death, Resignation or Inability, both the President and Vice President, declaring what Officer shall then act as President, and such Officer shall act accordingly, until the Disability be removed, or a President shall be elected.

The President shall, at stated Times, receive for his Services, a Compensation, which shall neither be encreased nor diminished during the Period for which he shall have been elected, and he shall not receive within that Period any other Emolument from the United States, or any of them.

Before he enters on the Execution of his Office, he shall take the following Oath or Affirmation:—"I do solemnly swear (or affirm) that I will faithfully execute the Office of President of the United States, and will to the best of my Ability, preserve, protect and defend the Constitution of the United States."

Section 2. The President shall be Commander in Chief of the Army and Navy of the United States, and of the Militia of the several States, when called into the actual Service of the United States; he may require the Opinion in writing, of the principal officer in each of the executive Departments, upon any subject relating to the Duties of

---

[5]This paragraph was superseded by the Twelfth Amendment.

their respective Offices, and he shall have Power to Grant Reprives and Pardons for Offenses against the United States, except in Cases of Impeachment.

He shall have Power, by and with the Advice and Consent of the Senate, to make Treaties, provided two-thirds of the Senators present concur; and he shall nominate, and, by and with the Advice and Consent of the Senate, shall appoint Ambassadors, other public Ministers and Consuls, Judges of the supreme Court, and all other Officers of the United States, whose Appointments are not herein otherwise provided for, and which shall be established by Law: but the Congress may by Law vest the Appointment of such inferior Offices, as they think proper, in the President alone, in the Courts of Law, or in the Heads of Departments.

The President shall have Power to fill up all Vacancies that may happen during the Recess of the Senate by granting Commissions which shall expire at the End of their next Session.

Section 3.　He shall from time to time give to the Congress Information of the State of the Union, and recommend to their Consideration such Measures as he shall judge necessary and expedient; he may, on extraordinary Occasions, convene both Houses, or either of them, and in Cases of Disagreement between them, with Respect to the Time of Adjournment, he may adjourn them to such Time as he shall think proper; he shall receive Ambassadors and other public Ministers; he shall take Care that the Laws be faithfully executed, and shall Commission all of the Officers of the United States.

Section 4.　The President, Vice President and all civil Officers of the United States, shall be removed from Office on Impeachment for, and Conviction of, Treason, Bribery, or other high Crimes and Misdemeanors.

Article III

Section 1.　The judicial Power of the United States shall be vested in one supreme Court, and in such inferior Courts as the Congress may from time to time ordain and establish. The Judges, both of the supreme and inferior Courts, shall hold their offices during good Behaviour, and shall, at stated Times, receive for their Services a Compensation which shall not be diminished during their Continuance in Office.

Section 2. The judicial Power shall extend to all Cases, in Law and Equity, arising under this Constitution, the Laws of the United States and Treaties made, or which shall be made, under their Authority;—to all Cases affecting Ambassadors, other public Ministers and Consuls;—to all Cases of admiralty and maritime Jurisdiction:—to Controversies to which the United States shall be a Party;—to Controversies between two or more States;—between a State and Citizens of another State;[6]—Between Citizens of different States;—between Citizens of the same State claiming Lands under Grants of different States, and between a State, or the Citizens thereof, and foreign States, Citizens or Subjects.

In all Cases affecting Ambassadors, other public Ministers and Consuls, and those in which a State shall be a Party, the supreme Court shall have original Jurisdiction. In all the other Cases before mentioned, the supreme Court shall have appellate Jurisdiction, both as to Law and Fact, with such Exceptions, and under such Regulations as the Congress shall make.

The trial of all Crimes, except in Cases of Impeachment, shall be by Jury, and such Trial shall be held in the State where the said Crimes shall have been committed; but when not committed within any State, the Trial shall be at such Place or Places as the Congress may by Law have directed.

Section 3. Treason against the United States, shall consist only in levying War against them, or in adhering to their Enemies, giving them Aid and Comfort. No Person shall be convicted of Treason unless on the Testimony of two Witnesses to the same overt Act, or on Confession in open Court.

The Congress shall have power to declare the Punishment of Treason, but no Attainder of Treason shall work Corruption of Blood, or Forfeiture except during the Life of the Person attainted.

Article IV

Section 1. Full Faith and Credit shall be given in each State to the public acts, Records, and judicial Proceedings of every other State. And the Congress may by general Laws prescribe the manner in

---

[6]See the Eleventh Amendment.

which such Acts, Records and Proceedings shall be proved, and the Effect thereof.

Section 2. The Citizens of each State shall be entitled to all Privileges and Immunities of Citizens in the several States.

A Person charged in any State with Treason, Felony, or other Crime, who shall flee from Justice, and be found in another State, shall on demand of the executive Authority of the State from which he fled, be delivered up, to be removed to the State having Jurisdiction of the Crime.

No Person held to Service or Labour in one State, under the Laws thereof, escaping into another, shall in Consequence of any Law or Regulation therein, be discharged from such Service or Labour, but shall be delivered up on Claim of the Party to whom such Service or Labour may be due.[7]

Section 3. New States may be admitted by the Congress into this Union; but no new States shall be formed or erected within the Jurisdiction of any other State; nor any State be formed by the Junction of two or more States, or parts of States, without the Consent of the Legislatures of the States concerned as well as of the Congress.

The Congress shall have Power to dispose of and make all needful Rules and Regulations respecting the Territory or other Property belonging to the United States; and nothing in this Constitution shall be so constructed as to Prejudice any Claims of the United States, or of any particular State.

Section 4. The United States shall guarantee to every State in this Union a Republican Form of Government, and shall protect each of them against Invasion; and on Application of the Legislature, or of the Executive (when the Legislature cannot be convened) against domestic Violence.

Article V

The Congress whenever two-thirds of both houses shall deem it necessary, shall propose Amendments to this Constitution, or, on the Appli-

---

[7]Obsolete. See the Thirteenth Amendment.

cation of the Legislatures of two-thirds of the several States, shall call a Convention for proposing Amendments, which, in either Case, shall be valid to all Intents and Purposes, as part of this Constitution, when ratified by the Legislatures of three-fourths of the several States, or by Conventions in three-fourths thereof, as the one or the other Mode of Ratification may be proposed by the Congress; Provided that no Amendment which may be made prior to the Year One thousand eight hundred and eight shall in any Manner affect the first and fourth Clauses in the Ninth Section of the first Article; and that no State, without its Consent, shall be deprived of its equal Suffrage in the Senate.

Article VI

All Debts contracted and Engagements entered into, before the Adoption of this Constitution, shall be as valid against the United States under this Constitution, as under the Confederation.

This Constitution, and the Laws of the United States which shall be made in Pursuance thereof; and all Treaties made, or which shall be made, under the Authority of the United States, shall be the supreme Law of the Land; and the Judges in every State shall be bound thereby, any Thing in the Constitution or Laws of any State to the Contrary notwithstanding.

The Senators and Representatives before mentioned, and the Members of the several State Legislatures, and all executives and judicial Officers, both of the United States and of the several States, shall be bound by Oath or Affirmation, to support this Constitution; but no religious Test shall ever be required as a Qualification to any Office or public Trust under the United States.

Article VII

The Ratification of the Conventions of nine States shall be sufficient for the Establishment of this Constitution between the States so ratifying the Same. Done in Convention by the Unanimous Consent of the States Present the Seventeenth Day of September in the Year of our Lord one thousand seven hundred and Eighty seven and of the Independence of the United States of America the Twelfth. In Witness whereof We have hereunto subscribed our Names

Go. Washington
Presid't and deputy from Virginia

Delaware
Geo: Read
John Dickinson
Jaco: Broom
Gunning Bedford jun
Richard Bassett

Maryland
James McHenry
Danl Carroll
Dan: of St. Thos Jenifer

Virginia
John Blair
James Madison, Jr.

North Carolina
Wm Blount
Hu Williamson
Richd Dobbs Spaight

Pennsylvania
B. Franklin

New York
Alexander Hamilton

New Jersey
Wil: Livingston
David Brearley
Wm. Paterson
Jona: Dayton

South Carolina
J. Rutledge
Charles Pinckney
Charles Cotesworth Pinckney
Pierce Butler

Georgia
William Few
Abr Baldwin

New Hampshire
John Langdon
Nicholas Gilman

Massachusetts
Nathaniel Gorham
Rufus King

Connecticut
Wm. Saml Johnson
Roger Sherman
Robt. Morris
Thos. Fitzsimons
James Wilson
Thomas Mifflin
Geo. Clymer
Jared Ingersoll
Gouv Morris

Attest:
William Jackson, Secretary

Amendments[8]

AMENDMENT I

Congress shall make no law respecting an establishment of religion, or prohibiting the free exercise thereof; or abridging the freedom of speech, or of the press; or the right of the people peaceably to assemble, and to petition the Government for a redress of grievances.

AMENDMENT II

A well regulated Militia, being necessary to the security of a free State, the right of the people to keep and bear Arms, shall not be infringed.

AMENDMENT III

No Soldier shall, in time of peace be quartered in any house, without the consent of the Owner, nor in time of war, but in a manner to be prescribed by law.

AMENDMENT IV

The right of the people to be secure in their persons, houses, papers, and effects, against unreasonable searches and seizures, shall not be violated, and no Warrants shall issue, but upon probable cause, supported by Oath or affirmation, and particularly describing the place to be searched, and the persons or things to be seized.

AMENDMENT V

No person shall be held to answer for a capital, or otherwise infamous crime, unless on a presentment or indictment of a Grand Jury, except in cases arising in the land or naval forces, or in the Militia, when in actual service in time of War or public danger, nor shall any person be subject for the same offense to be twice put in jeopardy of life or limb, nor shall be compelled in any criminal case to be a witness against himself, nor be deprived of life, liberty, or property, without due process of law; nor shall private property be taken for public use, without just compensation.

---

[8]The first ten Amendments were adopted in 1791.

AMENDMENT VI

In all criminal prosecutions, the accused shall enjoy the right to a speedy and public trial, by an impartial jury of the State and district wherein the crime shall have been committed, which district shall have been previously ascertained by law, and to be informed of the nature and the cause of the accusation; to be confronted with the witnesses against him; to have the compulsory process for obtaining witnesses in his favor, and to have the Assistance of Counsel for his defence.

AMENDMENT VII

In suits at common law, where the value in controversy shall exceed twenty dollars, the right of trial by jury shall be preserved, and no fact tried by a jury, shall be otherwise reexamined in any Court of the United States, than according to the rules of the common law.

AMENDMENT VIII

Excessive bail shall not be required, nor excessive fines imposed, nor cruel and unusual punishments inflicted.

AMENDMENT IX

The enumeration in the Constitution, of certain rights shall not be construed to deny or disparage others retained by the people.

AMENDMENT X

The powers not delegated to the United States by the Constitution, nor prohibited by it to the States, are reserved to the States respectively, or to the people.

AMENDMENT XI[9]

The Judicial power of the United States shall not be construed to extend to any suit in law or equity, commenced or prosecuted against

---

[9]Adopted in 1798.

one of the United States by Citizens of another State, or by Citizens or Subjects of any Foreign States.

AMENDMENT XII[10]

The Electors shall meet in their respective states and vote by ballot for President and Vice President, one of whom, at least, shall not be an inhabitant of the same state with themselves; they shall name in their ballots the person voted for as President and in distinct ballots the person voted for as Vice President, and they shall make distinct lists of all persons voted for as President, and of all persons voted for as Vice President, and of the number of votes for each, which lists they shall sign and certify, and transmit sealed to the seat of the government of the United States, directed to the President of the Senate;—The President of the Senate shall, in the presence of the Senate and House of Representatives, open all the certificates and the votes shall then be counted;—The person having the greatest number of votes for President, shall be the President, if such number be a majority of the whole number of Electors appointed; and if no person have such majority, then from the persons having the highest numbers not exceeding three on the list of those voted for as President, the House of Representatives shall choose immediately, by ballot, the President. But in choosing the President, the votes shall be taken by states, the representation from each state having one vote; a quorum for this purpose shall consist of a member or members from two-thirds of the states, and a majority of all the states shall be necessary to a choice. And if the House of Representatives shall not choose a President whenever the right of choice shall devolve upon them, before the fourth day of March next following, then the Vice President shall act as President, as in the case of the death or other constitutional disability of the President.—The person having the greatest number of votes as Vice President, shall be the Vice President, if such number be a majority of the whole number of Electors appointed, and if no person have a majority, then from the two highest numbers on the list, the Senate shall choose the Vice President; a quorum for the purpose shall consist of two-thirds of the whole number of Senators, and a majority of the whole number shall be necessary to a choice. But no person constitutionally ineligible to the office of President shall be eligible to that of Vice President of the United States.

---

[10]Adopted in 1804. Partly altered by the Twentieth Amendment in 1933.

AMENDMENT XIII[11]

Section 1. Neither slavery nor involuntary servitude, except as a punishment for crime whereof the party shall have been duly convicted, shall exist within the United States, or any place subject to their jurisdiction.

Section 2. Congress shall have power to enforce this article by appropriate legislation.

AMENDMENT XIV[12]

Section 1. All persons born or naturalized in the United States and subject to the jurisdiction thereof, are citizens of the United States and of the State wherein they reside. No State shall make or enforce any law which shall abridge the privileges or immunities of citizens of the United States; nor shall any State deprive any person of life, liberty, or property, without the due process of law; nor deny to any person within its jurisdiction the equal protection of the laws.

Section 2. Representatives shall be apportioned among the several States according to their respective numbers, counting the whole number of persons in each State, excluding Indians not taxed. But when the right to vote at any election for the choice of electors for President and Vice President of the United States, Representatives in Congress, the Executive and Judicial Officers of a State, or the members of the Legislature thereof, is denied to any of the male inhabitants of such State, being twenty-one years of age, and citizens of the United States, or in any way abridged, except for participation in rebellion, or other crime, the basis of representation therein shall be reduced in the proportion which the number of such male citizens shall bear to the whole number of male citizens twenty-one years of age in such State.

Section 3. No person shall be a Senator or Representative in Congress, or elector of President and Vice President, or hold any office, civil or military, under the United States, or under any State, who, having previously taken an oath, as a member of Congress, or as an officer of the United States, or as a member of any State legislature,

---

[11]Adopted in 1865.
[12]Adopted in 1868.

or as an executive or judicial officer of any State, to support the Constitution of the United States, shall have engaged in insurrection or rebellion against the same, or given aid or comfort to the enemies thereof. But Congress may by a vote of two-thirds of each House, remove such disability.

Section 4.   The validity of the public debt of the United States, authorized by law, including debts incurred for payment of pensions and bounties for services in suppressing insurrection or rebellion, shall not be questioned. But neither the United States nor any State shall assume or pay any debt or obligation incurred in aid of insurrection or rebellion against the United States, or any claim for the loss or emancipation of any slave; but all such debts, obligations and claims shall be held illegal and void.

Section 5.   The Congress shall have power to enforce, by appropriate legislation, the provisions of this article.

AMENDMENT XV[13]

Section 1.   The right of citizens of the United States to vote shall not be denied or abridged by the United States or by any State on account of race, color, or previous condition of servitude.

Section 2.   The Congress shall have power to enforce this article by appropriate legislation.

AMENDMENT XVI[14]

The Congress shall have power to lay and collect taxes on incomes, from whatever source derived, without apportionment among the several States, and without regard to any census or enumeration.

AMENDMENT XVII[15]

The Senate of the United States shall be composed of two Senators from each State, elected by the people thereof, for six years, and each

---

[13]Adopted in 1870.
[14]Adopted in 1913.
[15]Adopted in 1913.

Senator shall have one vote. The electors in each state shall have the qualifications requisite for electors of the most numerous branch of the State legislatures.

When vacancies happen in the representation of any State in the Senate, the executive authority of such State shall issue writs of election to fill such vacancies: Provided, That the legislature of any State may empower the executive thereof to make temporary appointments until the people fill the vacancies by election as the legislature may direct.

This amendment shall not be so construed as to affect the election or term of any Senator chosen before it becomes valid as part of the Constitution.

AMENDMENT XVIII[16]

Section 1. After one year from the ratification of this article the manufacture, sale, or transportation of intoxicating liquors within, the importation thereof into, or the exportation thereof from the United States and all territory subject to the jurisdiction thereof for beverage purposes is hereby prohibited.

Section 2. The Congress and the several States shall have concurrent power to enforce this article by appropriate legislation.

Section 3. This article shall be inoperative unless it shall have been ratified as an amendment to the Constitution by the legislatures of the several States, as provided in the Constitution, within seven years from the date of submission hereof to the States by the Congress.

AMENDMENT XIX[17]

The right of Citizens of the United States to vote shall not be denied or abridged by the United States or by any State on account of sex.

Congress shall have power to enforce this article by appropriate legislation.

---

[16]Adopted in 1919. Repealed by the Twenty-first Amendment in 1933.
[17]Adopted in 1920.

AMENDMENT XX[18]

Section 1.   The terms of the President and Vice President shall end at noon on the 20th day of January, and the terms of Senators and Representatives at noon on the 3d day of January, of the years in which such terms would have ended if this article had not been ratified; and the terms of their successors shall then begin.

Section 2.   The Congress shall assemble at least once in every year, and such meeting shall begin at noon on the 3d day of January, unless they shall by law appoint a different day.

Section 3.   If, at the time fixed for the beginning of the term of the President, the President elect shall have died, the Vice President elect shall become President. If a President shall not have been chosen before the time fixed for the beginning of his term, or if the President elect shall have failed to qualify, then the Vice President elect shall act as President until a President shall have qualified; and the Congress may by law provide for the case wherein neither a President elect nor a Vice President elect shall have qualified, declaring who shall then act as President, or the manner in which one who is to act shall be selected, and such person shall act accordingly until a President or Vice President shall have qualified.

Section 4.   The Congress may by law provide for the case of the death of any of the persons from whom the House of Representatives may choose a President whenever the right of choice shall have devolved upon them, and for the case of the death of any of the persons from whom the Senate may choose a Vice President whenever the right of choice shall have devolved upon them.

Section 5.   Sections 1 and 2 shall take effect on the 15th day of October following the ratification of this article.

Section 6.   This article shall be inoperative unless it shall have been ratified as an amendment to the Constitution by the legislatures of three-fourths of the several States within seven years from the date of its submission.

---

[18]Adopted in 1933.

AMENDMENT XXI[19]

Section 1. The eighteenth article of amendment to the Constitution of the United States is hereby repealed.

Section 2. The transportation or importation into any State, Territory, or possession of the United States for delivery or use therein of intoxicating liquors, in violation of the laws thereof, is hereby prohibited.

Section 3. This article shall be inoperative unless it shall have been ratified as an amendment to the Constitution by conventions in the several States, as provided in the Constitution, within seven years from the date of the submission hereof to the States by the Congress.

AMENDMENT XXII[20]

Section 1. No person shall be elected to the office of the President more than twice, and no person who has held the office of President, or acted as President, for more than two years of a term to which some other person was elected President shall be elected to the office of the President more than once. But this Article shall not apply to any person holding the office of President when this Article was proposed by the Congress, and shall not prevent any person who may be holding the office of President, or acting as President, during the term within which this Article becomes operative from holding the office of President or acting as President during the remainder of such term.

Section 2. This article shall be inoperative unless it shall have been ratified as an amendment to the Constitution by the Legislatures of three-fourths of the several States within seven years from the date of its submission to the States by the Congress.

AMENDMENT XXIII[21]

Section 1. The District constituting the seat of Government of the United States shall appoint in such manner as the Congress may direct:

---

[19]Adopted in 1933.
[20]Adopted in 1951.
[21]Adopted in 1961.

A number of electors of President and Vice President equal to the whole number of Senators and Representatives in Congress to which the District would be entitled if it were a State, but in no event more than the least populous State; they shall be in addition to those appointed by the States; but they shall be considered, for the purposes of the election of President and Vice President, to be electors appointed by a State; and they shall meet in the District and perform such duties as provided by the twelfth article of amendment.

Section 2.   The Congress shall have power to enforce this article by appropriate legislation.

AMENDMENT XXIV[22]

Section 1.   The right of citizens of the United States to vote in any primary or other election for the President or Vice President, for electors for President or Vice President, or for Senator or Representative in Congress, shall not be denied or abridged by the United States or any State by reason of failure to pay any poll tax or other tax.

Section 2.   The Congress shall have power to enforce this article by appropriate legislation.

AMENDMENT XXV[23]

Section 1.   In case of the removal of the President from office or his death or resignation, the Vice President shall become President.

Section 2.   Whenever there is a vacancy in the office of the Vice President, the President shall nominate a Vice President who shall take office upon confirmation by a majority vote of both houses of Congress.

Section 3.   Whenever the President transmits to the President pro tempore of the Senate and the Speaker of the House of Representatives his written declaration that he is unable to discharge the powers and duties of his office, and until he transmits to them a written declaration to the contrary, such powers and duties shall be discharged by the Vice President as Acting President.

---

[22]Adopted in 1964.
[23]Adopted in 1967.

Section 4.   Whenever the Vice President and a majority of either the principal officers of the executive departments or of such other body as Congress may by law provide, transmit to the President pro tempore of the Senate and the Speaker of the House of Representatives their written declaration that the President is unable to discharge the powers and duties of his office, the Vice President shall immediately assume the powers and duties of the office as Acting President.

Thereafter, when the President transmits to the President pro tempore of the Senate and the Speaker of the House of Representatives, his written declaration that no inability exists, he shall resume the powers and duties of his office unless the Vice President and a majority of either the principal officers of the executive department or of such other body as Congress may by law provide, transmit within four days to the President pro tempore of the Senate and the Speaker of the House of Representatives their written declaration that the President is unable to discharge the powers and duties of his office. Thereupon Congress shall decide the issue, assembling within 48 hours for that purpose if not in session. If the Congress, within 21 days after receipt of the latter written declaration, or, if Congress is not in session, within 21 days after Congress is required to assemble, determines by two-thirds vote of both houses that the President is unable to discharge the powers and duties of his office, the Vice President shall continue to discharge the same as Acting President; otherwise, the President shall resume the powers and duties of his office.

AMENDMENT XXVI[24]

Section 1.   The Right of Citizens of the United States, who are eighteen years of age or older, to vote shall not be denied or abridged by the United States or by any State on account of age.

Section 2.   The Congress shall have power to enforce this article by appropriate legislation.

---

[24]Adopted in 1971.

Case Index

Subject Index